The Autobiography of Thomas Witherow

1824-1890

The boy from Aughlish, near Dungiven, who became Presbyterian minister of Maghera and then first Professor of Church History in Magee College, Londonderry

A centenary edition by

Graham Mawhinney & Eull Dunlop

Foreword by the Rt Rev Principal Finlay Holmes

Moderator of the sesquicentenary General Assembly;
Magee Professor of Christian History & Doctrine,
Union Theological College, Belfast

Commentary by the Rev John Brown

sometime Presbyterian minister of Draperstown;
former Lecturer in History, Magee College, and the
New University of Ulster, Coleraine

Afterword by Rowan Witherow Hamilton

Ballinascreen Historical Society
Draperstown, 1990

ISBN 0-9511759-5-5

Published by
Ballinascreen Historical Society,
c/o 7 Tobermore Road, Draperstown,
County Londonderry, Northern Ireland,
BT45 7AG

Launching 'the wee Witherow', an illustrated reprint of 'Three Prophets Of Our Own', on 2 January 1990: (left) Eull Dunlop, Peter McAlary (then Chairman of Ballinascreen Historical Society), Graham Mawhinney and Finlay Holmes

Typeset by Muriel Barr: telephone 0266-656211

Coleraine Printing Company: telephone 0265-54873

Foreword
by the Moderator of the sesquicentenary General Assembly

The year 1990 is one in which many significant events in Irish history are being remembered and it is good that, among them, the life and work of Thomas Witherow have not been forgotten. The publication of his 'Autobiography', hitherto available only in manuscript or typescript, and the earlier re-publication of his valuable 'Three Prophets of Our Own' mark the centenary of his death in an appropriate and useful way.

Witherow's own careful historical works, in particular his 'Derry and Enniskillen in 1689', his biography (in collaboration with Thomas Croskery) of A P Goudy and his 'Historical and Literary Memorials of Presbyterianism in Ireland', as well as his collection of important primary documents, continue to place students of Irish and especially Presbyterian history in his debt. His 'Autobiography' is invaluable for those who wish to understand the ethos of Irish Presbyterianism in the nineteenth century. He is of particular interest as an evangelical churchman who was conservative in his theology, but liberal in his politics, as was Richard Smyth MP, his colleague on the Faculty of Magee College, whom he succeeded as editor of the 'Derry Standard' in 1878.

'Three Prophets of Our Own', a lecture which Witherow originally gave in 1855, when he was minister in Maghera, on three significant churchmen with local associations (Alexander Carson, the Baptist polemicist, Adam Clarke, the Methodist polymath, and Henry Cooke, the Athanasius of Irish Presbyterianism), was first published in 1855, with a second edition in 1880. The re-publication of this lecture in January 1990 has introduced these important nineteenth-century figures to a wider public and has been welcomed by many.

One hundred years after the death of Thomas Witherow, I congratulate the Ballinascreen Historical Society on their fitting and useful tribute to a careful and patient Irish Presbyterian historian and humble man of God.

Finlay Holmes

Dr Holmes is Principal of Union Theological College, Belfast, where he is Magee Professor of Christian History and Doctrine. Formerly Lecturer in Church History and Systematic Theology in Magee Theological College, he is the author of 'Magee: 1865-1965', 'Henry Cooke' (1981), 'Our Irish Presbyterian Heritage' (1985) and various papers on local religious history.

Ballinascreen Historical Society

Ten Years On

It was during September, 10 years ago, that the idea of forming a local historical group in Draperstown was first mooted.

When Ballinascreen Credit Union decided to sponsor a written quiz on local history, the event was highly successful and it brought together a group of people who shared an interest in the past.

TheFederation for Ulster Local Studies was contacted and a few of their members came along to a meeting in Draperstown, where the decision was taken to form a local historical society.

A Steering Committee was then set up and a draft constitution was formulated which set out the following objectives for the society.

(a) The study and encouragement of public interest, in the history, folklore, archaeology and antiquities of the region, in and around, Ballinascreen.

(b) The publication of research papers on the above topics, and the establishment of a society archive.

A public meeting was then held to publicise the proposed aims of the society. Following this there was a general meeting of members which was preceeded by a session of local poetry and song, prompting a large attendance.

The society was formally set up in February 1980, and the Annual General Meetings take place every year at that time.

From the beginning, the Committee decided against the practice adopted by most other socities to publish a regular journal and instead opted to have occasional publications.

Since the founding of the Society, publications of all kinds have been produced on an annual basis. All have been best sellers and most of them are now unobtainable. One of the most significant publications, was the reprinting of Alfred Munn's "Notes on the Place Names of Parishes and Townlands of the County of Londonderry", from the 1925 original.

The Society's current publication "Looking Back on Ballinascreen" is a collection of local lore that has been compiled by the Secretary, Angela O'Keeney. Copies of the 80 quarto page book are selling very well in local shops at £4.00.

The Society is unique, in that it is the only one in the whole of Ireland which has successfully produced a record of songs and music, and also a hour long documentary video film, "Images of Ballinascreen".

Since February 1980, membership has remained at around 80, and monthly meetings are usually well attended.

One particularly interesting activity for members is the annual one-day outing to places of historic interest throughout Ireland. There have also been many outings for the committee, and a few years ago there was a very successful three day trip to Edinburgh.

In recent years the work of the society has been augmented by the use of three A.C.E. employees. Black and white photographs have been taken of every house in the Ballinascreen parish and these have been filed and indexed according to their townland. Other tasks carried out by the A.C.E. workers has been to organise the Society archives, transcribing gravestone inscriptions and mounting public displays of local historical artifacts.

Over the years, the Committee has successfully striven to get the right blend of activity, with considerable emphasis being placed on in-depth research projects and topics. Maximum use has been made of the local press and other media to maintain a high profile for the Society.

With interest in local history still growing, a hard-working and relatively young Committee, continues to plan for the future, as the Society heads confidently towards its first decade.

List of Publications

1980 - "The Wee Black Tin" (Poems by George Barnett and John Paul Kelly) - out of print.

1981 - "Ordnance Survey Memoir for Ballinascreen 1836-37" - out of print.

1982 - "The Meetin' House" (Draperstown Presbyterian Church History) - out of print.

1983 - "Statistical Reports of Six Derry Parishes, 1821" (Balinascreen, Kilcronaghan, Desertmartin, Boveva, Banagher, Dungiven). - £3 including p. & p.

1984 - "Songs and Music of Ballinascreen" (L. P. Record and Cassette) - £5.50 including p & p (Records only)

1985 - "Notes on the Placenames of Parishes and Townlands of the County of Londonderry" by A. M. Munn, 1925. (Limited Edition reprint) - out of print

1986 - "Ordnance Survey Memoirs for the Parishes of Desertmartin and Kilcronaghan. 1836 - 1837" - out of print

1986 - "Images of Ballinascreen" (V.H.S. Video Cassette) - £10.75 including p. & p.

1987 - "Famous Maghera Men" by Eoin Walsh - out of print

1988 - "The Heart of Ballinascreen" Poems by Nora Ni Chathain - £2 including p. & p.

1989 - "Looking Back on Ballinascreen" by Angela J. O'Keeney - £4 including p. & p.

All enquiries about publications should be addressed initally to the Society at 7 Tobermore Road, Draperstown, BT45 7AG

> The Rev Thomas Witherow, professor of Magee College, writing later, recalled his family's first and rather mysterious meeting with a youth, later identified as John MacCloskey (David O'Kane, 1983).
>
> Thomas Witherow has imprinted his name on the history of our denomination (Sidlow McFarland, 1985).
>
> Thomas Witherow was one of the most remarkable ministers of the Irish Presbyterian Church in the nineteenth century (Douglas Armstrong, 1985).

Many years ago, and for reasons which the memory now renders indistinct, I had the pleasure of attending a function in Maghera Presbyterian Church. It was a fine summer evening, and, following the main event, I found myself exploring the building, its annexes and surrounding graveyard. My companion, who felt justifiably proud of 'his' meeting-house, ushered me from room to room and, like any good guide, kept up an informed commentary. As we entered the Session Room, my attention was immediately gripped by a gallery of former clergy - each portrait clearly labelled and dated. Here was history coming alive! For the very first time, I was coming face to face with people like Glendy, Witherow and Dickey, not to mention those of more recent times, such as Marshall and Haire. I was impressed by the number of these gentlemen who had reached the highest academic office in their denomination, becoming professors, or who had otherwise excelled themselves. Maghera Presbyterian Church had surely a proud pedigree! I mention this incident, not only because it was the first time that I became aware of Thomas Witherow, but also because it heightened my appreciation of the importance of preserving old documents and old photographs. In more recent times I have 'copied' from my Maghera friends and now Draperstown Presbyterian Church has photographs of all its former incumbents.

In 1980 Ballinascreen Historical Society was formed and every year since then it has produced at least one publication. There has been a wide variety of topics. In the first year a collection of local poetry quickly became a best-seller. This was followed by an edited version of the Ordnance Survey Memoir for the parish of Ballinascreen. In 1982 'The Meetin' House', my own history of the Presbyterian congregation in Draperstown, was printed and the fourth item to reach the bookshops was a transcription (1983) of John MacCloskey's 'Statistical Reports' of six Derry parishes (1821). The editor, (now Rev) David O'Kane, quoted Witherow in his introduction to that book and this made me aware of the relevant microfilm in the Public Record Office. At that time I thought that Mic 161 would be worth further perusal, but other projects came along and they, of course, got preference.

The MacCloskey book was well received and enthusiastically reviewed, not only on my own side of the mountain (Ballinascreen, Kilcronaghan and Desertmartin), but also in the more northern parishes of Dungiven, Banagher and Boveva. The Sperrin range which isolates the southern part of the county can be more than a physical barrier. To some extent, it maintains a mutual ignorance of the topography, history and traditions of neighbouring parishes. As a result of reading MacCloskey's report for the North-West Farming Society, I became more enlightened and my numerous sales-trips 'over the hill' made me realise that Banagher wasn't really far away.

To try to maintain some chronological order, I must mention that around 1983-84 my occasional meetings with Rev Sidlow McFarland led me to believe that he was industriously gathering material for what I thought would be a history of Maghera Presbyterian Church. In 1985 'Presbyterianism in Maghera' was published and it certainly was much more than a mere congregational history. Richly illustrated, and written with great style, it was a wide-ranging social history of Maghera and district over three centuries. Each chapter was carefully researched and concluded with a list of footnotes. Witherow was often quoted and his "unpublished autobiography" frequently appeared in the references. The document which was in typescript in the Presbyterian Historical Society would have to be seen - urgently!

Around about the same time, by a strange co-incidence, Rev Douglas Armstrong of Greenisland had written a booklet entitled 'The Life and Work of the Rev Prof Thomas Witherow LLD, DD, of Maghera and Magee College, Derry, 1824-1890'. This booklet was published by the Presbyterian Historical Society and so, when I next visited Church House in Belfast, I was able to buy multiple copies of this new item and also inspect their typescript. Scanning through the 'Autobiography' for the first time really aroused my interest. Here were details of Witherow's growing up and being educated in the next parish, of twenty years being spent in Maghera, including Famine and Revival times, and of his lecturing in the newly-opened Magee College. I thought that this record of a long and distinguished life, spent entirely in this county, would be of great interest to the general reader a century after it had been written.

On another day, while checking cross-references on the index cards in the Presbyterian Historical Society, I was led to look up various issues of 'The Irish Presbyterian' from 1936 to 1938. I found, with somewhat mixed feelings, that the 'Autobiography' had already gone into print. Further detailed checking, however, revealed that these monthly journals contained only extracts from the original work and I was heartened to realise that, half a century earlier, the Rev D B Knox had received the same inspiration as myself.

Ballinascreen Historical Society has a committee which takes decisions regarding future meetings, activities and publications. My colleagues warmly supported me when, in 1988, I suggested that the Society should purchase a complete photocopy of the original 'Autobiography' from the Public Record Office in Belfast. Considering my usual impatience in these affairs, I was pleased that it was not many days before a large heavy envelope filled with countless glossy photocopied pages arrived in Owenreagh. It was a thrill to see this complete life-story written in Witherow's own hand. I could mentally picture every scene as I turned the pages and noticed his changes of pen or where he doodled in the margins! I didn't even pause to consider who would publish, when or by what means. I just felt it would have to be done and so transcription started immediately. For an hour or two most weeks I would copy out every detail and after about nine months the job was complete. The committee were again consulted and, without hesitation, agreed that "Witherow" would be the 1990 publication from the Society.

It is always good to mark anniversaries. In 1990 the Presbyterian Church in Ireland commemorates the 150th anniversary of the General Assembly. Witherow, who was Moderator of that Assembly in 1878, would, I feel, have been proud to be associated with such a celebration. More important, though, is the fact that Thomas Witherow died on 25 January 1890; so what better way to mark the centenary of his death than by, first, the re-printing of his earliest work and, then, the publication of his 'Autobiography'? As 1989 came to a close, it had become obvious to Eull Dunlop, who had been helping to edit the manuscript, and myself that we could not possibly have the 'Autobiography' ready for January 1990, as orginally intended. Consequently, our efforts were hastily turned to Witherow's first publication. On 3 January 1855 Witherow had delivered a lecture in Maghera, outlining the lives of three very significant churchmen with South Derry connections: Adam Clarke, Alexander Carson and Henry Cooke. Soon thereafter he was encouraged to publish the text of that lecture as 'Three Prophets of our Own'. A second edition was printed in 1880, but copies of either edition are not easily obtainable, except in a few library collections. Eull and I therefore decided to publish, under our own auspices, a facsimile edition with introduction and illustrations and to launch it in January 1990 to mark the centenary of the author's death. On Tuesday, 2 January 1990, in Draperstown, Rev Principal Finlay Holmes addressed the Ballinascreen Historical Society on the subject of the 'Three Prophets', the book was launched and the centenary of Thomas Witherow's death was fittingly commemorated.

Acknowledgements

My co-editor, Eull Dunlop, Ballymena, is deserving of the highest possible praise. From the outset, he encouraged, enthused and generally assisted me in every way. He scrutinised my original transcription and spent countless hours amending the punctuation and lay-out, so that this final version would conform with modern conventions. His experience of book production was invaluable when it came to the arranging of photographs, reading of proofs and final design. From the commencement of the project, he was involved at every possible stage and numerous trips were made, in both directions, across the Bann. I offer him sincere thanks for his advice and practical support. Throughout the summer of 1989 Jennifer Johnston also spared no effort, to take photographs to illustrate this book. Many journeys had to be made, sometimes to the most unusual of places, and very often, if the light was not right, a return trip was necessary. Hundreds of miles were covered and Jennifer deserves all the credit for bringing this text to life.

I would like to thank the Right Rev Principal R F G Holmes, whose support for the 'Three Prophets' has already been recorded, for contributing the present Foreword. We congratulate the Magee Professor of Church History on his election as Moderator of the historic Assembly of 1990. Another Ballymena man, the historian of the Magee Colleges, whose roots lie further north in Kilraughts, Principal Holmes has a natural interest in any colleague of Professor Richard Smyth of Ganaby. Mr Rowan Witherow Hamilton, representing the family, very kindly offered further words of commendation on the work of his great-grandfather. The Rev John Brown has very graciously provided us with a lengthy, detailed and scholarly commentary on Witherow's personality, career and contribution to nineteenth-century Presbyterianism. A third (and, indeed, Third) Ballymena man, this former minister of Draperstown, and then Lecturer in History at Magee and later at the New University of Ulster, Coleraine, is offered our sincere thanks for his distinctive contribution. The Rev Sidlow McFarland, now of Carrickfergus, the historian of Maghera Presbyterianism who favourably reviewed 'Three Prophets', forwarded material on Witherow which had been gathered by the late Eoin Walsh, that lifelong student of famous Maghera men. Some of that material has been appended. Mr Robert Bonar of the Presbyterian Historical Society has also been most helpful.

The support and encouragement of my colleagues on the committee of Ballinascreen Historical Society and the financial support of the Magherafelt Arts Advisory Committee must be acknowledged. Both Mrs Muriel Barr, 4 Inishowen Park, Ballymena, who did the typesetting (and, she says, enjoyed getting to know Witherow), and Coleraine Printing Company are to be congratulated on the fruit of their efforts. It was the late Col M Witherow who originally allowed PRONI to microfilm the 'Autobiography' and the Deputy Keeper of the Records, Northern Ireland, who granted us permission to use Mic 161. To the many others who lent photographs, offered advice or helped with this project in various ways I offer thanks. A particular word of gratitude goes to the lady who, at an advanced stage of preparation, suddenly and generously made available much new material which requires intensive analysis on another occasion. I sincerely hope that the reader will get as much pleasure from perusal of this book as I have got from its preparation. Finally, I take the personal liberty of dedicating this volume to the memory of my father, Sam Mawhinney (1909-1989).

Owenreagh, Draperstown, 1990 Graham Mawhinney

This likeness of Witherow hangs in Maghera meeting house

The Witherow homestead at Aughlish, Dungiven

Stevenson's of Knockan, Feeny

(1) Boyhood

My grandfather, James Witherow, was born, I often heard him say when I was a lad, in the year (1759) that Thurot landed at Carrickfergus. He held a small farm at the foot of the mountains in Aughlish, four miles south of Dungiven, in the County Londonderry. He married Jane Chambers, one of the three daughters of Hugh Chambers of Upperland whose tombstone is still to be seen in the old churchyard at Maghera. They had four sons and three daughters. In early life James met with an accident when dressing timber; the axe glanced from the wood and struck him on the leg. Though the wound healed and he lived to be an old man, he was rendered practically useless for life.

My father, Hugh Witherow, born, as nearly as I could make out, about 1787, was the eldest son and was only thirteen when my grandfather was disabled, and, from that time, the care of the farm and the household fell on him and his mother. He held the plough the very first spring after the accident. Instead of contending with his brothers and sisters, as to what portion of duty should fall on the one and what should fall on the other, Hugh early made up his mind to attend to everything about the farm, as if he alone was responsible, let the others do as they might. He laboured very industriously and saw most of his brothers and sisters married or settled, before he himself took a wife. One day Thomas, my grandfather's second son, who afterwards emigrated to America and died at New Orleans, came home from playing in the glen at Cushcappul, a romantic spot about a mile from my grandfather's house, saying that he had met a very nice lad of thirteen or fourteen years of age, who had come from Belfast and who appeared to have no home and no friends, and that he admired him very much. My grandmother told him to bring him home, that she might see him. This was done and the young stranger soon became a favourite with all. His name was John MacCloskey, about the same age as my father and well educated for his years. He became an inmate of their dwelling and lived for several years as one of the family.

Aughlish was at the time badly off for education. My grandfather got up a school for him in an old kiln upon the farm, and, as some of the pupils were as old as the Master, my grandfather attended once a day, to administer corporal punishment to any who proved disobedient or refractory. My grandmother had charge of his purse and any fees the young schoolmaster received were brought home and deposited in her kindly hands. At a little later stage he continued to pick up some knowledge of Latin and Greek from a classical teacher who lived a little farther down the country; and, at last, through the influence of my grandmother, he was accepted as a tutor in the family of Mr Stevenson of Knockan. When Mr MacCloskey was able to save a little money, he went for a year to the Belfast Institution and, for more than forty years afterwards, he conducted a

John MacCloskey's old school at Tirgarvil

Statistical Report

of the Parishes of

Ballinascreen, Kilcronaghan, Desertmartin, Banagher, Dungiven and Boveva

in the

County of

Londonderry

by

John Mac Closkey

1821

Edited by David O'Kane

Ballinascreen Historical Society
1983

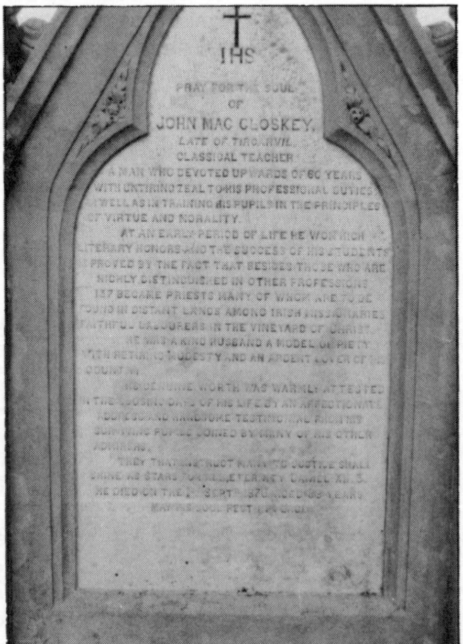

classical school at Tirgarvil, near Maghera, where he educated many young men for the Presbyterian ministry or the Roman Catholic priesthood. Mr MacCloskey was a most intelligent man of high moral character. His conversation and example were useful to my father and impressed him with the great importance and value of education. The ideas received from him probably suggested to my father the project of obtaining for me a classical training.

In those early years, when brothers and sisters were springing up to maturity, the family must have had difficulties enough. But, when my father was still a young man, a mountain of rough land comprising nearly two thousand acres adjacent to his own farm fell vacant and he, taking courage, ventured to rent it and to stock it with Scotch sheep. A ten-pound note given him by his mother's sister, Mrs Wilson of Agivey, was the beginning of his fortune. From that day and hour he prospered. When my grandfather divided the thirty-acre arable farm between Hugh and his third brother, James, it seemed to be little better than poverty for both. But Finglen, to which additions were subsequently made, compensated for all. It grazed five hundred sheep and a large stock of cattle. From that time my father was more of a grazier than a farmer. He attended the neighbouring fairs and markets and easily made as much profit as kept his family in comfort. His farm for years after did little more than supply the wants of the household.

Tamlaghtard Parish Church (Aghanloo), burial-place of the Martin family

Then and now: the Martin homestead at Ballycastle, near Limavady

Drumachose Presbyterian Church,
Limavady

Kindred buried at
Tamlaghtard churchyard

On 22 May 1823 my father was married to my mother, Elizabeth Martin, the elder daughter of Thomas Martin of Ballycastle, in the parish of Aghanloo, three miles north of Newtown-Limavady. The minister who officiated was the Rev Richard Dill, who had lately resigned the charge of Drumachose, the congregation in which my mother's family belonged, and was about to remove to Ballykelly. Four children were the issue of their marriage, but only two, my brother Robert and myself, survived into manhood. I was the eldest of their children, being born on 29 May 1824, at Ballycastle, the residence of my mother's father. It seems that, as she felt that the hour of her sorrow was near, my mother went to her father's, that she might have the help and comfort of her own mother in her trial. My grandmother, Mrs Martin, did not long survive; and probably it was owing to her own declining strength that she did not go to Banagher, but sent for her daughter to come to her. My grandmother had been an Episcopalian prior to her marriage and the Episcopal clergyman of the place called occasionally to see her. He called one day, soon after I was born, and before my mother had returned to Aughlish. The old lady took advantage of the occasion and had me baptised then and there a member of the Protestant Established Church of Ireland. How my father liked it, I never heard, but the thing was done without his knowledge, and by a lady with whom he could not afford to be angry, so there was nothing for it, but submission and silence.

Cruckenroe school, before recent renovation

The new bridge at Aughlish

Ralliagh school (right) today

Though I remember various little incidents of my childhood, I know of none worthy of record till I was six years of age. It must have been in the spring of 1830 that I was sent to school at Cruckenroe, about a mile or more distant from home. My father would often carry me on his shoulders over the new bridge at Aughlish and encourage me to learn. The teacher at Cruckenroe was one Henry Maclosky, the youngest son of Harry Hamish, a man who had great celebrity in his day as a pugilist. It was in the school taught by his son that I learned to read. Owing to the teaching of home, I had learned to spell words of two syllables before going to school. Manson was the school-book used. According to my recollection of it, a recollection not refreshed for nearly sixty years, the first part of the book consists of spelling-columns, commencing with words of one syllable and ending with words of six or seven. The second portion consists of reading lessons, arranged also on a progressive system, from the easy to the more difficult. By the directions of the teacher, I took the book in order, so that I could spell long words like "unrighteousness", and pronounce them too, before I was asked to attempt any reading at all. When I had finished the spelling portion and commenced the other, I read so fast the opening sentences ("All's well that ends well"; "the best may mend"; "look before you leap") that the Master had to restrain me and compel me to take time.

Mr Maclosky took ill towards the end of the summer and, after lingering a few months, eventually died. I attended his funeral, my father leading me by the hand. Two chairs were brought from the house and deposited on the street before the door. The coffin was then carried out and laid upon the chairs. Six women, three standing on each side of the coffin, raised loud lamentation and prolonged a monotonous howl, for fully fifteen minutes, over the ashes of the dead. I was frightened very much, but eventually the noise stopped as suddenly as it had begun. The coffin was then taken up and conveyed to the last long home. This was the Irish "caoine". It was the only instance of the kind at which I was ever present.

Early in the summer of 1831, my mother took me down to Ralliagh Church School and put me in the charge of the teacher, one William Ross, instructing him to flog me well, for she knew "I was in need of it". This part of the instruction, to do him justice, he did not neglect. He often administered discipline in a sharp and, as I thought, somewhat capricious style. His mode of teaching was peculiar. He seldom or never gave any explanation. So much Dictionary or so much Grammar was prescribed and, if this portion was not repeated correctly from memory, the birch was called in to supply the want. Nevertheless, I picked up a very considerable knowledge of Geography and English Grammar. Of Arithmetic I never knew anything, except what I learned in that school. The penmanship that I acquired was very bad.

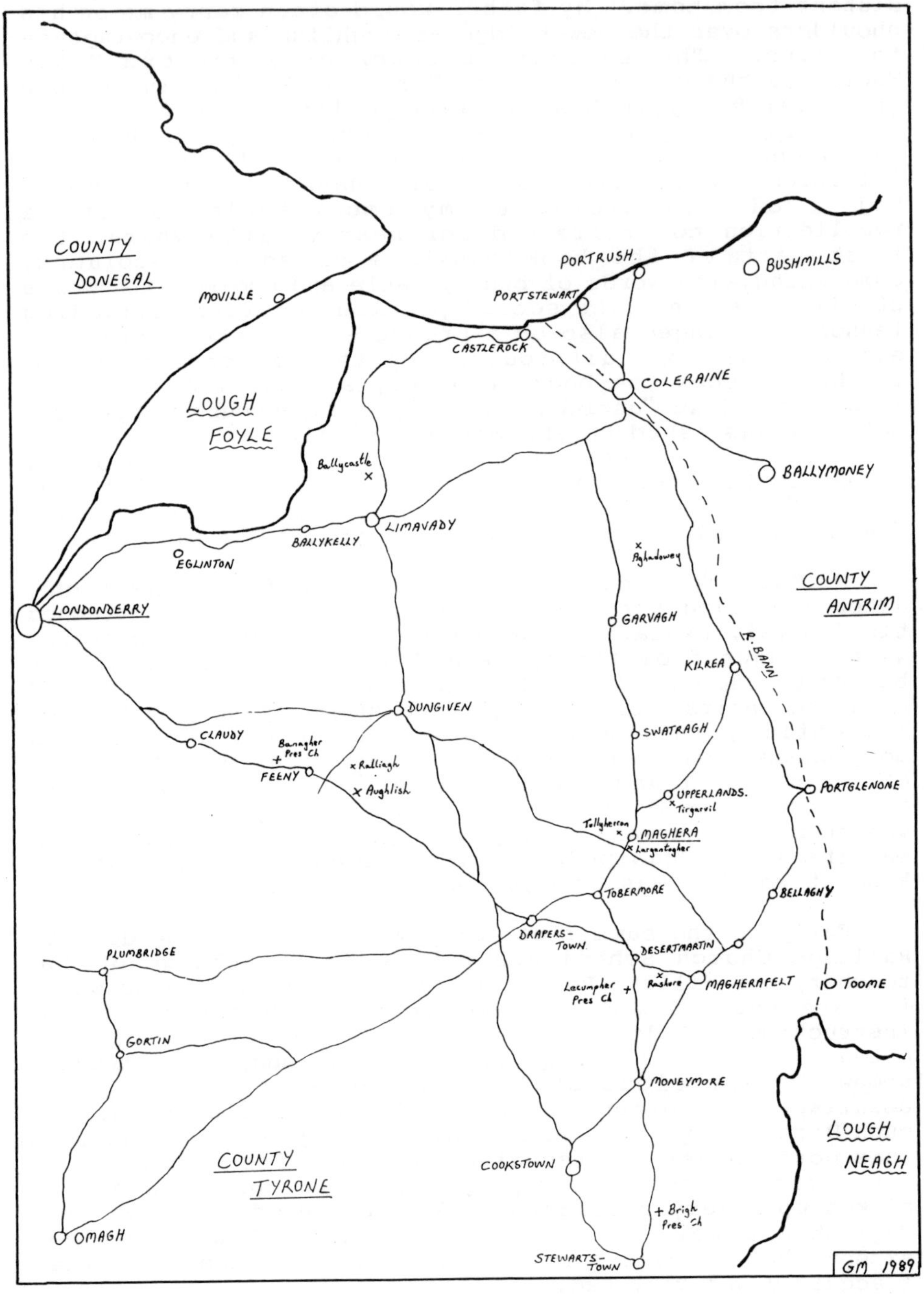
COUNTY DONEGAL
MOVILLE
LOUGH FOYLE
PORTRUSH
BUSHMILLS
PORTSTEWART
CASTLEROCK
COLERAINE
Ballycastle
BALLYMONEY
LIMAVADY
BALLYKELLY
EGLINTON
Aghadowey
COUNTY ANTRIM
LONDONDERRY
GARVAGH
R. BANN
KILREA
DUNGIVEN
CLAUDY
Banagher Pres Ch
Ralliagh
FEENY
Aughlish
SWATRAGH
UPPERLANDS.
Tirgarvil
PORTGLENONE
Tullyheran
MAGHERA
Largantogher
TOBERMORE
BELLAGHY
DRAPERS-TOWN
PLUMBRIDGE
DESERTMARTIN
Rashere
MAGHERAFELT
TOOME
Lecumpher Pres Ch
GORTIN
MONEYMORE
LOUGH NEAGH
COUNTY TYRONE
COOKSTOWN
Brigh Pres Ch
OMAGH
STEWARTS-TOWN
GM 1989

What I did learn thoroughly was to spell and the attainment was of great advantage to me ever after. The last school lesson of the day was Orthography. The whole school stood up in line. The Master went round and compelled each candidate to deposit a pin on the book. He then selected the most difficult words in the lesson and, as any person spelled correctly, he removed to a place above all who had missed that word. After the lesson was exhausted, four difficult words were chosen, from any part of the dictionary at the Master's pleasure, and then came the trial of strength. Whoever was at the head of the class, when the ordeal was passed through, was said to "lift the pins". The Master divided the pins, giving about one half to the head boy and giving the remainder, half and half, to the second and third. At first I had no pins. The Master was obliged himself to stake one in my name and I was for days or weeks at the foot of the class. Often I gave expression to my inability to make way against such formidable opposition, but my father always encouraged me to persevere and said that I would one day put them all down. So it came to pass. For more than a year before I left the school, I stood at the head of the spelling-class and no old soldier, coming home from the war with the medals on his breast, attesting his prowess, could be prouder than I was of the row of pins that adorned the sleeve of my jacket. The pleasant result was that never afterwards did I run any risk of a mistake in the spelling of any ordinary English word.

Newspapers sixty years ago were so expensive, each costing five pence or six pence a copy, that they were not often taken in by farmers in remote parts of the country. In those days (1830-1834), I never saw any, except when Mr John MacCloskey sent one from Maghera, or when my father, returning from the Derry market, brought with him a 'Journal' or 'Sentinel' that he bought at the office. The earliest events that I remember to hear read from the newspaper, for I can scarcely think that I was then able to read the narrative for myself, were the wreck of the emigrant ship, the 'Lady Sherbrooke', on the coast of Newfoundland, and the Coronation of King William IV. But I remember distinctly seeing cars taking voters to the county election after the passing of the Reform Bill. Sir John Byng, in the Liberal interest, endeavoured to unseat the Tory member, Sir Robert Bateson. The forty-shilling freeholders alone had the right to vote. From the most extreme point of the county, all the voters had to come to Derry to poll. The election lasted for a fortnight. During that time the public houses were kept open for the voters to eat and drink at the expense of the candidates. When the successful candidate was declared, the victor drove in triumph down the street, showering handfuls of small silver among the mob. As might be expected by those who know the constituency, the Conservative was returned and no Liberal tried the county again, until Mr Samuel McCurdy Greer came forward on Tenant Right principles in 1852.

Tyrglasson school, where Robert Thompson taught

BANAGHER PRESBYTERIAN CHURCH Dallas, Garvagh and Kilrea

Though access to the newspaper was rare, I was not left in my boyhood without other means of instruction. Through the friendship of my father with Mr Robert Thomson, the teacher of Tyrglasson school, maintained by the Fishmongers' Company of London, some four miles away on the other side of the parish, I had access to the excellent little library provided for the scholars by the kindness of the Company. I read everything attractive that I could find there, in addition to any books in our own house. My father and mother were both fond of reading and often borrowed from their friends. I cannot now recount all the books which I had devoured, so to speak, while I was under ten, but I remember distinctly to have read, before I went to Classics, the 'Seven Champions of Christendom', 'Valentine and Orson', 'Prince Lee Boo', the 'Voyages of Christopher Columbus', Cook's and Anson's 'Voyages', 'Robinson Crusoe', 'Pilgrim's Progress', McSparran's 'Irish Legend or Story of Dunluce', 'Roderick Random', 'Peregrine Pickle', Miss Edgeworth's 'Patronage' and 'Don Quixote'. To these I must add the 'Fool of Quality', known to me then in John Wesley's edition as the 'History of Henry, Earl of Moreland', which was a special favourite of mine.

My religious training, I regret to say, was not much attended to in those days. There was no Sabbath school at that time in that part of the country. The Presbyterian population is thin, and, even for secular knowledge, it had to depend on Roman Catholic or Episcopalian schools. I was taught indeed to repeat the Lord's Prayer, the 23rd Psalm and the 'Mother's Catechism', often printed at the end of the 'Shorter'. Occasionally I read a chapter at home and a chapter in the school at Ralliagh, but this was a measure of my religious knowledge at this time. The want of being well drilled in the 'Shorter Catechism' was a great loss to me during all my College days and it was not supplied till long after, when I was well advanced in my theological studies.

The simple childish faith of those times strikes me now as something wonderful. Having read in the Bible about Elisha drying up the waters of Jordan, by smiting them with the mantle of Elijah, I remember taking off my jacket and smiting a little stream on the way to school, in hope that I could walk through the middle of it, without wetting my feet. But it suprised me not a little to find that, in spite of my command and adjuration, the brook babbled on as before. That I was seriously disappointed at the time there can be no doubt; but, on a little reflection, I accounted for the mishap by remembering that, after all, I was not Elisha and that the jacket of a schoolboy was not the mantle of a prophet.

(2) The Classical School: 1834

At ten years of age, I had received all that Ralliagh could do for me and my father had made up his mind to send

Killeag (above) and Bryce's home at Ballyclough

me to a classical school. But where, was the question. Mr MacCloskey offered most kindly to do his part gratis, should I be put under his care at Maghera. My father, however, determined to put me under the instruction of the Rev James Bryce of Killeag. He was determined in his choice by the fact that his sister, Nancy, was married to Alexander Baird of Ballynacally, a member of Mr Bryce's congregation, with whom I could lodge.

On Monday, 16 June 1834, I made my first appearance before Mr Bryce at his residence at Ballyclough and received my first lesson in the Latin Grammar. There were, on an average, some twelve or fourteen pupils in attendance, of whom two were his youngest sons, William and Archibald Hamilton Bryce, both apparently two or three years older than myself. I remained there four years in all, and, during that time, read two books of Ovid , two of Caesar , the 'Eclogues' and six books of the 'Aeneid' of Virgil and all Horace, except the 'Epodes'. In Greek I read the 'Gospel of John', eight books of the 'Iliad' of Homer, two books of the 'Cyropaedia' of Xenophon and some few 'Dialogues' of Lucian. These, I think, are all. Mr Bryce was a painstaking and careful teacher, taking us over the grammar of both languages again and again and drilling us in the minute points of the language; but he did not ask the pupils to do exercises or to make any attempt to translate English into Greek or Latin. Nor did he undertake to teach Mathematics or the rudiments of Science. It was not till long after, that I discovered the loss I sustained by not being required to carry on the two departments of study together.

Mr Bryce, under whom I received my classical training, had a history of his own. He was a native of Airdrie and had acted as a minister at Caithness in the Antiburgher section of Seceders, before leaving Scotland. Tradition said that he had been up before his Synod for broaching some eccentric opinions on the subject of marriage and that the censure, expressed or implied, hurt his feelings and led him to resign his congregation. However this may be, he and his family came to Ireland in 1802, and he was chosen minister of the Antiburgher congregation of Killeag, five miles south-west of Coleraine, on the outskirts of the parish of Aghadoey. A misunderstanding with his brother ministers in regard to Regium Donum, fully explained in a 'Narrative' which he published in 1816 and which is now a very rare pamphlet, led to his withdrawal from the Synod and his proclaiming himself a Voluntary out and out. Perhaps the first representative of the principle that it is a sin for a Christian minister to receive money from the State, as payment for the discharge of any religious service, who had yet appeared in Ireland? He not only retained his congregation, after being suspended by the Synod, but sent supplies of preaching to sections of dissatisfied people, until he was able first to educate and then to ordain ministers for them.

Mr Bryce was the founder of what is called the United Presbyterian Presbytery. He lived for fifty years after separating from the Synod and, although all that time the minister of a congregation who did not pay him very liberally,* he never touched a farthing of Regium Donum to the last hour of his life. A small income of about thirty pounds a year was supplemented by the fees of his pupils. He held a farm for the convenience of the household, but, as he took nothing to do with its management; it probably was not a source of any emolument. Yet he reared and educated a large family, who made their way in the world very well. His eldest son, Dr Reuben Bryce, was Principal of the Belfast Academy; another of his sons, James Bryce, was Mathematical Master in the High School of Glasgow; my school-fellows, William and Archibald, became the former a medical gentleman in good practice at Dalkeith and the latter a learned classical author and teacher in Edinburgh. James Bryce MP, author of 'The Holy Roman Empire', is the grandson and namesake of my old teacher at Ballyclough.

Mr Bryce was a little eccentric in some of his opinions, for he followed no master and thought on every subject for himself, but he was a good man, sincere and upright, honest and true. He treated his pupils very kindly and my connection with him as my teacher was in every way pleasant and profitable. Among the pupils who attended Mr Bryce, I need only name my dear friend, David Hanson, who in after years was minister successively at Drumkeen, Fahan and York Street, Belfast; John Wilson, afterwards minister at Killymurris; Joseph Caskey, who joined the Church of Scotland and was settled in the Orkney Islands; John Gilmour, who emigrated to Australia; Samuel Fulton, who emigrated to the United States; John Law, who became a minister at Richibudo in Canada; Andrew Law, who died when only a theological student and is buried at Ballywillan; Alexander Kennedy, who became an MD; James Clark, who married Mr Bryce's youngest daughter; and John Leslie and Charles Brewster, of whose subsequent careers I know nothing. My intercourse with these young men in school and out of school was very pleasant and I regard the time I spent in their society as among the happiest of my life.

Aunt and Uncle Baird, with their family of two sons and two daughters, were very kind to me, but they were scarcely so well off, in a worldly point of view, as my father and mother, and I was not surrounded with the rough plenty to which I was accustomed at Banagher. But the surroundings amid which I found myself placed were entirely new. In Aughlish I lived in what was virtually a Roman Catholic neighbourhood and was environed with Roman Catholic notions all around me. Here I was in the centre of a Presbyterian population, most of them weavers,

---

*See my article on Mr Bryce, in 'Evangelical Witness', 1864, p 152.

bleachers and artisans. Aghadoey had originally been settled by a Scotch immigration and I found that my new neighbours spoke as pure Scotch as a man might hear in any part of Ayrshire. The people were industrious, their houses cleanly and orderly and themselves more civilized. But, outside the routine of daily work, they had nothing to engage their attention, so as to expand the intellect, except the Bible and the instruction given from the pulpit. They were religiously intelligent, but not so on any other subject. I never saw a newspaper during my residence in Ballynacally, except one copy of the 'Derry Standard', a new paper recently started in the county town. Of course it is not so now, in these days of penny papers, but I speak of a period more than fifty years ago. Books also were rare. During these four years I do not remember to have read anything outside the daily lessons, except Goldsmith's 'Histories of Greece and Rome', Ramsay's 'Gentle Shepherd', 'Ringan Gilhaize', 'Ivanhoe' and 'Don Juan'. How these came into my hands I do not now remember, but that I read them at this time is certain. Mr Bryce had a collection of perhaps two or three hundred volumes and would have lent me some of them if I had asked him, but I was shy and did not take the liberty.

In February 1837 I took a sharp attack of typhus fever, which interrupted my studies and brought me almost to the point of death. I was attended on the occasion by Dr Fullerton, then stationed at Garvagh, who afterwards emigrated to New South Wales, and who some years ago bequeathed £2,000 to found the Fullerton Scholarships for the sons and grandsons of ministers in Magee College. Through the divine blessing on the means used, I recovered; but, when I was able to stand, I was removed to my father's and spent that summer in Aughlish. The sensations of returning health are delicious and I felt it a pleasure all that summer to run about and to do any little work I could do on the farm. I think I would then have even renounced my studies and consented to devote myself entirely to agricultural operations; but, fortunately for me, my father would not hear of it, and, at the end of the season, I was sent back to Mr Bryce.

I mentioned that, when I left Ralliagh to go to the classical school, I was a very poor penman. At a point earlier than that which I have now reached in my narrative, the defect was remedied. In December 1834 I returned from Aghadoey to Banagher, for a brief Christmas holiday. A gentleman employed on the Ordnance Survey was lodging for a month or two in my father's, and, observing the wretched scrawl I wrote, he volunteered to teach me to write a good hand after twelve lessons. He set to work and succeeded; and I wrote a fair hand ever after.

Four years at Classics, before going to College, may seem a long time to young men who now pass on to matriculation without passing half that time in preparation. But the truth is that I never gave half my

The Quay Londonderry

GLASGOW STEAMER IN HARBOUR, PORTRUSH Nº1.

strength to study, not feeling the importance of it. The summer afternoons were given to play; the winter nights were not turned to account for want of light, not being available in the ordinary farmhouse, except what was afforded from the blaze of the kitchen fire. To handle lexicon and textbook under such circumstances was difficult. The only time that I gave to study was the time spent in the schoolroom under the eye of the teacher, and, as this was five hours daily, for five days in the week, I was able to get over a good amount of ground. Early in the spring of 1838 I began to think that I should go to College at November, as the Laws and others had done the preceding year, who were not, as I knew, as far advanced as I was. Someone suggested that the Rev John Brown, then minister of Aghadoey, ought to be consulted on the subject, as one competent to give good advice. David Hanson and I reached Droghead one morning in summer, before the Doctor (for soon after he was made Doctor in Divinity and I may give him the title from the first) had come downstairs. We were told that, except we found him before he went forth upon his daily pastoral rounds, our journey would be in vain.

The Doctor received his two young visitors most kindly. He compelled us to sit down and take a second breakfast. He inquired minutely into our family connexions, our ages, our time at school, the books we had read and what we proposed to do. We told him that we proposed to go to College at November, if he thought we were fit for going. He then examined us minutely, both in Latin and Greek, and said at the close that we had satisfied him that we had not idled our time, but that we were both young and could enter College with more advantage to ourselves a little later. His advice upon the whole was that we should go for at least a year to a public school and carry forward our knowledge to a higher point before entering the university. This was most excellent advice, and, when it became known to our fathers, both of them determined to act upon it. It was this that decided us to go for a year to Belfast, before presenting ourselves at the Entrance Examinations. Ever after I felt grateful to Dr Brown, for his kind reception of two young country lads and for the good advice he gave us, the very best in our circumstances which could have been given.

I was the more ready to act on the Doctor's opinion, because I was now thoroughly cured of my wish to go to sea. From reading the glowing account of the voyages of Columbus, Cook and Anson, I had early cherished a boyish fancy for being a sailor. In September 1837, when I was at home after recovering from my attack of fever, my father was taking over some cattle to the Glasgow market and I insisted on going with him. We sailed from Derry in a steamer, as steerage passengers, and all went well till we passed out of the lough into the channel. A strong gale was blowing, which made the vessel heave tremendously and in a very short time I was the victim of 'mal de mer'. As the vessel passed Portrush, I would have given a heavy

Banagher
Presbyterian Church

ANNALS

OF

MY LIFE, LABOURS, AND TRAVELS

BY

REV. JONATHAN SIMPSON, J.P.,

PORTRUSH

purse, if I had had it, to be one of those happy people whom I saw walking on the hill and beholding our misfortune. Had the vessel called at the pier, she would have left, I feel convinced, with one passenger fewer than had come in her from Derry. But she did not call and I had to submit to my fate. The horror of that night in the steerage, myself sick and everyone sick about me, except my father, I can never forget. After disposing of his cattle in Glasgow, we returned home by the same route and got better weather than on the passage outward. This little experience was useful to me. From that hour to this, I never dreamt of being a sailor. Seldom have I crossed the channel since, even in the calmest weather, without being sick.

My Uncle Baird was a member of Mr Bryce's congregation and, of course, I attended with him and his family at Killeag. The floor was earthen; stones and sods were placed in the pews for hassocks; and the general fitting-up was far inferior to that of our church in Banagher, which was a fine edifice, built for the use of the congregation by the Fishmongers' Company. Mr Bryce was a plain, instructive preacher, brimful of information, which he used to edify the congregation in a lecture in the morning and a sermon in the afternoon of every Sabbath during the summer months of the year. Plain as he was in his address, I scarcely understood a word; it was only in the last year of my attendance that I began to follow the preacher with any intelligence. There was no congregational Sabbath school, so far as I can remember, but, if there was, I did not attend. The historical parts of the Old Testament I read through for my own entertainment. The 'Catechism on the Government and Discipline of the Presbyterian Church' was put into circulation by Dr Brown in his congregation and I got a copy; but, although it seems to me now so clear and so easy to be understood, I did not then comprehend a word of it. How I puzzled over the question, What kind of officers were Timothy and Titus? My notion of an officer was one who possessed military or naval rank, and I could never imagine Timothy to be the captain of a ship or Titus as a colonel in a marching regiment. I remember Mr Simpson, now the worthy minister of Portrush, then a theological student, coming round and reading to the assembled villagers the 55th chapter of Isaiah and offering prayer. Some person put into my hand Dr Brown's 'Sermon on the Reformation'. I read it over carefully, and, as I read, turned up in the Bible all the texts referred to in the sermon.

During this interesting period of life, I am not aware that any other religious book fell into my hands; and, at the close of my residence in Aghadoey, I was still dark as to the glory of the Gospel salvation, not through any fault of the venerable pastor whom I heard on Sabbath, but because I was so far destitute of the spiritual faculty necessary to discern spiritual things.

The Hillhead, where Witherow boarded the coach for Belfast

The Old Bridge and High Street, Belfast

(3) The First Year in Belfast: 1838-39

Belfast fifty years ago was a very different town from what it is now. The population then was about 70,000. The town ended at the head of Donegall Street and on the south side of the Linen Hall there was little but green fields. A long, old, ugly, stone bridge united the town with Ballymacarret. An unsavoury dock from the river ran up High Street, to the point where the Albert Memorial now stands. No cars plied for hire on the street. No railway line came to the town. The ordinary way of approaching the place from a distance was by stage-coach; and, when the coach drew up on the street, it was beset by a crowd of hungry porters, who seized upon the stranger's luggage and carried it off, sometimes in opposite directions. When the stranger following in the wake of the porter reached his destination, it was no easy matter to satisfy the rapacity of the man who rendered this piece of service. Now a man and his luggage are both carried to any part of the town for half the sum which in those days a porter would have rejected with disdain.

About 11 o'clock on the night of 31 October 1838 my father and I left Aughlish and passed across the mountain. We had but one horse between us and we rode and walked in turn. As might be expected, most of the walking fell to my father, who, though beyond fifty, was still an active man. We passed through Tubbermore and reached the Hillhead, near Castledawson, about five in the morning. There, by concert, I met with my school companion, Mr Savage, who was about to enter College for the first session. Having put me in the charge of Mr Savage, who was some years my senior, and having seen us safely seated on the top of the stage-coach, when it came forward from Magherafelt, my father returned home. About eleven o'clock in the day we were set down in North Street, and, through the intervention of an old schoolfellow at Ballyclough, who had gone to Belfast a year or two before us, we found lodgings at 45 Joy Street, then a street not fully completed and the buildings in which looked fresh and new. That evening or next morning we were joined by David Hanson, who had come to town on the same errand as myself.

The Academy which we purposed to attend occupied a range of old brick buildings, apparently much dilapidated, which ran along the left hand side of Academy Street, as you enter it from Donegall Street. The Principal's house opened into Donegall Street, but the Academy proper was in the rere of the dwelling and was entered by a broad wooden gate, more like that of a store or timber yard than the entrance to a seminary of education. We entered the Classical School, then taught by Dr Bryce in person, and the English School, then under Mr Abraham Hume. We both made the mistake of neglecting the Mathematical School and that too for the same absurd reason that Mathematics were not required for passing the Synod's Entrance Examination.

THE ROYAL BELFAST ACADEMICAL INSTITUTION

(From an old print)

Divinity classes were held here from 1815 till 1853 and during this period the majority of Irish Presbyterian ministers received their training here in both Arts and Theology.

The Divinity lectures were given in the small building to the right (the North Wing) except during the years 1849-53 when the classes were transferred to the main building.

This small building was afterwards popularly known in church circles as the 'Old College,' to distinguish it from the present building in Botanic Avenue. The statue in front of the Institution is that of the Earl of Belfast, the original 'Black Man.'

Reproduced by permission from Robert Allen, 'The Presbyterian College, Belfast, 1853-1953'

I was now out in the world for the first time, far from home without father and mother, uncle or aunt, or any one to speak to, except my two companions, whose knowledge of the world was not much better than my own. I had none outside to whom I could speak, or with whom I could consult. I was a total stranger, under fifteen years of age, mixing with strangers in a strange town. Of all the sports of which boys are fond, I was doubly fond, up till the day I left my father's house; but now I was shut up, day after day, in a close room, and, when I went out on the street, I had to maintain the demeanour and gravity of a gentleman. I grew homesick. I began to count the days to the Christmas holidays. I longed for Ballyclough and Aughlish, and thought I could gladly enter on any kind of work, however mean or laborious, if only permitted to flee from this dreary and lonely wilderness. At the end of a month, this homesickness began to wear away and fortunately did not return.

Dr Bryce did not succeed as a teacher in winning my affection or respect. He was vain, pedantic and imperious in no ordinary degree. I was a rude country lad, uncouth in manners, shy and timid among strangers, but inwardly sensitive, and, I fear, somewhat proud besides. For nearly four years I had been under the training of his father, and regarded at Ballyclough as one of its best pupils, but, from the day I entered the Academy, the aim of the Doctor seemed to be to show me that I knew really nothing at all, and that a lad who had studied only a few months under himself was much my superior. He began with me from the beginning. He kept me for a full week on one sentence of Sallust. When I, or indeed any of my class-fellows, made a blunder, however slight, he had no other terms in which to speak of us than: Well, you are an egregious ass! You have no more brains than a pin-head! I suspected, perhaps wrongly, that his denunciations were showered on us rough country lads and fell very gently on the sons of rich merchants and gentlemen in town; but, although that was my feeling at the time, I am inclined to believe now that this was not the outcome of partiality or respect of persons, but because he was really grieved by our greater ignorance. I would have borne all without complaint, had I really been making progress, but, at the end of the first quarter, I had only read two chapters of Xenophon and about one half the 'Jugurtha' of Sallust. At this rate I foresaw that I could not expect to read the lengthened course of Classics, on which I had to be examined at October. Had my purse or my circumstances enabled me to spend four or five years more at school, I have no doubt Dr Bryce would have made me a fair classic; but unfortunately I was shut up to enter College at next November.

Mr Hume, the English Master, a few years after conformed to the Anglican Church and became one of the clergymen of Liverpool. At the time of which I speak, he had finished his curriculum at Belfast College and was understood to contemplate the Presbyterian ministry. I

Caldwell's house at Rashure, Desertmartin

Mullaghbuoy Hill

profited considerably from his instructions; he taught me to read and pronounce with more accuracy, to express my thoughts in written composition, and to take an interest in works of standard literature. He put into my hand Chambers' small 'History of the English Language and Literature'; and this of itself opened up to me a wide field of reading and thought, from which I have since derived many an hour of delight. I never saw or spoke to Mr Hume after I left his school, but he is certainly one of the teachers to whom I feel myself under deep obligations.

When the Christmas holidays came, I gladly returned to Aughlish. The man who met me at Magherafelt brought me the sad intelligence that my grandmother, my father's mother, was no more and was to be interred the next day. She had been friendly to me; she had given me my first lessons in the alphabet; she had read with me verse about in the New Testament; she had told me the story of the Siege of Derry and of the Battle of the Boyne, over and over again, and favoured me with many a wise and useful advice. She had now passed away at the age of seventy-five or thereabout. It was the first time death had come so near to me. It was with sorrow that I saw her remains deposited in the dust.

At the end of the holidays, on 5 January 1839, I left my father's to return to Belfast to school. This I regret to have to record, for there was no necessity, not the smallest, that I should travel on the Sabbath day. That night I stayed at Mr John Caldwell's residence at Rashure, near Desertmartin. He was an intelligent and good man and a warm friend of my father's, but I am sure he must have been surprised at seeing me come to his house on the Sabbath afternoon. Next morning he woke me at three-o'clock, with the view of having me forward in Magherafelt, in time to catch the five-o'clock coach for Belfast. But he told me that it was a terrific storm, that no coach could travel, and he advised me to keep abed. But I was headstrong, would have my own way and insisted in going in to Magherafelt, which lay at the distance of a mile and a half. We started about four. The storm was terrible and the aged trees that lined the avenue waved fiercely as we passed along. More than once we were blown off the road into the ditch and had to hold on by the thorn bushes. When we came to the hollow of the road, before ascending Mullaghbuoy Hill, we found the road covered with water for a great distance and impassable. To advance was out of the question and to return was the difficulty, for we had now to face the storm. After some time we succeeded, although trees, standing when we passed at first, had been blown down in the interval and now lay across the way. The journey to town had therefore to be postponed till Tuesday; that day, as I passed along on the top of the stage, it was dismal to see the dismantled houses, the broken chimneys, the fallen trees and the desolation produced everywhere by the tempest of 6 January 1839.

While at home during the holidays, I had taken the

Henry Montgomery

and Henry Cooke

The Rev. HENRY MONTGOMERY. LL.D.
1788 - 1865.

THE REV. HENRY COOKE, D.D., LL.D.

The Belfast Institution, behind Henry Cooke, the Black Man

precaution of telling my father what I thought of the Academy and of obtaining his consent for leaving it at the end of the quarter and entering at the Academical Institution. It was not very long till I was afforded what I considered a fair pretext for doing so. In the last week of January the words "No Pope" were chalked one morning on the door of one of the schoolrooms. This was regarded as a very serious offence. All the boys were congregated forthwith in the English School and addressed by the Principal on the enormity of this wickedness. An investigation was instituted, or rather a fishing inquiry was started, with the view of detecting the criminal who was rather slow to respond to the invitation to confess his guilt. The Masters sat in conclave in another apartment and called in the boys, one after another, for private examination. While this was going on, the boys were held together in the English room, doing nothing but looking at each other and forbidden to speak or communicate with each other. One boy was detected in spelling on his fingers to another boy on the opposite side of the room; for this offence he was called up and punished severely. At the close of the day, Dr Bryce came in and said that the culprit had confessed his offence and would be punished accordingly. The culprit's name was not revealed and we did not witness the punishment.

At the close of the day's proceedings, David Hanson discovered that, while the investigation was in progress, some person unknown had cut the tassel off his cap. He complained to the Principal. Next day, when we all assembled at ten, the business of all the Schools was suspended again and another fishing inquiry set on foot, to discover the new transgressor. While the investigation was going forward, and after the boys had sat for hours in silence looking at each other, something amusing caught my attention and I was detected laughing. The usher in charge reported me to Mr Hume at the close of the investigation. I was called up and received four severe strokes of a cane on the hand for doing what I could not help and what I did not understand previously to be any offence. Though it was still two or three days before the end of the quarter, I did not return to the Academy, but went to the Academical Institution the next morning. My departure undoubtedly left the impression that I had gone in consequence of the punishment and the report that Mr Hanson carried of my words spoken in private must have strengthened that impression. But, the fact was, I did not care about the beating; it was only the occasion, not the cause, of my leaving. The true cause felt by Mr Hanson as well as by myself was that we were not getting on in our Classical Reading with the rapidity that we required to advance. But we did not care to say this, for Dr Bryce was the son of our old teacher and we did not wish to cast upon him any blame. Mr Hume was a stranger to us and I thought that his readiness to punish me, without previous reproof or warning, who had never offended before, entitled him to bear the odium. Of course I was wrong in all this, but I

Cooke's meeting house in May Street, Belfast

The Gun of the Gospel: Andrew Todd, Finvoy

am only telling now the motives, whether good or evil, by which I was actuated then.

On the third day after I had entered the Classical School of the Institution, the Head Master (the Rev Hugh Wilson BA) took me aside and said that he had received a letter from Dr Bryce, saying that I was a pupil of his who had left on some slight offence and requesting that I should not be admitted until he would have time to communicate with my father. Mr Wilson added that I should stay at home for a few days, till my father's wishes were known, but that, should he consent, it would afford him pleasure to have me in his School. This caused me much annoyance. I at once called on Dr Bryce and asked him what demands he had on me, and when had my father ever put me under his care? He answered me very cavalierly and said that he had written to my father, describing my disobedience. I was so indignant that the tears burst into my eyes with passion, but I controlled myself and without saying a word hurried to the street. For three days I remained in my lodgings, in no pleasant mood of mind. If my father should order me back to the Academy, and thus humiliate me before the whole school, it would be the greatest trial of my life; if he should consent to my removal, I made up my mind to show by my attention to business, that I was grateful for his consideration. During that dark hour of life, my future destiny was in the balance. At the end of the three or four days I waited on the Principal and he told that he had a letter from my father, saying that he would not compel me to go to the Academy against my will, but that, if I chose to return to it, he would offer no objection. "That being so", said I, "I know what to do", as I hurried out of the door. Never again had I occasion to speak to Dr Bryce. Once afterwards, when I was minister of Maghera, I met him at a funeral, but, though he knew who I was, he took no notice of me. Long afterwards, when I occupied the Moderator's Chair in the General Assembly, I saw him sitting in the House, but, of course, the opportunity was not favourable for his entering into conversation with his runaway pupil. Mr Hanson, at the end of the quarter, also removed to the Institution; but the Doctor had now learned something and did not appeal to Maclary [Hanson's home]. I have often heard since, from persons admitted to his friendship, that, in spite of a manner somewhat repulsive in dealing with inferiors, he was not bad at heart; and often since have I thought that if I had had, before taking the extreme step, the moral courage to go and tell him modestly what was the matter, the whole thing might have been arranged in a manner satisfactory to both.

From the time I went to the Institution I set about to learn in earnest. The teachers from the highest to the lowest were genial and attractive. The lads in attendance were not looked down upon or abused, but treated as gentlemen and friends, so long as their conduct deserved it. Very rarely indeed was there any degrading punishment and never any general investigations. The whole atmosphere of the place was pleasant. The lessons were indeed lengthy, such as it was worth a man's while to sit down and prepare; but this was the very thing I desired. I attended the Institution from 1 February till 1 October 1839 and I do not think that I ever made so much progress in the same time. One motive that activated me, I confess, was that my father might have no cause to regret his permitting me to leave the Academy. My progress was still more marked after Mr Savage and Mr Hanson went home at the close of the College session in the end of April and left me remaining behind. I was no longer under temptation to spend time in conversation or in running about and I wrought with all my might. During that quarter I attended no fewer than eight separate classes in the Classical School and won honours in them all.

Mr Wilson, the Head Classical Master, was a native of Banagher as well as myself, being one of the Wilsons of Derrychrier, about a mile from Dungiven; but I had never known or seen him till I went to his school. He had been a Scholar of Trinity College, Dublin, and, some short time after that at which I have now arrived, he resigned the Mastership in the Institution and became an incumbent in the Ards. He was a genial man and a good teacher. One of his assistants was Andrew Todd, from whom I received much useful instruction; he afterwards became the minister of Finvoy and, after I became a member of the Presbytery of Magherafelt, he was my very intimate friend. The most distinguished man, however, in office at the Institution was Dr Montgomery, well-known to all the North of Ireland as the representative of Arian theology and the most formidable antagonist of Dr Cooke. For one quarter I was under him as Master of the English School; but I did not come much under his personal tuition, as I was consigned to the care of Mr John Montgomery, who afterwards became Unitarian minister of Limavady. Dr Montgomery was a man of fine physique. It was said he corrected sharply, if a boy deserved it, but I never saw him correcting anyone. His whole air showed him to be a man who could not be trifled with; a deep hush fell on the whole school if he was even seen entering at the gate. Dr Montgomery retired from the charge of the school at that Midsummer. The boys in attendance subscribed and made him a present of a gold watch as a parting gift. In return, he asked the teachers and pupils of the Institution to a picnic on the slopes of Divis mountain. The day was charming, the scenery delightful and the good cheer abundant. To all of us, it was a very pleasant day. Nearly all the teachers made speeches or tried to do it. Dr Montgomery made half a dozen and the boys cheered vociferously. He was in every way an able and estimable man, a man whom I could have loved as well as admired, had it not been that his Arian opinions made me afraid of him.

Passing along May Street one day, on my way from school, I noticed a large company of ministers standing in the porch and on the steps leading up to Dr Cooke's church. I wondered what brought so many of them together and, stealing into the gallery, I looked down for the first time on the Synod of Ulster. Dr Denham of Derry, a man of noble and impressive appearance, filled the Chair; he gave me the first idea of what a Moderator ought to be, dignified, courteous, gifted with readiness of speech and power to control the House. The debates and the business interested me very much and, as often as my necessary engagements allowed, I was never absent from their meetings while the Synod sat.

When the Entrance Examinations drew on, I went home and, as the rules required, was introduced to the Presbytery of Glendermot by my minister, Rev Thomas Ellison. A day or two after, I attended for examination at the schoolroom of the First Church, Londonderry, where, for about eight or nine successive hours, I, with a number of others, including Mr Moran, afterwards of Belmont, and Mr Josias Porter, afterwards President of Queen's College, Belfast, was examined before the Synod's Committee. It would have been a shame for me, if, after all my privileges, I had not passed respectably. Mr Moran, in my opinion, made the best appearance before the Committee, but he insisted that that honour belonged to me. I had never met any of the candidates nor any of the examiners before. A copy of the 'Derry Standard', posted to Mr Andrew Todd, Academical Institution, Belfast, according to a prior agreement, for postage was then dear, conveyed to him the news of my success.

(4) College Days: 1839-42

I entered the Collegiate Department of Belfast Institution in November 1839 and finished its curriculum of literary and scientific study in April 1842. I cannot now look back on those precious years, turned by me to so little profit, without a feeling of sorrow and humiliation.

The Professors were, without exception, men of ability and learning, under whom it was a pleasure to study and to whom no blame could justly be attached, if their students did not progress. The opportunities of study were favourable, but there were no rewards to encourage effort. There was neither scholarship nor bursary about the place; only the Tennent Exhibition, so called, I suppose, in irony, of five pounds given at the General Certificate Examination to the foremost man of the candidates. The result was that nobody was enabled to stay long enough at the college or encouraged to make sufficient exertions to acquire learning. But, so far as I was concerned, the fault was not in the system; the fault was in myself. No doubt I attended the classes with great regularity. I listened to the lectures and noted their substance with care. I wrote the essays and handed them punctually in. But I made no exertions at home and never put forth my whole strength on any subject. My ambition was simply to be an average student; to do what was necessary and to pass respectably, but to do no more. The consequence was that in my first session I took only the Third Class Prize in Latin and the Hall Prize at the public examination; but no honour, so far as I remember, in Greek or Logic. Most in the class were older than I was, but few of them had received nearly so good preliminary training, so that, if I had made any effort such as I ought to have made, the result might have been very different.

In my second session, while I attended Mathematics and Moral Philosophy, my career as a student touched its lowest point. Owing to want of good advice, I sought no mathematical instruction on my first coming to Belfast. The result was that I entered on my second year's studies without knowing the first proposition of the First Book of Euclid and without being able to do a single question in Algebra. When it was too late, I discovered my radical mistake. I was not able to keep up with the class or follow the demonstrations of the Professor. I lost heart and would have withdrawn from the class altogether, had it not been for Mr Young, the Professor, who encouraged me and who at the end kindly gave me a ticket; although I knew in my heart that I was unworthy of it and of his forbearance. I did better in the Moral Philosphy, which met that year in the Linenhall Street lecture-room, under care of Professor Robert Wilson. He was a keen, sharp man, who lost no time in useless words and gave us time to take notes. In the third session (1841-42), I attended Natural Philosphy and Hebrew. But there was not much improvement. For a good part of the session I was afflicted with sore eyes, which gave me some excuse for want of ordinary application. I did what was necessary to carry me through. I did no more.

What lay at the root of all this intellectual indolence? It was an unwise economy. My father constantly pressed on me the necessity of spending as little money as I could. In order to accomplish this, it was necessary to live with a companion. This was understood to be cheaper. The same room, the same fire, the same light and the same bed served both. My companions, David Hanson, Alexander Savage and William A Russell, afterwards minister of Second Strabane, were as good men as any student could have. But the temptation when two live together is to talk and to go into society. Each is visited by friends outside and then has to visit in return. This wastes time. Each one of us would have been a far more successful student, had he lived alone. It would scarcely be believed now, but it is true that, for each of the four sessions I passed in Belfast, except one, twenty pounds paid all my expenses. Washing clothes was done at home and, when the box of clean shirts and stockings came up, my mother always found a corner in it for eggs and butter.

One year I exceeded the twenty pounds so far that I had to borrow two pounds from one of my companions, but my father showed so much ire, when enabling me to pay my debt, that I never ventured again to repeat the experiment. This, I think now, was false economy. A few pounds more would have enabled me to live by myself. My father made a mistake in not insisting that this should be done. Had he only said so, it would have been done. All my life, from the time I was a child six years old, I made it a rule never to disobey him in anything. Here again, nobody but myself was really in fault. My father would readily have undertaken the extra expense, had I shown him the advantage. How could he be expected to know my temptation and the best way of escaping from the snare? I did not tell him, because I did not wish him to know, that I was idling so much time that might have been profitably spent.

Notwithstanding this inattention to anything like severe study, I made it a point to comply scrupulously with everything that the law of the Church required from a student. From the day I was taken under care of the Presbytery, till the day I was licensed, I never missed attending any of its meetings at which I was required to be present. I never failed at an examination. On every occasion I made what was regarded as a fair appearance. This was simply owing to the fact that, however I may have misspent the College session, I always turned the long summer vacation to good account. At home in my father's house, at the foot of the Derry mountains, I was far outside the reach of any persons that had power to draw me away. No student known to me lived within a distance of many miles. Association with uneducated people, whose ideas and habits were so different from mine, had no charm for me. I was thrown back on myself. My plan was to sit down, copy out the lectures of the session and take a fresh survey of the old ground. I did so with the lectures on Logic and Moral and Natural Philosophy. I think now it would have been better, instead of copying out old notes very imperfectly taken, had I mastered some standard work on each of the subjects; but I was not provided with the book and did not think of it at the time. Still, the practice gave me strength; and possibly I went up at the commencement of each new session as well acquainted with the business of the past year as some who had been more laborious students. A prize offered by Dr Cairns at the end of the first session, for the best answering on Chambers's 'History of the English Language and Literature', I succeeded in winning at the beginning of the second session, from several competitors of the year before.

My reading during these College days became so abundant and miscellaneous that I cannot now recall anything like the number of books which passed through my hands. During my first session, I read with delight the 'Republic of Letters', borrowed from the class library; during vacation, at the end of the second session, I read the 'Plea of Presbytery'; and it was, I think, in my third session that I read the first two volumes of the English translation of

Merle D'Aubigné, the Reformation historian, whom W D Killen and John Edgar travelled to Geneva to persuade that he should open the Presbyterian Assembly's College in Belfast

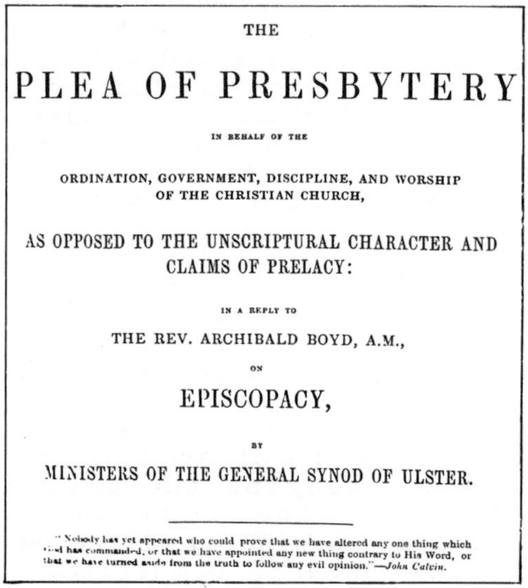

THE

PLEA OF PRESBYTERY

IN BEHALF OF THE

ORDINATION, GOVERNMENT, DISCIPLINE, AND WORSHIP OF THE CHRISTIAN CHURCH,

AS OPPOSED TO THE UNSCRIPTURAL CHARACTER AND CLAIMS OF PRELACY:

IN A REPLY TO

THE REV. ARCHIBALD BOYD, A.M.,

ON

EPISCOPACY,

BY

MINISTERS OF THE GENERAL SYNOD OF ULSTER.

"Nobody has yet appeared who could prove that we have altered any one thing which God has commanded, or that we have appointed any new thing contrary to His Word, or that we have turned aside from the truth to follow any evil opinion."—*John Calvin.*

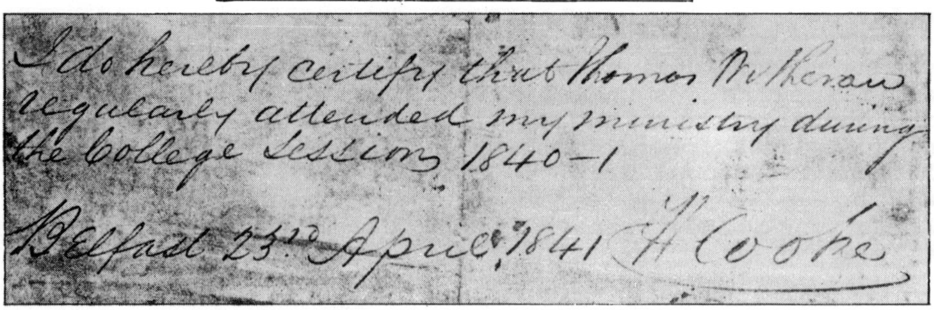

I do hereby certify that Thomas Witherow regularly attended my ministry during the College Session 1840–1

Belfast 23rd April 1841 H Cooke

Proof of attendance

D'Aubigne's 'History of the Reformation'. These are all I remember. They represent the three departments of study, which have all my life given me most satisfaction, Literature, Theology and History. From the time my school education ended, down till the present, I was always fond of knowing what was afloat in the country where I lived and of course this could not be done without reading the newspaper. My favourite paper was first the 'Derry Standard'; after I settled at Maghera, the 'Banner of Ulster'; and, after it passed away, the 'Northern Whig'. But I have often taken in and read other papers, to enable me to take a fair honest view of both sides of the question.

I do not know that, after the summer of 1840, I ever could fairly be called a Conservative. My sympathies were with progress, not stagnation; with justice and fair play, not with privilege;, with wise and gradual reforms, rather than with stupid and unreasoning opposition to all change. My sympathies have always been with the great party led in succession by Lord John Russell, Lord Palmerston and Mr Gladstone, but I never went so far as to hope for anything from extreme radicals who would overturn the Crown, the Constitution, the Christian system and almost everything else that is worth preserving. I could never believe that either Repeal of the Union or Home Rule would be any advantage to Ireland, but I have always thought that Irish Roman Catholics should be treated with justice and even with kindness by the State, considering the seven hundred years of suffering and humiliation through which they have passed. These views would now be accepted by all except the most rabid Orangemen, but, when I gave expression to them so early as November and December 1840, some of my fellow-students regarded them with horror, even men who, a few years after, proved more advanced Liberals than I ever was.

The ministry of Dr Cooke, the addresses of the Deputations sent to Belfast to represent the case of the Non-Intrusionists in Scotland and the debates in the General Assembly, when it met in Belfast during the College session, did much to excite my interest in religious matters. But now, when Sabbath schools in abundance were at hand, I did not attend; from which I infer that it would have been much the same if a similar opportunity had offered in Aghadoey. Still, I was advancing a little in religious knowledge. I understood better what fell from the pulpit and picked up facts and lessons which strengthened my principles and gradually modified my course of life. At no time did I ever feel sympathy with people who magnified other churches and disparaged their own. No church, I knew even then, is perfect; the very best has much in her constitution that needs to be improved. But, so far as I could judge then, and I hold the same opinion at this day, the Presbyterian Church was the purest in her principles of any church in the world; and, if I had not thought so, I would have been ashamed to sit in her sanctuaries or to enter her ministry. No honest man, as I thought and still think, could believe any other church to be better than his own.

Sincerity in religion is essential and without this persuasion no Christian can be sincere. This being so, truth has claims on men of sincerity not to be shaken off. We are bound to give it all the support and encouragement in our power, and, although our influence be small, that does not make personal duty anything the less. I wish no harm to any man, however much I differ from him in religion, but would on the contrary do him good, if it were in my power; but that is no reason why I should look with favour on a form of religion that I regard to be corrupt or give it any countenance, while a purer faith, standing at its side, claims from me hearty and loyal support. During the four winters and one summer that I spent in Belfast, I never heard a Unitarian sermon, never witnessed the celebration of Mass and was present only at one Episcopalian service, on which occasion Dr Drew preached in Sandy Row Church from the words in Revelation: "Whosoever will, let him take the water of life freely". At that time I was under nineteen, living in a large town without parent or guardian and free to go where I pleased; but I was satisfied with the true and had no yearning for the untrue. Hearing Dr Cooke or Dr Morgan every Sabbath, I was under no temptation to go anywhere else.

At May 1842 I had completed attendance in the undergraduate classes and nothing now remained, but to pass what was called the General Certificate Examination. Up till 1840, the General Certificate was a literary honour, given after a careful examination by the Faculty of the College, stating that the receiver of it had passed through all the classes, literary and scientific, and had made an amount of proficiency satisfactory to the Professors. It was awarded to a student by the men who had trained him and were best acquainted with his capacity and his attainments. It had been from the foundation of the College accepted by the Synods as equivalent to a degree in Arts. But in 1841 a quarrel, between the Synod of Ulster and the Managing Board of the College, led to a withdrawal of the Arts students from all the public examinations. The General Assembly appointed a Committee to examine students at the end of the third year and to issue General Certificates. Some of us did not attach much literary value to this Certificate. It was issued by persons who had no prior acquaintance whatever with those whom they examined and who could only certify under their hands that the student had passed one examination. Nobody who knew the facts could attach much importance to what it represented, but Dr Cooke, to whom somebody stated this objection, quieted our scruples by assuring us that his signature alone to our Certificate would weigh more with the outside public than that of the whole Faculty. There was a sense in which, as we knew, all that was quite true.

There was no portion of the time given to College studies in which I read so closely as the summer of 1842. Greek and Latin gave me no uneasiness. Logic and Moral Philosophy were indeed thorny subjects, but Mathematics and Natural Philosphy were my special dread. For these last subjects I had no aptitude and no taste; still, I sat down doggedly to both and, by private study alone, I made up before the end of the summer such an amount of Algebra and Euclid that, had I only possessed it during the College session, would have made me a prizeman. The result was that I passed the General Certificate Examination with credit. Of the fifty-five who presented themselves for examination, fifteen passed with the unanimous consent of the Committee; and, of these fifteen, I was one, and my friend, Russell, another. The remainder were examined a second time and of these sixteen were allowed to pass. Twenty-four were absolutely rejected. I do not know that I ever experienced a deeper feeling of joy than when I heard my name read out among the successful candidates. The main cause of my joy was that I was done with Mathematics and Science for ever, and that they would never more cause me any anxiety. I left the presence of the Committee, clutching the tin box that enclosed my parchment certificate as a precious casquet and, from that hour to this, I am not aware that I ever wrought out a question in Algebra or read a proposition in Euclid.

(5) Theological Studies: 1842-44

Had I entered College with the definite object of studying for the ministry, there were some subjects such as Modern Languages and Elocution to which I ought to have given some attention in my undergraduate years. But, the truth is, I thought nothing of the matter. My father never spoke to me on the subject. He never said in my hearing that he intended to make me a minister. His invariable answer to any who inquired was that he intended to give me a good education. At the beginning of my fourth year I entered on the study of Theology, because my companions and friends were about to do so, not because I felt any very strong predilections in that direction. My tastes had been for some time turning towards the Church, but two difficulties lay in my way. One was that I was very defective in the early training that now seemed so essential. I was very inferior in knowledge of the very alphabet of Christianity, as compared, for example, with my friends, Savage and Russell, the former a member of a Covenanting family, the latter reared in the religious atmosphere of a Secession household. The other, in my case, was the more than ordinary defect of presence of mind and self-confidence, when it was necessary, without premeditation, to express myself in words. Before that session ended, I had more than one painful reminder of my disqualification for being a theological student in any proper sense. A preliminary examination on the elements of Christianity was required before entering the Divinity

JOHN EDGAR

Samuel Hanna,
the Kellswater man who was Moderator
of the first General Assembly (1840)

William Dool Killen

NEW BOOKS AND NEW EDITIONS.

DERRY AND ENNISKILLEN IN THE YEARS 1688-9: The Story of some Famous Battlefields in Ulster. By Professor WITHEROW, *Magee College, Derry.* Illustrated with Steel Engravings and with Maps of Derry and Enniskillen as they appeared in 1689. Cloth, elegant, 5s.

M'CRIE'S LIFE OF JOHN KNOX. New edition, with Illustrations. Post 8vo, cloth extra. 3s. 6d.

THE HUMAN MIND: A System of Mental Philosophy for the General Reader. By JAMES G. MURPHY, D.D., Belfast. Crown 8vo. 5s.

"The Notes are capital, condensed, clear, and decisive."—*Publishers' Circular.*
"His literary style is neat, and, indeed, what may be called elegant."—*Scotsman.*
"Always clear and interesting."—*Morning Post* (London).

THE DOCTRINE OF ETERNAL PUNISHMENT VINDICATED AGAINST RECENT ATTACKS. By the Rev. Professor WATTS, D.D. Demy 8vo, sewed. 1s.

THE FAITHFUL PASTOR AND HIS FLOCK: A Sermon preached on the occasion of the Death of the late Dr. Morgan, by the Rev. Professor Wallace, Belfast. Demy 8vo, sewed, 3d.

CUYLER'S (Rev. Theodore) HEART LIFE. Cloth, 1s. 6d.
„ „ *HEART CULTURE.* „ 1s. 6d.
„ „ *HEART THOUGHTS.* „ 1s. 6d.

THE FLOWER FADED: A Memoir of Clementine Cuvier, Daughter of Baron Cuvier; with Reflections. By JOHN ANGEL JAMES. With portrait. Cloth, 1s.

"We earnestly commend the volume to our readers."—*Londonderry Standard.*

REID'S HISTORY OF THE PRESBYTERIAN CHURCH IN IRELAND; comprising the Civil History of the Province of Ulster, from the Accession of James the First; with a Preliminary Sketch of the Progress of the Reformed Religion in Ireland during the Sixteenth Century, and an Appendix, consisting of Original Papers. By JAMES SEATON REID, D.D., M.R.I.A. A New Edition; with additional Notes, and continued to the present time, by W. D. KILLEN, D.D. 3 vols., Crown 8vo, 15s., or strongly half-bound, 18s.

"The very best book, in my opinion, which has ever been written on these matters."—FROUDE, *vide Fraser's Magazine, January, 1873.*

LIFE OF THE REV. JOHN EDGAR, D.D., Professor of Theology in the Assembly's College, Belfast. By W. D. KILLEN, D.D. Crown 8vo, neatly bound in cloth. Reduced to 2s. 6d.

"It is a delightful record of benevolent enterprise, inspired by an ennobling Christianity, sustained by the richest and most exalted eloquence, and carried on with unconquerable energy. This choice volume ought to be in every household library throughout the United Kingdom."—*Londonderry Standard.*

WILLIAM MULLAN, BELFAST.

classes. At this examination, Dr Cooke asked me a question out of the Shorter Catechism: "What is effectual calling?" or something of that sort. To the surprise of all, and to my own great shame, I stuck fast and was not able to answer.

Hitherto I had, on one pretence or another, avoided taking my turn at family worship; however, one night, Savage and Russell would not be put off, but insisted that it was my night to pray and pray I must. When the chapter was read, all went down upon their knees and I thought that one or other of them would pray as on former occasions. To my horror, on this occasion they carried out their threat and neither of them spoke a word. I commenced, but at the end of the second sentence I stuck fast and could not utter another word. "Gentlemen, I told you that I could not pray" was what I stammered out, as I rose from my knees in confusion. But the worst had not yet come. Professor Wilson, in the Criticism class, called upon me one morning unexpectedly to open with prayer. Had I known beforehand that this was to happen, I would have had a few sentences arranged; but I was taken by surprise. "O Lord, pardon our sins and bless us in our studies, for Christ's sake. Amen" was all I could say, and then I sat down with crimson cheeks and buried my face in my hands. All this shows how much I had to learn in November 1842 and how ill-prepared I was in every way for entering a theological class.

Dr Samuel Hanna, who had been Professor of Divinity for the Synod of Ulster, and Dr John Edgar, who had been Professor of Divinity for the Secession, now worked together under the General Assembly. They arranged between themselves to take charge of the class, month about, and each followed his own plan, without any regard to the plan pursued by the other. Dr Hanna would lecture on some Christian doctrine, dividing the whole into sections and semi-sections and supporting each statement by chapter and verse at full length. He appeared to have a system, though, in a course of three months' lecturing which fell to him, very little of the whole system came into view. Dr Edgar had no system. Today he was lecturing on Temperance, the next day on the Romish controversy; this week he was debating on Scripture Geography; the week after he was busy in giving a synopsis of Calvin's 'Institutes'. His purely theological lectures, such as those on Justification, sounded to me like a sermon addressed 'ad populum', while on every subject he spoke so rapidly that to take any satisfactory notes was impossible. Both were good men. Dr Hanna had in his time held up the lamp of truth in Belfast, but, at the time I speak of, he was now in extreme old age. Dr Edgar was an eloquent speaker and had a high reputation outside. But I cannot say that I derived much benefit from the prelections of either.

Dr Wilson was regarded by the public as somewhat dry in the pulpit, but he was an excellent professor, a man of correct taste, sound judgement and ability to put the student in possession of the main facts of his subject. His subject was, in the session that I attended his class, the method of reaching a correct text of Holy Scripture, which of course led him to speak very much of manuscripts, versions and Fathers. This introduced me to an entirely new science, of which I knew nothing before, and I listened with great interest to a series of lectures, in which, from the first sentence to the last, there was not perhaps a single useless word. The principles laid down in these lectures have ever since made a portion of my intellectual life. It was Dr Killen's second year as Professor of Church History. His subject had peculiar charms for me and I listened to him with great attention. His lectures were ever calculated to interest and instruct, as well as to communicate an impulse.

Friday and Saturday in each week were spent in the Theological class in preaching sermons before one of the Professors. Each student was assigned half-an-hour for his discourse and each had to deliver a sermon and a lecture in the course of the session. As it so happened, Dr Hanna assigned the subjects, but it fell to my lot on both occasions to preach before Dr Edgar. The composition of the piece was comparatively easy; the whole difficulty was in the delivery, for any attempt to use a manuscript would result in an immediate order to come down from the pulpit.

The subject of the sermon I now entirely forget, but the lecture was on the martyrdom of Stephen, founded on the closing verses of Acts Chapter VII. To one so timid and unready, as I naturally was, this was no ordinary trial, and made all the more so, because I had never attempted to speak without paper to people on any previous occasion. All I had to say was well prepared and well committed and I took my place on the rostrum at the appointed time. I got on better than I expected. I never looked in the face the students who formed my congregation, for, had I done so, I would most certainly have lost the thread of my discourse; but, fastening my eyes steadfastly on the Cavehill, which was visible from the rostrum, looking through the window, I went on without a stumble from the first line to the last. Dr Edgar listened attentively and at the close honoured me with a criticism of a more gentle kind than that which he sometimes offered. On one occasion he told a student who commenced a sermon with a few magniloquent sentences and followed them up with a series of rather tame observations that "he rose like an eagle and sank like a goose". He treated me with more mercy; nevertheless, I was glad to have my discourse over and to escape out of his hands.

The summer which followed is one that I have good cause to remember. Early in these months the Disruption occurred in the Church of Scotland, an event that excited my deepest regret. I regarded it as a wound to religion, a disaster to Presbyterianism and a terrible blow to the cause of truth and God. All my feelings were in favour of Dr Chalmers and those noble men who in the hour of trial stood firm to their profession and to the time-honoured principles of Presbyterianism, the principles of Knox and Melville, of Henderson and Gillespie. This was the only period of my student life in which I took part in tuition, for, during this summer, I went down daily and instructed the younger members of the family of Mr Michael Ross of Banagher Cottage in the rudiments of English. At the same time, unknown to all the world, I was passing through an experience that gave a new turn to my opinions and feelings in regard to personal religion.

That all men are sinners and that the Lord Jesus is in some sense the only Saviour, I had from reading the Scriptures long been aware. But, in my inmost heart, I cherished the idea that, in the Day of Judgment, the Omniscient Being would balance the good in a man's conduct and character against the evil, and that, according to which would predominate, so would be his destiny. I held firmly the hope that, although I was a sinner, God would be merciful to me, because I knew multitudes of people, counting on salvation, whose outward behaviour was worse than my own, and because I thought that, upon the whole, my life had not been immoral. This was salvation by works, without doubt, although at the time I did not recognise it as such. But one day, when reading in the third chapter of Galatians, I hit upon the tenth verse where the words are written: "Cursed is every one which continueth not in all things that are written in the book of the Law to do them". This passage shut me up under sin. This, and the other of the great commandments of the Law, I had never consciously transgressed; but I could not in truth and in conscience say that I had continued in all things. I must therefore be a sinner in the sight of God; not only so, but I must be under the curse and how could a man under the curse of a Law holy, just and good, be taken into the Divine favour and admitted to the Divine presence. This caused me much distress, for it showed me that, although I may not have committed such heinous sins as others, I was nevertheless under the curse, fallen, lost and guilty, and that, if I perished, it made little matter to me whether others perished still more deplorably. The first thing that gave me a little light on the subject was a verse of the same chapter a little farther down: "Christ hath redeemed us from the curse of the Law, having become a curse for us". I saw that our deliverance from the consequences of sin is somehow due to the Lord Jesus, who put Himself in our place. This idea I followed up. I found it stated that "Christ Jesus came into the world to save sinners"; that "He gave His life a ransom for many"; that He "bore our sins in His own body on the tree"; that "God so loved the world that He gave His only-begotten Son, that whosoever believeth on Him should not perish, but have everlasting life"; that "God hath made Him to be sin for us who knew no sin, that we might be the righteousness of God"; that "if any man be in Christ, he is a new creature"; and that "to as many as received Jesus, to them gave He power to become the sons of God, even to them that believe on His name".

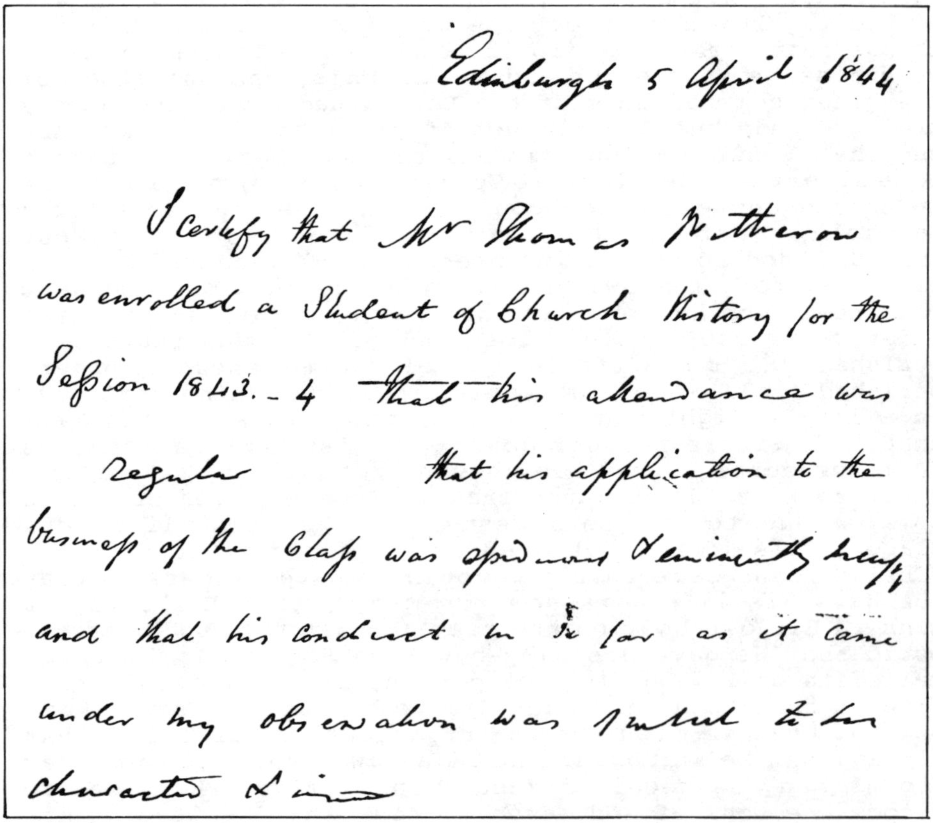

Edinburgh 5 April 1844

I certify that Mr Thomas Witherow was enrolled a Student of Church History for the Session 1843.-4 his attendance was regular that his application to the business of the Class was assiduous & eminently successful and that his conduct in so far as it came under my observation was suited to his character & [illegible]

Certificate of Witherow's attendance at Edinburgh

From these and various other kindred passages I was convinced of the following facts: (1) that the Son of God became incarnate with the consent of the Father; (2) that His errand into the world was to save sinners; (3) that, by dying on the cross, He paid the penalty of our sins; (4) that substitution of the Just for the unjust lies at the root of the Gospel; (5) that, as He took our sins, we receive His righteousness and the benefit attaching to righteousness the moment we receive Him as our Saviour; (6) that it is faith only which brings us into communion with Jesus and secures righteousness; (7) that any sinner is made welcome who comes to Jesus and repents; (8) that faith, not works, brings us into a condition wherever God can, without sin, justify the ungodly; (9) that if a sinner believes in Jesus, he becomes regenerate and a new creature; and (10) that no obedience of the creature is acceptable to God, except it spring from faith and love, and that such obedience every believer is to render. These are the main principles of that plan of salvation which I then regarded as revealed in the Word of God; these are the truths I have ever since held and to which I hope to testify with my latest breath. I have since often doubted whether the full effect of these blessed truths was either felt in my heart or made manifold in my life as it ought to have been, but I feel thankful that never for one moment have I doubted that this is substantially the plan of salvation set forth in the Gospel.

I was confirmed in this view of salvation, springing from the grace and love of God and intended as the climax of Divine benefit to men, when I found, a little after, that the Lord commissioned His apostles to "preach the Gospel to every creature" and that, in compliance with this order, I found Peter, on the basis of the great facts to which I have referred, more particularly the Divine mission, miracles, death, resurrection and exaltation of Jesus, saying to a vast congregation: "Repent and be baptized every one of you in the name of Jesus Christ unto the remission of sins" and John, the apostle of love, asserting that "the blood of Jesus Christ, His son, cleanseth from all sin" and Paul answering the question, "What must I do to be saved?", with the words, "Believe on the Lord Jesus Christ and thou shalt be saved". The work of a minister, among those of his people who are already children of God, seemed to me set forth in the words: "Teaching them to observe all things whatsoever I have commanded". The epistles written by the apostles show how they fulfilled this command. The discovery of these things in the Word of God, for it was a discovery to me, took away nearly all my objections to the work of the ministry. It pleased God by His grace to make a revelation of saving truth to my own soul and to enable me to receive it. He had pointed out the message that I was to carry to the unsaved, the precious Gospel, showing them the way of remission. He had pointed out my pastoral work in the congregation of His people: instruction in the things that Jesus had commanded. The only thing I now needed was more of the Divine Spirit to bring my own heart and life still more under the influence of the truth of God and take away my personal timidity and unreadiness of speech. I was indeed of slow speech and of slow tongue, but I was encouraged much by the words that God spake to Moses and Jeremiah.

As the summer drew toward a close, I resolved to change my place of study and to spend my last College session in Edinburgh. Dr Chalmers and Dr Welsh were then at the height of their fame. Every newspaper of that time was full of the sayings and doings of the new Free Church. Edinburgh was the capital of Presbyterianism and associated in my memory with John Knox and the martyrs. Accordingly, at the first of November, I set out. The steamer from Derry called at Portrush and there I met, without any previous concert, William Smyth of Garvagh, who afterwards married my cousin, Martha McKay, bent, it appeared, on the same errand as myself. We made it up to be "chums" for the session and, when we reached Edinburgh, found lodgings at 12 Roxburgh Street, only a very short distance from the University. The impression made upon me by Edinburgh was what is made on every stranger who sees it; that, whether for buildings, for situation or for historic associations, it was the noblest and most interesting of all cities. I soon grew familiar with all its prominent scenes and sights: the Castle, the Carlton Hill, Salisbury Crags and Arthur's Seat; then Holyrood Palace, John Knox's House, the Canongate and Grassmarket; St Giles Cathedral and the Greyfriars Church and Churchyard. Dr Johnston felt his piety warm as he trod the sacred soil of Iona, but Iona had no such charms for me as the Grassmarket and the Greyfriars. The former only suggested thoughts of monks and monkery, but the latter spoke to me of Covenanters and martyrs, men who had shed the last drop of their heart blood for the love they felt for Christ.

It was the winter of the very year of the Disruption (1843-44) and Chalmers and Welsh, who had withdrawn from the University, lectured in a building in George Street, temporarily fitted up for the reception of students. The Theological Class of that year contained all the students in Scotland who had withdrawn from the Church of Scotland and had signified their adhesion to the Free Church. In Dr Chalmers' class the number was about 230, of whom about thirty were from Ireland, many of whom I had known in Belfast. The Scottish and Irish students kept at a great distance from each other. At the close of the session, there were not half a dozen students whom I knew by name and there was not one with whom I had become intimate.

Dr Chalmers was one of those colossal men about whom there was nothing little or mean, but every thing fitted to win admiration and love. He was a stout, middle-sized man with broad, square countenance, a large forehead and fine grey eye, suggesting at once genius and power. His subjects during the session were mainly Natural Theology and the Evidences, apparently the opening portion of an extensive course of instruction. I could not say that he communicated any very large amount of knowledge; his object seemed rather to place the subject in a new and original light and to create in us a taste for the subject. This was the effect he produced on me. That session I acquired a fondness for every branch of theological science, which has ever since been a part of myself and which has made study in that line not a weariness and a toil, but a solace and a delight. To persons who knew Dr Chalmers only by his writings, his style seems ponderous and verbose, but, to us who heard him read his own compositions, every word seemed to fall naturally into its place and not one clause could be dropped without weakening the effect of the whole. Often and often again did I linger, the last of the class, that, unobserved, I might, going out at the door, take a look at that great and noble man who towered so high above all the preachers and theologians of his age and whose life was so spotless above all other public men of his time. None was superior to him.

Dr Welsh, without pretension to oratory, was a man of taste and learning. His subject during the session was the external history of the first three centuries of Christianity and the lectures were in substance the same as those printed in the 'Church History', the first and last volume of which he issued that year. What struck me most about him was his familiarity with the writings of the Christian Fathers, which evidently he had studied minutely. He died the following session and Dr Chalmers also in about three years after I studied under him. Both men were therefore verging then to the end of their earthly career, but their minds were in full vigour. I cannot adequately express how much I owe to the fine spirit, to the example and to the teaching of these great men.

During this my last session, though not altogether idle, I cannot say that I was a very laborious student. Heavy work was not exacted from Irishmen. The preparation and delivery of sermons were voluntary and, that being so, I did not prepare any. But, in addition to taking ample notes and making abstracts of the historical lectures, I bought the four volumes containing Chalmers on 'Natural Theology and the Evidences' and made them up as well as I could. I made it a practice to attend every important public meeting in the city, whether religious in its object or not, in order to get acquainted with the ideas of the time and with public men of whom I had often heard. Dr Guthrie, who, for a year or two after the Disruption, till a new church was built for him, known afterwards as Free St John's, occupied the Methodist Chapel in Nicolson Square, was the minister whom I heard every Sabbath and I took copious notes of his sermons, the most telling and eloquent I had ever heard; but I went sometimes to hear Dr Candlish, Dr James Buchanan and Dr Beggs. I was present at a meeting in the Mission Hall to raise funds for erecting the Scott Monument, now standing in Princes Street, but only a model of which then existed in plaster of Paris, exhibited on the platform. I heard on this occasion Lord Cockburn, Professor John Wilson (Christopher North), Sir Thomas Dick Lauder and others.

Christopher North was the most striking figure of them all. When on my way to George Street from my lodgings, I often met him on the South Bridge. He stalked along, tall, erect, stately, his collar open and spreading out over the cape of his coat, and his hair streaming down in ringlets on his broad shoulders. Physically he was a magnificent man. On passing him, a stranger could not resist the impulse to turn round and look after him till he was out of sight. I once went to hear him lecture in the Moral Philosophy class in the University. His subject was Sympathy. He moved to and fro constantly, behind the long table that stretched across the classroom, looked out of the window, keeping the side of his head to his students, pulled occasionally a scrap of paper out of his pocket, as if to suggest to him another part of his subject, and then broke forth into another extemporaneous harangue, largely interspersed with passages from the poets and always ending with a burst of eloquence which elicited from the class the most rapturous applause. The only two men I did not see, whom afterwards I would have liked to know, were Hugh Miller and Sir William Hamilton; to whom perhaps I should add Lord Jeffry. Miller was then Editor of the 'Witness', but his duties were such as not to make his personal appearance very well known to the public. Sir William Hamilton had not then acquired his reputation as a philosopher. Edinburgh people, in general, only knew him as a learned gentleman who had written a spiteful pamphlet against the leaders of the Free Church. Lord Jeffry was celebrated as the critic who had given vigour and character to the 'Edinburgh Review'. I might have seen them all, had I taken a little trouble, and I afterwards regretted that I did not, but, in the circle in which I moved, the reputation of Chalmers and Cunningham and Guthrie and Candlish eclipsed that of everybody else, and, knowing them, I felt satisfied.

I returned home in the end of March, very much the better in every way of my five-month sojourn in Edinburgh. I now set vigorously to work to complete my trial pieces before the Presbytery and to prepare for my final examination before the Theological Committee of the General Assembly. In the first trial piece before the Presbytery, after coming home from Scotland, I gave proof, without intending it, of my intense admiration for Chalmers. The discourse was so full of elaborate sentences, Latinized expressions and repetitions of the same thought in a variety of forms, that one of the ministers took me aside at the close of the Presbytery meeting and told me candidly that such a style would never do. That I must write in a simple, natural, unambitious manner, as being more adapted to myself and more intelligible to the people. I was very grateful to Mr McConnell for this advice and from that day forth did my best to act upon it.

The impending Theological Examination was not, as it is now, purely academic, but an enquiry into those subordinate, but useful, branches of knowledge that College classes are so apt to overlook. The nature of it may be judged from the way which I took in order to prepare for it. First I committed the 'Shorter Catechism', now I am ashamed to say, for the first time and discovered to my delight the grand theological system which it contains. Then I read over two or three times carefully the 'Westminster Confession of Faith', the 'Form of Presbyterian Government' and the 'Directory for Public Worship'. Next I selected a dozen or two of the main doctrines, appended to them three or four passages, by way of proof to each, and committed them to memory, so as to be able to repeat them accurately and state the chapter and verse where they are found. After this, I took up the 'Companion to the Bible' and made myself familiar with the information, particularly in regard to the component books of Holy Scripture. Lastly, I made an abstract of Dick's 'Theology', which gave a more scientific exposition of theological science than any I had yet received.

During this, as well as the preceding summer, I taught diligently in the Sabbath school which had recently been organised in Banagher Presbyterian Church and I found the exercise most beneficial, not only for making me better acquainted with the English version of the Bible, but for enabling me to speak to others with more freedom. The result was that, when the time came, I had no difficulty whatever in passing the Theological Committee. The Rev James Wilson of Magherafelt was my Examiner and I acquitted myself to his satisfaction and to that of the other members. I returned home from Belfast, having passed successfully through my five sessions, and all my examinations, preparatory to being licensed to preach the Gospel; and without having lost a day more than was absolutely required by the law of the Church.

(6) Life as a Probationer: 1845

In the ordinary course of events, I should have been licensed to preach at the first meeting of Presbytery after passing the Theological Examination, but I persuaded the minister to postpone it for three months. The fact was, I had no sermon ready to submit to a popular audience and I thought it would be a prudent thing to prepare at least five or six, to lay up a small stock of goods before going forth to submit them to the public. I soon discovered that this was not so wise a plan as I had supposed. I found that committing a sermon was no dfficult thing, if it was done immediately after it passed through the mind when writing it; but, if written two or three months before being committed, it was almost as difficult to transfer it to the memory as if it had been composed by another man. It was impolitic in another point of view. The most desirable vacancies, of which there was a considerable number, had been nearly all picked up by my fellow students who were licensed at November and few remained for any of us who deferred entering on our work till February. I improved the three months in writing sermons and eventually was licensed on the first Tuesday of February 1845.

As I rode home from the meeting in company with Mr Ellison, he stopped to tell every member of the congregation whom he met between Claudy and his own residence that "Thomas had got his mouth opened today and that he was likely to say a word to the congregation on the following Sabbath". This was the only announcement, but the news ran over the parish like wildfire that I was about to preach and, at twelve o'clock on Sabbath, there was an overflowing congregation. There were my father and mother sitting in their own pew at the upper end of the house, directly facing the pulpit; a number of Roman Catholic neighbours, who had come, I suppose, from curiosity to witness my first appearance as a public speaker; and a great number of others, who all knew me, if I did not know them.

To add to my difficulty, I had no natural fluency of speech and, outside a classroom, had never attempted on any previous occasion to address a congregation without a manuscript. The text was one given me in the Presbytery for a trial sermon and which I had dressed up for the occasion. It was Revelation XXII 16, "I am the root and offspring of David and the bright and morning star". It was a very plain and simple discourse, one that, except on a very few occasions, I never preached again; but it took an hour in the delivery and was pronounced without stumble and without hesitation, from the first word to the last. That I did not come to a full stop, long before I reached the end, was for me a triumph; but, over and above this, all my friends were pleased to express their satisfaction. Next to my father and mother, nobody was so pleased with my performance as our minister, Mr Ellison. He was almost frantic with joy, for he esteemed me as his own son.

That very night my grandfather died. From the time that he lost his wife (1839), he had lived apart from his two sons in a house built specially for his own use. The last six years of his life were given to the study of the Scriptures. He had not been what I would call a very pious man, even in his later manhood, but, in the last years of his life, he made a great advance in piety and knowledge and, before he died, he had become strong in faith and intelligent in the Scriptures, far beyond what is common. He was eighty-six years old at his death. He loved me very much and had often expressed an earnest desire to live till he would see me a minister of the Gospel. He had been wearing down and confined to bed for several weeks before his death, but his mind was clear on to the last. He ardently inquired from those who had been at church how I got on with my sermon and, when they told him, he expressed his thankfulness and joy. That day was his last on earth. Before the light of the next day dawned, he had passed away.

The practice at that time in the Presbytery was for each licentiate to preach first for his own minister, then for his licenser and then for the Clerk, after which he went over the whole Presbytery in order, devoting to the purpose every Sabbath on which he did not preach for supply or in a vacancy. I conformed to the practice and had completed the whole Presbytery, except three or four congregations, when I was called to Maghera. Near the end of March, Mr Wilson of Magherafelt wrote to say that he thought it strange he had not heard of me since the Theological Examinations, that some of the best vacancies were now settled, but that, if I wished it, he thought that he could even yet have me heard in Brigh and Maghera. I wrote to say that I felt much obliged for his kind offer and that, as I could not expect him to speak of me intelligently, without hearing me preach, I would with his permission occupy his pulpit in Magherafelt. Accordingly, I preached there on the Sabbath named, which happened to be Easter Sunday, and, as I often heard afterwards, preached morning and evening with acceptance.

Mr Wilson and the people received me very kindly. I was scarcely home from Magherafelt, till an invitation came to me through Mr Leslie, Clerk of Tyrone Presbytery, to preach in Brigh on the first Sabbath of April. Mr Wilson, through his brother, Mr Thomas Wilson of Corglassen, a member of the congregation, had put my name before the people, but the list was filled up and it was only through the accident of one of the invited not being able to come that my name at the last moment was put on to fill the vacant place. At the same time, I was given to understand that my going was a forlorn hope, for the minds of the people were bent on one of the gentlemen whom they had already heard. I went nevertheless and preached at Brigh in the morning and in Lord Castlestuart's private chapel at Stuart Hall in the evening. The result was that none on the list received a call, but the congregation selected two or three for a second hearing and of these I was one. I preached a second time, I think in May; during the interval a party had risen in the congregation against me, not strong in point of numbers, but very influential and determined. My friends on the other hand were numerous and enthusiastic and I began to fear that I might really receive a call and, with that sheepish distrust of myself, which has followed me like an evil genius all through life, I thought that, not being yet twenty-one years of age, I would never be equal to two sermons every Sabbath and a prayer meeting every week.

The Committee of Presbytery was to meet the congregation to moderate in a call on the Monday after I preached. That morning, without assigning any reasons, I wrote asking the Committee to withdraw my name as a candidate. The congregation was somewhat surprised, but, thinking it, I suppose, a piece of clever management on my part, they were equal to the occasion. My friends were numerous enough to poll out all the other candidates and

Brigh Presbyterian Church

Smylie Robson

Maghera Presbyterian Church

then carried a proposal to bring me back in July, in order to take a poll for myself alone. By that time I had acquired a little more confidence and, I suppose, would then have accepted the congregation, had I succeeded at the poll. When the poll was taken, I wanted, however, some six or seven votes of having two-thirds of the electors on my side, the number necessary to give a legal Synodical call. My two warm friends, Thomas Wilson and Hugh Robson, were deeply mortified, but I bore it with equanimity. The congregation, after this unfortunate difference of opinion, remained vacant for more than a year. My friends during that time polled out a most excellent man, John Moran, afterwards of Newry and Belmont, but they would have done the same thing to the Apostle Paul, had he appeared as a candidate brought forward by the opposition. Each side had now obtained a victory and suffered a defeat. Being thus in a measure satisfied, they had less difficulty in giving a call to my friend and fellow-student, John Maxwell, who lived among them nearly forty years and proved to be an able and excellent minister.

Meanwhile I preached my first sermon at Maghera on 8 June. The congregation had been vacant for upwards of a year, since the time that the Rev Smylie Robson resigned, in order to go as a missionary to the Jews at Damascus. They had had a warm dispute over the choice of a minister and had agreed to give a call to Rev Alexander Russell, a probationer who afterwards joined the Free Church of Scotland and settled in Ayrshire; but Mr Russell, understanding that some opposition had risen to his settlement among the people, returned their call. They then disposed of another list of candidates and, at the end of all, the people, stimulated as I believe by an exaggerated report of my popularity in Magherafelt, overlooked the objection to my youth and consented to give me a hearing. On the day named I lectured there on the 17th of Numbers and preached on Romans V:1. The fact was that, although I preached in compliance with their request, I did not wish to accept a call from them, as my thoughts at the time were turned to Brigh, which did not reject me till a month after. I was desired to announce that the congregation would remain for a few minutes after the Benediction was pronounced. I did so and withdrew from the house as soon as I could, but, before I reached the head of the avenue that opens upon the street, one of the elders followed, overtook me and told me that the congregation had agreed unanimously to give me a call. I was very much astonished.

It was a fortnight afterwards, before the Presbytery could arrange to give the call an official form, and a little longer delay occurred before the Presbytery of Glendermot could meet to put the call into my hands. By that time all hope from Brigh was at an end and therefore I was free to consider the call. I consulted with various friends, Mr Wilson of Magherafelt, the Rev Hugh Rodgers of Kilrea, Mr Todd of Finvoy, all of whom thought I ought to accept it. Mr Ellison was opposed to my acceptance. My father would give no advice; he left the matter to myself. After serious consideration and prayer for Divine guidance, I consented to accept and was ordained there as junior minister on 1 October 1845. My friend Mr Todd preached from 1 Corinthians IX:16, "Woe is me if I preach not the Gospel". The congregation entertained the Presbytery and other friends at dinner. To my great relief, it had been agreed that there should be no toasts and no speeches. The rule was strictly observed by all but the rector, the Rev J Spencer Knox, who made a great flourish and proposed my health in very magniloquent terms indeed. I had no speech prepared and therefore could only say that I felt deeply the kind acts and kind speeches of all with whom I had come into connexion at Maghera, and that the best way to show my sense of their kindness was to perform my duties as a minister among them as well as I could. No notice of the day's transactions was taken, except in a short paragraph of eight or ten lines written by the Editor of the 'Coleraine Chronicle', who had been asked to the dinner. The event of that day brought my short life as a probationer to an end. The more laborious work of the pastorate now opened before me.

(7) Maghera, 1845

The town of Maghera, in which I was now settled as a minister, is a market town on what was once the coach road direct between Derry and Belfast, being about twenty-five miles from the former and thirty miles distant from the latter. It is rather stationary in point of population, containing then, as now, something about fifteen hundred inhabitants. It was about eleven miles distant from my father's residence by the mountain road, being situated on the eastern side of the ridge of hills which runs through the County Derry from north to south, the water-flow on the east being to Lough Neagh and the Bann, that on the west to Lough Foyle.

The Presbyterian congregation of the town dates from the Commonwealth and has had a long succession of ministers, of whom, so far as is known, I was the tenth.* My immediate predecessor was the Rev Smylie Robson, who, after holding the pastorate for only a year, resigned in 1844 to go to Damascus as a missionary to the Jews. I was studying in Edinburgh as a theological student when I saw in the newspapers the record of his appointment and I had no idea at the time that I should succeed him. The senior minister, the Rev Charles Kennedy, was still alive and I was appointed his assistant and successor at a salary promised by the congregation of sixty pounds a year. The prospect was not bright; neverthless, I entered on the work with spirit, resting on the help of God.

---

*See my history in the 'Evangelical Witness'.

The congregation consisted, as I ascertained, of three hundred and seventy-five families or very nearly two thousand individuals, whom I was expected to visit and instruct. They had called me when I had barely completed my twenty-first year and I was set to guide men and women, some of whom had far deeper spiritual experience than I had, and that at a time when, under ordinary circumstances, I would have needed somebody of wisdom to act as a guide to myself. But no minister ever received greater kindness and consideration from any people. They bore with my faults and weaknesses to an extent that was wonderful and never gave me a day's uneasiness for the whole twenty years that I lived among them. Their over-fondness was one of my troubles and the only trouble that they ever gave me. Many families were not satisfied, if I was not constantly going to see them and, should I fail, as no doubt I did, to go to see them often, they murmured in a kind, reproachful way that made me rather uncomfortable. But they never suspected that I felt it as I did.

There were about two hundred and forty or fifty families who contributed to support the Gospel. The others were poor and gave the minister very much to do; nevertheless, I was glad to visit them and instruct them as well as I was able. About fifty of the families resided in the town, the remainder in the country districts, more particularly to the north and east. The attendance on the whole was very good; the people filled the house, which was seated for five hundred. There was an excellent Sabbath school, consisting of three or four hundred children, who were attended to by a body of some thirty teachers, male and female, as intelligent and as devoted to their work as any body of teachers whom I ever knew. The school had been founded six or seven years before by Mr Joseph Barkley, who, while a student, had been an elder in the congregation, but who, some weeks before I was ordained, had been settled as minister of Carnmoney, near Belfast. His brother, my beloved and constant friend, Mr James Barkley, was superintendent of the school during all my ministry and is so at the present time (1888), having been in that office for very nearly fifty years.

Maghera is a congregation that gave many excellent ministers to the Presbyterian Church. Dr Cooke was born within its bounds; his father and family were members of it; and he was baptized by Dr Glendy, who stands seventh on the roll of its pastors. In the generation before me, it had produced the Rev Robert Gray of Burt; and, within my own time, the Rev Joseph Barkley; the Rev W C McCullough of Ballysillan; the Rev Hillis Kyle LLB of Markethill; the Rev Thomas Lyttle, founder of the congregation of Sandymount; the Rev John MacKeown of Waterford and Lismore; and the Rev John Macmillan of Dundalk; not to speak of my own relative, the Rev R G Milling BD, and others who were all the children of respectable families in the congregation.

At the time of my settlement, Maghera, as it still is,

Rosemount, Tullyheron: once the home of William Lytle

was connected as a congregation with the Presbytery of Magherafelt. This brought me into close connexion with several ministers whom I had not previously known, such as the Rev Hugh Walker Rodgers of Kilrea and the Rev John Radcliffe of Castledawson. My oldest acquaintance among the ministers of the Presbytery was the Rev Andrew Todd of Finvoy and Mr Wilson of Magherafelt was known to me for twelve months previously, as already described. These men I soon learned to love dearly and with all the members it was my happiness to live on excellent terms. Our intercourse as a body was very pleasant. There was never, so far as I remember, any bad feeling among us.

When I went first to Maghera I lodged at Tullyherron, in the family of a most estimable member of the congregation, Mr William Lytle of Rosemount, who himself and his respected wife (one of the most judicious and sensible of women) did all in their power to make me comfortable. Early in 1850 I took a house in town, formerly occupied by Mr John Hope, father-in-law to the Rev Smylie Robson, and I lived there till I resigned the congregation fifteen years after.

(8) Early Ministry: 1845-52

During my short career as a probationer, I always tried to produce one fresh sermon every fortnight, but I am afraid that I did not always succeed in doing so. At all events, the congregation drew upon me so often for supply, prior to ordination, that, when that event occurred, I had only one sermon which they had not heard. Very much to my relief, the winter was now setting in, when only one sermon had to be delivered. When summer returned, I had grown stronger and the two sermons were not so great a burden.

The sermons produced in the first years of my ministry were much inferior to those written while I was in the probationary state, or at a later stage, when my mind was more developed and my resources had multiplied; the main reason being that they had to be prepared with greater rapidity. They were alike meagre in thought and jejeune in expression. But, as I became better acquainted with my work, I fell into the following method of preparation, the design of which was to give point and body to my public addresses. In a small notebook, kept for the purpose, I noted down (1) any passage of Scripture which seemed to me a suitable text and on which I had something to say; (2) any happy thought that I met with in my reading and that I thought I could make available for public instruction, always connecting it with some suitable text; (3) anything dropped in conversation, embodying, it might be, some popular prejudice or notion that it might be desirable to refute; (4) any sermon from the lips of a brother minister which seemed to me to offer a fine subject, a good division and which, by admission or omission, I thought I might improve; (5) anything in my theological reading which might in substance, with a little dressing, be available for the pulpit; and (6), if nothing better could be done, I fell back on a skeleton of some orthodox minister, altering it as much as I properly could so as to make it my own. Each of these points, so far as I was able, I followed out at the time, classing it under an appropriate text and writing it on a separate slip of paper. These slips I threw into a separate drawer and, when the time for actual preparation came on, I usually found that I had my choice of a subject. Then I usually read the text in the original, consulted any available comment and wrote out the whole, either in extended notes or in shorthand at full length, usually on a single sheet of notepaper. These sheets were all carefully preserved and, when they were enough to make a volume, I had them bound together. When the time came for me to leave Maghera, I had no fewer than twelve of these volumes of shorthand sermons, all written with my own hand. The tendency of all this was not to cultivate originality, it is clear; but there was in my case no time to produce a well thought-out discourse and the plan adopted was what I judged best for rapid production and popular instruction. It was a kind of preparation that I seldom found failing to produce variety and to create interest.

The people of Maghera had always been accustomed to the exposition of a Psalm, introductory to the main discourse of the Sabbath. It was a kind of work which it is difficult to do well and to perform in an instructive manner; still, I never like to oppose even popular prejudice, when it is innocent in its nature and runs in a beneficial direction. I commenced with the first Psalm and went through regularly, taking on the average two stanzas every morning, until I had completed the whole Psalter. I then told the people that I did not mean to return to the Psalms so long as there were other portions of the Divine Word that I had never been able to overtake. I did not know much about practical agriculture, but I knew this much, that it was not good policy for the owner of a large farm to give nearly all his attention to one field and to leave the rest uncultivated. I intended instead to comment on the chapter read at the morning service. I then began at the first chapter of Genesis and, when the time came that I resigned the pastorate, I had advanced to the middle of the Second Book of Samuel. This method enabled me to give a large amount of Scriptural knowledge to the congregation in which there were many young people trained in the Sabbath school to love the Bible and better able than they otherwise would have been to appreciate any attempt to help them to understand it better. It was specially useful to myself. It furnished me with a subject for constant meditation, without imposing upon me the trouble of selection; it made me better acquainted with the Word of God in its historical order and connexion; and gave me an opportunity of touching many minor topics which came up in their natural order, and which could scarcely be touched upon in a selected passage without suggesting remark and perhaps giving offence.

On the various subjects that came up for consideration I first made up my mind and then I spoke out honestly what I believed. To trouble a congregation of plain people, unprepared and unable for any elaborate inquiry, with doubts and difficulties seemed to me absurd. I never told a congregation a single sentiment in a ministry of more than forty years that I did not believe at the time to be the truth, and, although I dare not say that I never fell into a mistake, I have seldom altered any opinion on religious matters. On the contrary, more mature study has only deepened my earliest convictions. The sum and substance of my preaching always was Jesus Christ, the only Saviour of lost men. Making Christ the centre, I swept round the whole circumference of saving truth, avoiding profitless inquiries and barren speculation. If my subject was doctrine, I tried to show how it led up to Christ and bore more or less directly on human salvation and happiness; if my subject was duty, I began with Christ and showed how love to Him should be our grand motive for obedience to what He has commanded in His word. I always spoke with an air of authority, as became Him whose messenger and minister I was; never troubled the people with this or the other opinion broached by learned men, but, having made up my mind as to the true meaning, I endeavoured to impress this on the popular mind. Matters about which I was uncertain I passed over as lightly as I could. Of course, I do not profess to have brought out everything contained in the Bible. Who is sufficient for that vast work? But the whole truth, so far as it came within my range of vision, I did not fail to declare and more particularly the truth bearing on the present duty and final destiny of men. I never could understand people, who, standing in the place where they are to speak in the name of God, either contradict the Bible or suppress this or the other thing written in it, which they do not count it polite to announce. The Great Salvation was my main theme; anything bearing upon that, directly or indirectly, it was my delight to proclaim. Anything not bearing upon that great subject, but written in the Bible, I did not regard as unimportant, but not so important for a country congregation, consisting of merchants and farmers and labourers and servants.

The visitation of the people in their own homes was one of my great difficulties. The people insisted on it and were apt to complain if it was neglected. It involved a great waste of time and the benefit resulting scarcely seemed, at least so far as I could judge, an adequate compensation. I made it a rule never to neglect the visitation of the sick, but I found it difficult to get the people to inform me of any case of illness. The only annoyance that I ever received from the people, and it is true of a number, was that they appeared constantly to assume that I was quite well aware of any sickness or calamity which befell them and theirs, and that if I was not immediately in attendance it was owing to some intended disrespect. This was constantly occurring and it was the

The Rectory, Maghera, and St Lurach's

one thing only that ever made me uncomfortable at Maghera. The winter months were given to the regular visitation of the people at the rate of two days in the week and ten families each day. This took me over the whole congregation in less than half a year, but in the last years of my ministry, owing to a painful affection of the leg, I was not able to carry it strictly out. Some of the people complained that I had not been in their house for more than two years. There is nothing in regard to which the Presbyterian people seem to me so thoughtless and unreasonable as in the matter of pastoral visitation. Had many of them their wish, they would never let their minister away from their elbow.

The attention shown by the Episcopal clergy to their people in those Establishment days was constantly held up as an example. The clergyman of a neighbouring Parish told me that the Episcopalian people consisted of forty families. He and his rector arranged among themselves that the rector would visit them once every half year and the curate once a quarter. This secured the forty families six visits from a minister every year; in other words, two hundred and forty pastoral visits were paid them inside twelve months, eighty from the rector and one hundred and sixty from the curate. Each of them preached one sermon on the Sabbath, one of them in the morning and the other at the evening service. My people were not satisfied except I paid three hundred and fifty visits in the year and preached twice every Sabbath day. That is, I was expected to do more work than these two men and a little over besides, while, to add to my comfort, I was very liable to have the example of their superior industry quoted for my imitation. The regular churchgoers were the most unreasonable in this matter of visitation. Poor people, absenting themselves from church, were always willing to receive without murmur whatever I could give them. But people who attended me every Sabbath and who heard me from the pulpit state over and over again all I could tell them at the fireside, were, some of them at least, the most ready to find fault, though not, I must admit, very often in an unpleasant way.

The way in which I conducted a visitation was to enquire into the circumstances of the family, say a word by way of exhortation, read a few verses of Scripture and then end with a short prayer. On an average this took about twenty minutes; so, with the time spent in passing from one house to another, it required about five hours in the day to visit ten families. I always left a tract, mostly one published by the Religious Tract Society, in the hand of every person who could read. This was intended to make up for any defect of mine in preaching the Gospel, for I had the feeling throughout all my pastoral visitations that, after all, the butter was very thin on the bread. I found it necessary from the first to act on the total abstinence principle in the congregation. Had I accepted all the hospitality in the way of drink offered me by the people, my visiting would have soon come to an ignominious close; but, at the end of the first two days, when the people saw that I was firm, and could not be enticed to taste either wine or whisky, they never troubled me in that way again. To their great credit, they never practised the treating of people to liquor at funerals, so I had no trouble at any time in regard to a matter which has caused many other ministers great vexation.

The building in which the congregation worshipped was a plain substantial structure, erected, I think, about 1837, in the last years of Mr Kennedy's ministry. There was no minister's room, no session room, no gallery and the three doors of the building were uncovered and open to the air. The draughts were dangerous to health and, as there were no stoves, it was very cold in the winter time. I had long been of opinion that every minister in succession should do something either to improve or to provide the material machinery of the church. I persuaded the people to erect a gallery and tower, eventually to provide stoves and a few years after to erect a building to serve as a session room and minister's room. This covered all the outside doors and added much to the comfort of the congregation. One man, who occupied a corner-seat, stoutly maintained that, after all this was done, the house was now colder than before. I asked him how he accounted for that. He said that the heat of the stoves placed in the centre of the house drove back the cold and compressed it into the corners, the result of which was that pews, situated as his was, were more uncomfortable than ever! The gallery and tower cost £400, of which £250 were raised by the subscription of the members and £150 raised by the teachers and scholars of the Sabbath school. I attempted to raise something outside the congregation, but, after collecting a few pounds, I gave it up in despair.

In 1846, the year after my settlement at Maghera, the population of Ireland had reached its maximum. It was then supposed to be eight and a half millions. Within five years after 1846 it had fallen to about two millions. This was the result of the poverty and distress produced by the potato disease. About the Twelfth in that year, before the tuber had attained maturity, a blight fell upon the potato, upon which more than on any other species of crop the people of Ireland depended for life. The stalk was first affected, then the root. All growth was at an end and scarcely so many were saved as supplied seed for the following year. Some kinds of potato which before that time had been in universal use were swept entirely away and have never appeared among us since. Government made every possible effort to save the people from destruction. The corn laws were abolished and the ports were opened to admit foreign grain free of duty. Indian corn was sent into Ireland and Indian meal sold to the people by charitable societies at nearly half-price. Relief works were opened at which people went through the appearance of work, in order to be able to claim alms in the form of wages. After every effort was made, numbers died, if not by starvation, at least by the diseases that starvation entails and multitudes fled to America. The result was that the population was very perceptibly thinned. The Roman Catholics had most poor and, of course, suffered most keenly, but the local gentry and clergy over the country did all in their power to relieve distress, without distinction of sect or party. A local Committee was established in Maghera, of which Mr J J Clark JP was Chairman and I was Secretary, mainly for the purpose of deciding who was most in need and who should be put upon the public works. This we found to be a difficult and most invidious task. We did our best, but, owing to our imperfect knowledge, we were often imposed upon in the most scandalous way. Men would come and get orders for employment on the plea of starvation, who, as we learned a few days after, had cows and horses of their own. If one such person got on the work, about a dozen others of the same class made application and, if they were rejected, then the Committee was charged with favouritism and everything that was evil.

As the spring drew near, a soup kitchen was instituted and it was sad enough to meet bands of poor people coming into town, carrying their vessels in order to be replenished with as much soup or porridge as would keep off death for one day longer. We gathered subscriptions from all who were willing to give, made collections among ourselves and received from America most generous gifts from congregations and from personal friends. By such means, the population were kept alive, until the new crop of 1847 gave substantial relief. But the effects of the famine of 1846 were felt in Ireland for many a day. Ever since, there has been a partial failure of the potato every year in Ireland, but never to the same extent as in that memorable year. Had we known what was about to come so soon, we would not have entered on the erection of our tower and gallery. But we had advanced too far to recede. The famine broke out and all through that terrible year, 1847, the work proceeded. By the time the enlargement was finished, it was found not to be so much needed as it had been and it was several years before the space was filled up. Ultimately it was found insufficient and under my successor had to be enlarged again.

The next thing to claim my attention was the Sabbath school. It had proved in every way so beneficial that, as it appeared to me, it might be extended with advantage. There was no evening service in the church. The morning service was over at three and then came the long afternoon or winter night, during which the young people had nothing to do. Evening Sabbath schools were started over the country, held either in schoolrooms or in cottages which were given for the purpose. Each of these drew in the children of the whole neighbourhood and each was furnished with a superintendent and a staff of teachers belonging to itself. Without weakening the morning school, which still

The Parade, Portstewart.
15261 JV

Bathing Place.
Portrush Co. Antrim.

continued in its efficiency, this institution reached all the Protestant children in the district and gave me an opportunity of visiting and addressing them as often as I was able. Then, once a year in those days, we brought the country schools, of which at one time six or seven were in full flow, into the church of a week evening in summer and had them addressed by ministers. That was a sight worth seeing. Each school, its pupils walking in procession, two by two, and headed each class by its own teacher, marched into town and filled the church from end to end. A thousand children and sometimes more were packed into the house. The practice gave us a fitting opportunity of showing our strength and created the enthusiasm that numbers always excite. It made an impression on the whole neighbourhood and made it more difficult for the proselytizer to do us any damage. A curate who, it seems, had been trying his hand at this kind of thing, at last spoke to me and said that, if I would leave him alone, he would leave me alone. Affecting not to understand him, I merely said that I thought both of us were bound to do all the good in our power.

During these early years, the short holiday of a week or fortnight that I was able to take in the summer was usually spent at the seaside, with my ever kind and affectionate friends, Mr and Mrs Matthew Lytle. Mrs Lytle, in her unmarried days, had been a Miss Hunter of Cookstown. She was late in marrying and never had any children but one, a daughter, who died after reaching womanhood and when under engagement to be married. Mrs Lytle was left childless in the spring of 1845, some time before I went to Maghera. She was then in great sorrow and it seemed as if she looked upon me as another child, sent in Providence to compensate her for the daughter she had lost. At all events, she could not have lavished upon me more affection than she did. Up till her death in 1860 she treated me as her own son and could scarcely bear me to be more than a day or two at a time out of her sight. When she went to the shore, that was warning for me to prepare and she was seldom a week there till I had an invitation to join her. I was with her for a fortnight at Port-Ballintrae in 1846, then at Portstewart in 1847 and following years and then at Portrush from 1853 till 1859, after which time Mrs Lytle had grown very feeble and handed me over to the charge of the lady who in that year united her destinies to mine. Those pleasant days spent entirely in the company of two of the best friends I ever had, can never be forgotten. Theirs is one of the friendships that I hope to have renewed in the Better Land.

On these occasions I enjoyed opportunities of making acquaintances among ministers and others that I could not have had in Maghera. When stopping at Portstewart in the summer of 1851, I met an old gentleman named Dickson, who, with his wife and family, was spending his holiday at the seaside. He was a merchant, I ascertained, in Dungannon and an elder in the Presbyterian Church. I spent several

TO THE PRESBYTERIANS OF MAGHERA AND ITS VICINITY.

My Dear Friends,

In a very few days you will be required to vote for members to represent our County in Parliament. As you well know, it is parliament that makes the laws: these laws are binding on the whole people: we are all therefore deeply interested that you make such a use of your privilege of voting as to return men, who will state your grievances to Parliament, who will do their best to have those grievances redressed, and whose principles if carried into law will best promote the good of the Country.

Three Candidates are now before you, Mr. Greer, Mr. Jones and Mr. Bateson. With regard to the personal qualifications of all three to serve in Parliament there can be no second opinion. They are all intelligent, respectable, honourable men. But with regard to their political principles it appears to me that there is a very wide difference. Mr. Jones has represented Derry for twenty years—Mr. Bateson for nine. During all that time what good have those Gentlemen done the County? My opinion is that they have not only done us little good, but all the harm that it was in their power to do. When the Government brought in the Bill by which most of you have votes, these two Gentlemen opposed it with all their force. When Sharman Crawford brought in his Tenant-Right Bill, the object of which was to give you a legal right to be paid for the improvements you make on your farm, these two Gentlemen voted even against the principle of the Bill. Every thing that would benefit the landlords at the expense of the people, and put the poor tenantry more and more at their mercy, has found ready supporters in Messrs Bateson and Jones, the two Gentlemen who are now asking you to send them to Parliament that they may damage your interests once more. If such has been their practices, what must be their principles.

Mr. Greer on the other hand comes forward as the friend of the people. From an acquaintanceship of several years, I am able to say that I believe him to be a high-minded man, on whose principles and integrity the County may rely. He is the supporter of Civil and Religious Liberty. He is the advocate of Grand Jury Reform. If returned to Parliament, he will vote for having the Tenant-right custom made the law of the land. He will tell the wants and complaints of the tenantry to the House of Commons, and employ all his talents and eloquence to obtain for the people justice. And the very circumstance that his opponents allege against him namely, that the bulk of his property does not consist of land is the very reason why he will be better fitted to befriend you, for a great Landlord sent to Parliament usually looks for his own interests, and forgets those of the Tenant,

But what most of all recommends Mr. Greer to me is that he is a Presbyterian—a Ruling Elder in the Church—a member of the General Assembly. Presbyterians are often assailed in the House of Commons; we require to have there a member of our own communion to raise his voice on our behalf. Our principles are there misstated through ignorance if not misrepresented by design: the interests of truth demand that we should send a Presbyterian to Parliament to give voice to our principles in the high places of the land. The Catholics of Ireland have Members of their own Church in Parliament—why should they not? The Established Church has members of its Communion in Parliament—why should it not? But the Presbyterians of Ireland though they be 600,000 in number—fully one half the Protestants in the Country—have no member of their own Church to represent them there. Would that my native County were the first in Ireland to wipe off the deep disgrace that lies upon our name, and strike a blow that would thrill with joy every true Presbyterian's heart. The revised list of County voters comprises twenty-eight hundred Presbyterians, Eleven hundred Catholics, and four hundred Church-men: yet the Church party have held in their hands the representation of the County for generations. Presbyterians I ask you how long will the many submit to be trampled on by the few? Roman Catholics, notwithstanding their well known love for their own Church, have generally come forward to support a man, whose religious opinions are different from theirs, because they know him to be the advocate of popular rights—how much more should we record our votes for one who in addition to his sound political principles, is of the same religion with ourselves! Return Mr. Greer, to Parliament and you make all the enemies of your cause to quail; but if the Presbyterians of Derry fling one of the noblest of the Sons of their own Church away from them they deserve to wear the chain and collar of slavery till the bells of eternity ring. The glorious Constitution under which we live, and the laws of our Country give every elector the right of saying who is the man of his choice, but if Presbyterians rush to the poll to vote against the first Presbyterian who ever, so far as I know, offered himself to the Electors of Derry, they do a deed that will crown them with everlasting infamy. There may be traitors in the camp, but, Presbyterians of Maghera, I am far deceived if they be found among

→

evenings in his lodgings. Our conversation sometimes took a political turn and all the more so, when I discovered that he was a Conservative and he found out that I was a Liberal. His son, a lad of some fifteen or sixteen years, listened attentively as I descanted on the great shame of Presbyterians allowing themselves to be led captive by Episcopalians to vote for them at elections, to aid them in maintaining their ascendancy and to be rewarded in the end with their hatred and contempt. The young lad did not interfere in the conversation; he was only an interested auditor. That young lad was since the sitting Member for Dungannon and afterwards for the County Tyrone. Since that time the pupil has gone beyond the teacher. He is now a Home Ruler, representing in the House of Commons the St Stephen's division of Dublin, the very district within which at this moment I am, as it so happens, writing these lines.

In September 1850 I went up to Kerry, at the request of Dr Edward Dill, to supply his place for six weeks at a mission station near to Milltown. An Edinburgh lady who had long managed a successful boarding-school in that city was then spending her last days in conducting a school for the instruction of Irish lads in Kerry. This was the only appointment I ever held from the Mission Board and, at the request of the Rev George Bellis, I wrote on my return an account of the station in the 'Missionary Herald'. This was the only opportunity I ever enjoyed of seeing Killarney, Magillicuddy, Cork, Queenstown and the South. Beyond standing at Ross Castle and looking across the water, I could scarcely be said to have seen the Lakes at all. It rained all the time I was there. I came home impressed with two ideas, the magnificence of the country and the poverty of the people, to which I may be allowed to add the great difficulty of doing them any good in a religious point of view.

In the spring of 1852 there were indications that a General Election was not far away. An extension of the franchise to £12 occupiers in Ireland had put political power more largely into the hand of the middle class and, as the country had been long complaining of harsh treatment by the landlords, it was determined to give the farmers an opportunity of asserting their rights. Presbyterians were complaining, too, that the Episcopalian Conservative gentry who represented them cared nothing whatever about the religious interests of that large class of Protestants who had sent them to Parliament. It was determined to give the Presbyterian and Roman Catholic farmers of the County Derry an opportunity of showing their strength, but the difficulty was that all of them, with few exceptions, were tenants at will and of course completely in the landlords' power, while at that time the shield of the ballot was not thrown over them for protection.

Early in May, Mr Samuel McCurdy Greer of Springvale, Castlerock, came forward in the Presbyterian and Tenant you. Most of you plump for the Presbyterian Candidate; a few will split their votes for him and one of his opponents—an odd individual may refuse to vote at all; but I do not expect that a single man of you will register his vote against his Church, his Country, and himself. The almost universal unanimity that prevails among you, and the sturdy independence you are manifesting every day, combine to give joy to my heart, and make me proud of being your Minister. Were it otherewise—were I doomed to labour among a congregation of serfs, the very thought would make me hang my head for shame, and I would shut my door in silence to lament that from us the last vestige of Presbyterian Ireland had departed.

My dear friends and brethren, these are times that every man occupying the position as a teacher of the people, should point out the path of duty, and when danger comes in the distance should lift up a warning voice You will suffer therefore the word of exhortation, while I give you what I consider in times such as these very needful advice.

1.—*Vote in accordance with your Conscience.* When the law of the land confers on you the right to vote it bestows a sacred trust, which you as you shall answer to God are bound to use for His glory and the good of the community. Your vote is a talent for which you are responsible to God, and you should not let craft entice or power force you to employ that talent in any other way. than after a calm consideration of the matter you judge best for the welfare of the Country. The Landlord has a right to his rent, so long as you occupy his land; he he has a right to your respect so long as his conduct deserves it, but to lord it over your conscience and compel you to vote against the conviction of your own mind is what no man on earth has a right to do. Presbyterian doctrine it ever has been—it ever must be, that "God alone is Lord of the conscience." The rights of conscience are guaranteed to us by British law. It was for the right of conscience that our Covenanted forefathers shed the dearest blood of their hearts, and after winning their rights on the field of war and on the scaffold of the martyr their children will not be so degenerate now as to surrender them at the power of an Agent, or the summons of a Bailiff. If man were to punish you for voting as your conscience directs, the duty of a Christian is clear. He is to take joyfully the spoilings of his goods, remembering the words of the Master(Matt. V. 10.,) "Blessed are they which are persecuted for righteousness sake for theirs is the kingdom of heaven"—and you will have the consolation of reflecting that to the best of your knowledge you tried to do your duty to God and to man. But thank God you have no such suffering in prospect. I am led to believe that our resident Landlords beyond indicating their preferences and using their personal influence, as they have a legitimate right to do, have no intention of forcing any man to vote against his mind. You have a right to remember it to their honour for ever that not one word of compulsion, notwithstanding the rumours that are abroad, has escaped their lips; and I am very far mistaken in their manly and honourable spirit, if after the heat and hurry of the contest is over they do not pay more respect to independent men, who gave their honorable opposition, than to cringing slaves, who curse yet crouch and kiss their chains. Nothwithstanding all the prejudices of Education and class even they can distinguish between the respect of freemen, and the homage of serfs.

2.—*Beware of Bribery.* No contested election ever prospers without bribes flying about in all directions. At such a time, promises ofall kinds are made, situations of all kinds are held out, ardent spirts flow in streams: and for meat and drink, for place and person, for some petty personal gain a man is expected to give his vote and sell his conscience. Dear brethern, beware of temptation. Scorn a filthy bribe, come from who it may. Let me warn you that the Bribery Oath will be put to every man about whose conduct any suspicion is entertained and the Elector who takes that oath while he pockets his bribe votes for his man at the expense of his soul. It is a characteristic of the enemies of God that their right hand is full of bribes (Ps. XXVI. 10.) Again it is said. "He that despiseth the gain of oppression and shaketh his hands from holding of bribes. . he shall dwell on high; his place of defence shall be munitions of rocks, bread shall be given him, his, water shall be sure." (Isaiah XXXIII. 15-16.) And again it was said "fire shall consume the tabernacles of bribery."(Job. XV. 34.) Presbyterians of Maghera, you I am satisfied will scorn to receive a bribe come from what party it may. Give your vote to the man of your choice on public ground, without taking base personal profit into account. Let no man's meat or drink—let no man's money, let no man's smile bribe you to give a vote, but go to the polling booth, to vote for the man whose principles you believe if carried into law would benefit the country, with as much solemnity and determination as you engage in the most sacred duty you are ever called on to discharge.

3.—*Keep the Peace.* Let no taunt, no clamour, no bad language tempt you to break the Law. Depend upon it no good can come in the end to any party by violence and blows and bloodshed. The cause of the people is good, and it can only be retarded and disgraced, but certainly not advanced by riot and disorder. Let me see therefore that you act in strict accordance with the Law, that you pay due respect to the constituted authorities, and that you do your best to maintain peace and good order; but determine at the same time that by the blessing

Right interest. The canvass lasted from the first week in May till 20 July. It was a very hot struggle indeed. I stood warmly to Mr Greer, who ran against Sir Thomas Bateson and Admiral Jones. The congregation, considering their circumstances and the novelty of any political contest in the County, behaved nobly. The voters in the congregation were then ninety-six,out of which Mr Greer got eighty votes, about sixty of which were plumpers. We were beaten in the result, but the fight was so keen and well contested that neither of the victors ever ventured to offer themselves to the Derry electors again. On this occasion the Presbyterians who started the opposition were ably assisted by the Roman Catholics, both of them feeling that the battle in reality was their own. On the occasion of this contest, I issued an address to the Presbyterian Electors of Maghera which was printed, reprinted and largely circulated over the County.

The excitement of the time was great, so much so indeed that the reaction from it nearly cost me my life. The day after the issue was announced, I was sent for to attend the funeral of my mother, who for some time had been in declining health, but who was called away unexpectedly at last. A week or ten days were spent at the seaside, after which I went to the British Association which met that year in Belfast. I found it pleasant to see Sir David Brewster, Sir William Thomson, Sir John Ross (the Arctic navigator), General Sabine, Sir Roderick Murchison and other men of science of whom I had often read. On Saturday I came home, not ill, but excited with the meeting and the conversazione held in connexion with it. Next morning I felt pains in my joints and was reluctant to rise, but I had engaged to supply Bellaghy in Templeton's absence and rise I must. I drove to Bellaghy and preached. So long as I moved in the open air, I seemed all right, but when I returned, and sat down in my own house, I felt very ill indeed. My head was ready to split. Next day the Doctor came and pronounced my disease to be typhoid fever. Dr Moore came from Dungiven, bled me and shaved my head. The next three weeks I was virtually dead. I remember nothing that occurred. When I recovered consciousness, my dear friend, Mr Barkley, was reading and praying at my bedside. A day or two after, when I was able to bear it, Mr Lytle told me that the Presbytery had undertaken the supply of the pulpit for three months and that, since I took ill, the congregation had met every evening in the church, after the labours of the day were over, to pray for my recovery and that the whole house was full. That kindness I never can forget to the people of Maghera. I believe now, as I believed then, that my unworthy life was spared in answer to their earnest prayers.

(9) From Illness to Marriage: 1853-59

The idea of authorship haunted me from the first. My attention was turned to the subject of Establishment of of God you will use every privilege that the Constitution puts within your reach to advance the prosperity of your Country and good of your Church, and despite the force or flattery of power, you will vote for the man who promises to do his very best to secure the comfort and independence of you and your children.

My Dear Friend, you have now the state of the case fairly put before you let matters go as they may, I have the consolation of knowing that I have unburthened my conscience, and done my duty to you and myself—to the people who groan under heavy burthens and to a church which to me, and to many of you also, is dear as the very life. For the part I have taken I count on meeting much ill-will. Honours and emoluments await those who fight the battles of the great and rich; contempt and hatred to those who struggle for the weak and poor, but these things move me not. I have had a duty to discharge and I have tried to do it. I wish to keep a conscience void of offence toward God and man. Men may speak of me as they think I deserve, but I wish to leave in the power of no man—not even of an enemy—to say of me when I am dead, that my heart ever beat coldly to the cause of my Church and the cause of my people, or that from fear of men I forgot my principles.

My dear friends and brethren. I remain yours in esteem and affection, &c., &c.

THOMAS WITHEROW.

Maghera, 6th July, 1852.

Religion by reading the 'Report' of Dr Cooke's discussion with Dr Ritchie in Belfast, but especially by what seemed to me the injustice of supporting one form of Christianity at the expense of persons who did not profess it, but who had chosen another form in preference. In every part of Ireland this subject was forced on a man's attention, whether he chose it or not.

My private reading since my ordination was of a somewhat miscellaneous kind, but it had finally been directed to the line of English Literature, History and Theology. My thoughts gathered around the subject of Civil Establishments of Religion and finally assumed the form of a treatise. The composition of this treatise was begun in the second year of my pastorate in Maghera, but the work was copied over no fewer than four or five times, with the view of making it as perfect as it was possible for me to make it. The couple of months' rest, which, through the kindness of my brethren, I was able to take on my recovery from fever, was devoted to this object and the opening months of 1853 were spent in copying out this treatise for the fifth and last time. The idea of the treatise is this. The visible Church of Christ on Earth is not limited to any one section of the Christian name, but properly includes the professors of all forms of the Christian religion. To endorse any one of them, to the exclusion of the others, is simply to subsidize a sect, not to establish Christianity. The only just form of Establishment by a Christian government is to levy a tithe or other tax for the support of the Christian religion and then to hand over to each Christian sect that proportion of the tax which is paid by its own members. The purport of my essay was to expound this 'Theory of a Universal Establishment', to state arguments in its favour and to answer objections.

So enamoured was I at the time with this theory, that I certainly would have published it, had it not been that a young unknown writer had no chance of a publisher and that, with my small income, I could not face the risk of printing it at my own expense. I, therefore, had the manuscript bound up in a volume and put it on the shelf along with my shorthand sermons. For the last thirty-five years I have not read a chapter in that still-born book. Fortunately for myself, and perhaps for somebody else, it never saw the light. It being the first production of my hand, I cannot bear the thought of its destruction. Neither do I now desire its publication, for it would serve no good end. I prefer that my children should keep it as a memorial and a curiosity. As to the abstract justice of the theory, I am as firmly convinced as I was forty years ago. But I am now better acquainted with human nature and am satisfied that, in this wicked world, where nobody is satisfied to see his neighbour put on a level with himself, the plan would not work. At least it would not work very long.

My respected and earliest friends in the Presbytery of Magherafelt were now rapidly passing away. Mr Radcliffe

Three Prophets Of Our Own

Carson

Clarke

Cooke

A lecture on

Adam Clarke, Alexander Carson and Henry Cooke,

delivered in Maghera on 3 January 1855,
by Rev Thomas Witherow (1824-1890)

Republished on the
centenary of the author's death,
with Introduction and Illustrations

MEMORIAL CHURCH AND OBELISK, PORTRUSH

THE CLARKE MEMORIAL CHURCH, PORTSTEWART

in 1848 resigned Castledawson and was sent out by the Church of Scotland to be minister of the Scotch Church in Kingstown, Jamaica, where he yet (1888) resides and from which he sends me a much-valued communication now and again. Mr Rodgers of Kilrea died suddenly in Belfast, during the Assembly of 1851. My very dear friend, the Rev James Wilson of Magherafelt, died in 1854 and was succeeded in his congregation by a former fellow-student and friend of my own, the Rev Alexander Montgomery, who had, for some time before, been minister of Hillsborough. I was appointed to succeed Mr Wilson as Clerk of Presbytery, a position which I held till I left Maghera to remove to Derry.

Much about this time it became the common practice, in most of the towns in Ulster, to establish societies of young men for Christian work and intellectual improvement, popularly known as Young Men's Christian Associations. There was one set up in Maghera, before which clergymen and others were asked to appear and deliver an occasional lecture on non-political and un-denominational subjects. About the autumn of 1854 I was asked to deliver one of these lectures and I chose as the subject 'Our Local Celebrities'. It was a biographical sketch of Adam Clarke, the Methodist commentator, Alexander Carson, the Baptist theologian, and Henry Cooke, the Presbyterian orator. For two and a half hours of a cold winter's night, about the beginning of 1855, a large audience sat in the Market House of Maghera to listen to that address. It was listened to with much favour and was soon afterwards printed. At the end of thirty years, it has been reprinted in a second edition. This was the first of my productions ever offered in a separate form to the public and it was noticed so favourably in the Belfast and Derry newspapers, that I was encouraged in due time to try again. Under its title, as published, 'Three Prophets of Our Own', it has become well-known to the reading public of Ulster. A notice by Professor Gibson, giving copious extracts, which appeared in the 'Banner of Ulster', introduced it favourably to Presbyterian readers.

Since completing my 'Theory of a Universal Establishment', I began for the first time to read with a definite purpose in view and thus to turn my studies, which hitherto had been rather desultory and aimless, in one well-understood direction. I knew that, some day or other, professors would be needed for the Magee College and why, I asked myself, should I not read with that in view? My tastes ran strongly in the line of Church History. Why should I not qualify for the position, should an opportunity ever present itself? I was but an ordinary preacher, scarcely even that. Why should I not try to be useful in the line of authorship? I entered with avidity on the study of Church Government. The first fruits of this began to appear when, in the end of that year, Shepperd and Hutchinson of Belfast issued the first edition of 'The Apostolic Church'. It bore 1856 on the imprint,

Baptist churches,
old and new,
in Tobermore

TOBERMORE PRESBYTERIAN CHURCH. Photo by A. W. M'Whinney.

but it was published early in December 1855. My object in that little work was to put the argument for the Presbyterian polity in a simpler and clearer light than I had ever seen it put. Any exposition I had previously seen confused the mind of the reader, by going too much into detail and by dealing with principles in an unscientific manner. My idea was to touch nothing but great ecclesiastical principles, to refuse to consider mere details, to put the principles on a sound Scriptural basis, to range them in order, beginning with the simpler and easy and rising gradually up to the more difficult and important, and to cast the whole into a form that the people would understand. In doing so, I am led to believe that in some measure I succeeded. It has passed through a variety of editions and has been stereotyped for the use of Sabbath schools. It was reprinted at London, at Toronto, and at Philadelphia, by the American Board of Publication, and has found greater acceptance with the Presbyterian people than I could ever have anticipated when I sat down to write it in my humble study in the town of Maghera.

So far as I know, only two replies have been written to it, one by an Episcopalian clergyman who is settled somewhere in the backwoods of Canada, the other by an old friend and neighbour, the Rev Robert H Carson, Baptist minister of Tubbermore. The Episcopalian reply was written long after 'The Apostolic Church' had appeared and the feeble work of a writer, of whom I never heard before or since, did not seem to me to be worth the loss of powder and shot. Mr Carson's reply was more formidable and, as his counter-shot had been delivered at my own door, it seemed to me deserving of an extended refutation. Mr Carson's father, the Rev Alexander Carson LLD, had at one time been minister of the Presbyterian Church, but had left it first to become an Independent and subsequently a Baptist. To his high religious character and great abilities I did my very utmost to do justice in 'Three Prophets of Our Own', my recently-published lecture. 'The Apostolic Church' was not written with the design of attacking Independency, which is not much known in Ireland, but, as one of the three great systems of Church Government, which my subject required me to compare and contrast, it could not be entirely overlooked. I touched upon it, as I supposed, in the most inoffensive way. But my neighbour made this the cause of quarrel with me. He took the opportunity of attacking not only the Presbyterian system, but of attacking myself. He counted, I suppose, that he would escape as easily out of my hands as his father escaped from that most childlike and guileless of all Christian ministers, the Rev William Brown of Tubbermore. But he was mistaken in his calculation.

I sat down deliberately to the examination of his gratuitously offensive pamphlet. I not only tore his arguments into rags, but held them up to ridicule and derision. The whole country was set to laugh at a gentleman who came out to war with his father as his main

The Apostolic Church

Which Is It?

AN INQUIRY
AT THE ORACLES OF GOD AS TO WHETHER
ANY EXISTING FORM OF CHURCH GOVERNMENT IS
OF DIVINE RIGHT

BY

THOMAS WITHEROW

PROFESSOR OF CHURCH HISTORY, LONDONDERRY

"If a Divine plan of Church Government be extremely necessary, by what authority does any man reject the apostolical?"—*Dr Carson.*

EDINBURGH:
ANDREW ELLIOT, 17 PRINCES STREET.

HUDIE McGUIGAN

The "Quarter-Clift"

by

'Benroe'

Moyola Books

authority and who looked at everything with his father's eyes. Ever since the publication of the 'Defence of the Apostolic Church', the Baptists in that part of the country know that the Presbyterians have something to say for themselves and it is possible now to live quietly beside them, which had not been the case for fifty years before. A few days after the 'Defence' appeared, Dr Cooke wrote down to me from Belfast: "You have taken revenge for Hudy McGuigan". Hudy McGuigan had been an eccentric simpleton, well known in all that country, who had once attempted to fly from the summit of a cliff, Craignashook, with the wings of a goose tied to his arms, and the half-doors of a barn fastened to his limbs, and who, as the result of his mad experiment, fell and broke his leg. It was to this character that the late Dr Carson, in the heat of controversy, had shocked the religious public by comparing his respected and venerable neighbour, the minister of Tubbermore. Dr Cooke, who knew the neighbourhood well and the provocation the Presbyterian people had so long endured, commented on my performance by saying:"you have taken revenge for Hudy McGuigan". Mr Carson was, of course, furious at my keen rejoinder and he published a bulky pamphlet in reply to the 'Defence', but, as I never met anybody who read it through, I did not farther notice either it or him. He was taught a useful lesson which has made him a very quiet and peaceable neighbour ever since.

Ever since 1852 Mr S M Greer had entertained the idea of contesting the County again, and had been striving to prepare the electors for a new struggle. In the spring of 1857 an opportunity presented itself. A General Election was certain to occur and, five or six weeks before the expected dissolution, Sir Thomas Bateson resigned with the intimation that he did not mean to seek re-election. Mr Greer was a poor man and, should he be elected, it was known that he would not have more than time to take his seat, until the dissolution would compel him to face the expense of a second election. The result turned out very differently from what was expected. On the announcement being made that Bateson had resigned, the Conservative landlords met at Coleraine and chose my neighbour, Mr J J Clark of Largantogher, as their candidate. That night, before going home, Mr Clark called at my door to announce his selection by his party and to solicit my support. This put me into a difficulty. Mr Clark, though no longer a member of the Presbyterian congregation, had nevertheless claims upon me. He was perhaps the most unobjectionable of his party. He was a moderate Conservative and had never given encouragement to Orangeism or extreme politics of any kind. He was a good landlord, a just magistrate, and a sensible and kindly man. I told him, however, that I could not support him in opposition to a Liberal and Presbyterian candidate, but that I did not mean on this occasion, beyond giving my vote, to take an active part in the election.

Neither I did. I polled early and immediately after returned home to Maghera. In the afternoon some stone-

Broad Street, Magherafelt.

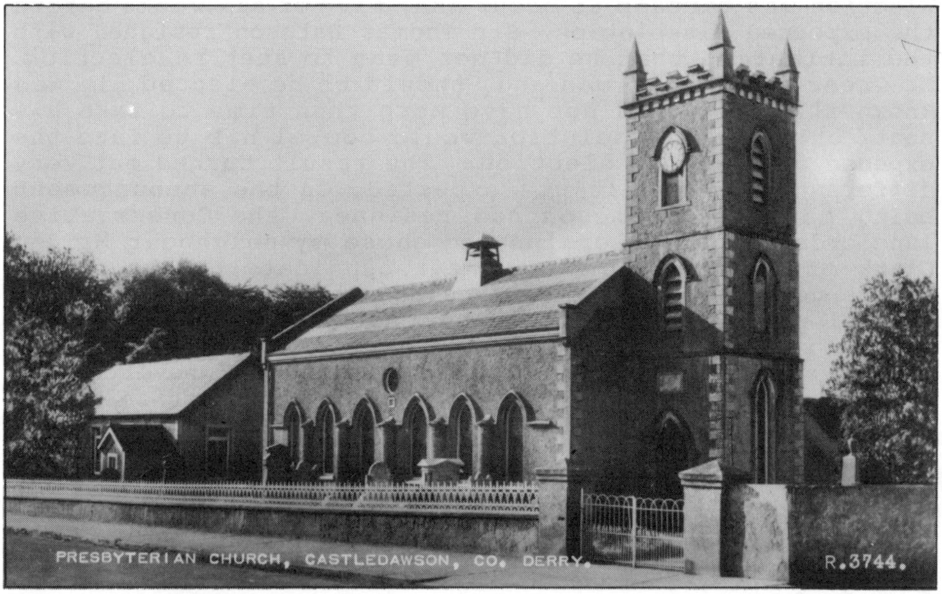
PRESBYTERIAN CHURCH, CASTLEDAWSON, CO. DERRY. R.3744.

throwing and rioting occurred on the street at Magherafelt, before the poll closed. The dragoons were sent, by the magistrate-in-charge, up through the crowd, and, seeing a gentleman in the garb of a minister in the midst of a riotous mob, they took him to be a ringleader and forthwith arrested him on the charge of being a stone-thrower and a rioter. The minister proved to be the Rev Robert Gamble of Castledawson, a man of kindly and peaceable spirit, but a man who knew no fear and who, having great influence with his party, had stepped in among them to stop the stone-throwing and riot. My wife's sister, Mrs Morrison of Magherafelt, who occupied the corner house of Broad Street nearest the Diamond, saw the whole affair from the first and could have testified, if necessary, that Mr Gamble, instead of breaking the peace, was, at the time of his arrest, doing all in his power to preserve it. He was taken down, however, as a prisoner to the Courthouse, which then stood at the foot of Broad Street; but the mob grew so indignant and threatening that the magistrate ordered his release. Informations, however, were sworn against him by the dragoons, and, next morning being Saturday, he was re-arrested in his house at Castledawson, and, as he refused to give bail, he was sent as a prisoner to Derry gaol. When he and his escort reached Derry, instead of lodging him in prison, the sub-inspector took him to a hotel. Mr Forrest Reid, a respectable solicitor, was sent for, and, by his advice, Mr Gamble gave bail to stand his trial; whereupon he was released. He did subsequently stand his trial at the Derry Assizes and was acquitted, there being no evidence against him, except that of the dragoons who arrested him under a mistake.

Meanwhile the indignation all over the country was very great, in consequence of the arrest of Mr Gamble and the loss of the election to the Liberal candidate. There was afterwards reason to believe that the arrest had occurred in consequence of the magistrate, sent by Government to take charge of the polling-place, being a hot-headed Tory, who wanted, under pretence of doing his duty, to strike terror to the opposite party. But the popular belief at the time was that the whole was a concerted thing among the local magistrates and landlords. The Presbyterians all over the county were deeply stirred. Ministers addressed their congregations on the Sabbath, hinted that the days of Claverhouse were at hand and asked how long Presbyterians would submit to be thus treated by a set of despots and oppressors. An elder at Castledawson, much respected in the neighbourhood, but who had worked for the Conservative candidate on the previous Friday, rose on Sabbath to lift the collection as he was in the habit of doing, but the first man to whom the box was presented lifted his foot and gave it a kick. The whole congregation, through whom an electric current of excitement ran, leaped to their feet and it took the utmost efforts of Mr Montgomery, who had come down from Magherafelt to conduct the religious service in room of the arrested minister, to soothe the congregation and preserve the peace.

That week Mr Clark started for London and, on the very night on which he took his seat in the House of Commons, Parliament was dissolved; and, at the very time when the Presbyterian electors were so highly excited over the arrest of Mr Gamble, the county was thrown into another election. This time there were three candidates for the two seats, Mr Clark, Mr Greer and Sir Hervey Bruce of Downhill. The last-named gentleman was an extreme Tory, who was not very acceptable, even to his own party. The opportunity for an effective opposition was the very best that could be desired. The Presbyterian blood was roused at last. The name of 'Gamble' everywhere stirred the feeling of the electors and, when the poll came, notwithstanding that the voters were almost all at the mercy of the landlords and unprotected by the ballot, Clark and Greer were returned. That was the first Liberal and Tenant Right victory in the County Londonderry. Mr Greer represented the County for two years, but, at the General Election of 1859, the popular enthusiasm had cooled. Mr Greer was beaten and two Tories were once more returned. We thought that the movement of 1857 in favour of the Liberals was a revolution. It proved to be only a revolt.

The excitement of the 1852 election had, in my case, been followed by such painful results as to deter me from taking a very active part in any of these later elections. During the contest between Mr Clark and Mr Greer, I contrived to be absent on a visit to Mr Waddell, a friend who resided near Ballybay in County Monaghan, and only returned in time to vote for Mr Greer. Roused by the harsh treatment extended to my brother Gamble, I threw myself heartily into the second election of 1857, when Greer was returned. At the canvass of 1859, I was away on my wedding-trip, returning, however, in time to vote. These bitter contests I found to be unpleasant in a high degree, but, when I was possessor of a vote, I regarded it as a talent that I was bound to use on the side of the political party in whose principles and action I had, upon the whole, most confidence.

It was in June 1857 that I saw London for the first time. Mr Todd and I went over to Manchester to attend a Temperance Convention and to see the Arts Treasures Exhibition. There we were joined by Mr Simpson, minister of Portrush, and then all three went on to London. We lodged at a private boarding-house in a court off Holborn, exactly opposite Chancery Lane. I was deeply impressed by the magnificent buildings, the interminable streets, the splendid parks, the vast multitudes of people and vehicles and the never-ceasing roar. We saw most of all the places usually visited by strangers, the British Museum, the National Gallery, the Tower, the Crystal Palace, St Paul's, Westminster Abbey and the Houses of Parliament. On the night I attended the House of Commons, I saw and heard Lord Palmerston, Sir George Cornwall Lewis, Sir Francis Thesiger, Sergeant Warren and Sergeant Kinglake (who made his maiden speech, lost the thread of his story and

Largantogher, home of J J Clark

suddenly sat down). Five years after, in 1862, I paid London a second visit to see the Great Exhibition held in that year, on which occasion Mr Montgomery of Magherafelt and I visited the Kensington Museum, Spurgeon's Tabernacle, Richmond, the Kew Gardens and Windsor Palace. I need scarcely say how much these two visits to the centre of the world's life added to my experience and enjoyment.

It would be now to me a matter of regret and shame if I had been for twenty years the minister of a large congregation without doing anything effective to encourage their growth in knowledge. There is a tradition that an old minister of Maghera once said, on the occasion of some brethren being troubled for putting their schools under care of the National Board, that he thanked God that he never took anything to do with education. Whether such words were ever actually used I do not know, but the state of things in regard to education was such, at the time when I settled in Maghera, that it was the embodiment of the spirit that these words expressed. The Episcopalians had in town a male and female school, both well attended and fitly lodged in a suitable building. The Roman Catholics had one mixed school at the upper end of the town, placed in connexion with the Vocational Board. The Presbyterians, who in a circle of three miles about the town were at least four-fifths of the Protestant population, had in town no school whatever. Most of their children went to the Episcopal and Roman Catholic schools. The only National School with a Presbyterian teacher was one established at Milltown, by Mr J J Clark of Largantogher, which, when I visited it, had eight pupils and no appliances whatever. Mr Paul, the precentor of the congregation, was the Master of a private school established in an outhouse on his own farm in Crew; but, owing to some objection that he entertained to the National Board, he had not put his school under its care. He drew no salary from it, and, of course, derived no advantages in the way of books or furniture. Still, his was the best school in the neighbourhood and he contrived to give the best lads in the country a good substantial English education. There was, in addition, a Church school in Carricknakielt, and a Company's school in Dunglady, but, not being under the Board, they were in other respects very inefficient.

The first step was to induce my friend, Mr William Lytle of Tullyheron, to fit up a vacant house for a female school, mainly for the use of his own children, but to which those of his neighbours were admitted; and this we succeeded in putting under the National Board. At the end of five or six years, a second step was taken. We induced Mr Clark to give us an old turfhouse, once connected with the Brewery. We ran up a partition, dividing it into two portions, and, at an expense of £200, fitted up the portions into a male and female schoolroom. The Milltown school, with consent of Mr Clark, was transferred to the one apartment and the Tullyheron school, with Mr Lytle's consent, was transferred to the other. This gave us at once a male and female school in town, each endowed by the Board. There was some little difficulty about transferring the endowment of Milltown school to the new quarters, mainly caused by the fact that Mr Knox, the rector, who had hitherto been antagonistic to the National System, had secretly applied for endowment for his boys' school; so that, when we sought a transfer of endowment, we discovered that he had anticipated us and the Board was reluctant, naturally enough, to plant a third male school in the same town. Mr Clark, however, rendered us powerful assistance and, after some little delay, we carried our point. Excellent teachers were appointed in these schools from the first and the whole district soon showed appreciation of them. Eventually Mr Paul was induced to connect his school with the Board and a mixed school, under a diligent female teacher, was established in Beagh. For some years before I left Maghera, four flourishing National Schools were in operation, carried on by Presbyterian teachers under my management. I took good care to have them well supplied with books and slates and maps, so that teachers were substantially helped and the parents satisfied with the growing intelligence of their children. The money required for fitting up the two schools in town to the amount of £140 was raised by subscription in the congregation and the remaining £60 was the product of a charity sermon preached by Dr Cooke.

A little physical infirmity which followed me for five and twenty years need not here be noticed, were it not that for some years it disabled me from pastoral visitation and made me long more ardently for a position in which I would not be expected to undertake so much physical exertion. In the summer of 1859 I noticed the appearance of a red itchy spot about the size of a shilling on the narrow part of my right leg, two inches above the ankle. When scratched, it exuded water and at a later period blood. Eventually it crept upwards and finally settled in the upper part of my calf. It developed in breadth, until it became somewhat broader than a five-shilling piece. Sometimes it gathered into a boil or small tumour, which, till it broke, gave me extreme pain. In 1858 it did not close for several months, but finally did so, on my applying the cold water cure. Sometimes it would dry up for several months at a time, making me believe that it had disappeared, but would break out again, as virulently as ever. Heat irritated it and when, at the end of the sermon, I sat down in a state of perspiration, I would often have to scratch it till it bled. Once for six months I knelt on a chair inside the pulpit and every sermon throughout the summer was preached on my knees. At ordinary times it was not painful, but it was at all times a trouble and vexation, a thorn in the flesh. Most of the physicians admitted honestly that it was beyond their skill to remove. Some tried it and failed. By the advice of Sir Robert Christison of Edinburgh, I used an arsenical solution diluted in water and this kept it in check. After afflicting me for more than twenty-five years, it passed away at last, as unaccountably as it came,

and now, for eleven years or so, I possess the privilege of a whole and healthy skin. The doctors called the complaint psoriasis, but it afforded me small comfort that they could do nothing but fix upon it a learned name.

On 13 April 1859 I was married at Castledawson by my friend, the Rev Alexander Montgomery, to Catherine Milling, second daughter of Thomas Milling, woollen-draper of Maghera. We kept our intention to get married a secret until the very day it came off, and, when the ceremony was over, we did not return to Maghera, but passed on to Sandymount, Dublin, where we stayed for a fortnight. There was no important step of my life in which I had so much reason to rejoice as this. Catherine made one of the best of wives. She bore me, during the twenty years that God permitted her to gladden my home, no fewer than ten children, three sons and seven daughters. Two of the sons died early; all the other children are alive at this date (August 1888). During the twenty happy years we spent together, time passed rapidly away. I could scarcely bear her out of my sight and, when business required me to be absent, as it sometimes did for eight or ten days at a time, I wrote to her regularly every day during all the time. She must have had some faults such as are common to humanity, but I can honestly say that in all these twenty years I never found one of them out. She was always cheerful, prudent, intelligent and good. We had no secrets from each other. Each understood thoroughly the other's affairs. We never differed on any subject. We consulted together and always acted for the best. If I acted at any time against her advice, I always found out at last that I was wrong. She was truthful, pious, sensible and pure, her only object in life being to please God and be useful to her husband and children. In all my acquaintance with women I never met any morally her superior. Her supreme delight was to deny herself in order to make her husband and children happy. All the time she lived, she multiplied my comforts and made my house a pleasant home. The separation that death made between us was the one great sorrow of my life.

MAIN STREET. MAGHERA.

THE YEAR OF GRACE:

A HISTORY OF

THE ULSTER REVIVAL OF 1859.

BY

THE REV. WILLIAM GIBSON,

PROFESSOR OF CHRISTIAN ETHICS, AND
MODERATOR OF THE GENERAL ASSEMBLY OF THE PRESBYTERIAN CHURCH IN IRELAND.

EDINBURGH:
ANDREW ELLIOT, 15 PRINCES STREET.
LONDON: HAMILTON, ADAMS, AND CO.
BELFAST: C. AITCHISON.
M.DCCC.LX.

Another work on
nineteenth-century life:

Buick's Ahoghill

❖

edited by Eull Dunlop

❖

- A filial account (1901) of Seceders in the Mid-Antrim village where Rev. Frederick Buick had been minister since 1835.

-An interesting insight into denominational customs of a century ago.

-A report on the 1859 Revival in Ahoghill.

-113 quarto pages, extensive footnotes, maps and photographs.

❖

Published by

Mid-Antrim Historical Group
1987

(10) From Marriage until the end of my Ministry: 1859-65

When my wife and myself returned from our wedding trip, we found the County Derry in the excitement of the election in which Mr Greer lost his seat. The agitation had scarcely quieted down until the religious movement known as the Revival of 1859 reached Maghera. The particulars of that movement in the congregation were written by me at the time and appeared in full in Professor Gibson's 'Year of Grace', published the following year. They need not therefore be repeated here. The account there given, so far as I am concerned, is true to the letter and the same statement might with truth be affirmed, as I believe, of the accounts written by the other ministers. I have only to add that there were, as it appeared to me, two classes of phenomena, physical and spiritual, of a very extraordinary kind. In the first place, there was a nervous affection of a powerful kind, by which the subject was often prostrated suddenly, accompanied by a sense of pressure on the heart, followed up by deliverance and freedom. Along with this physical affection, there was usually an amount of spiritual feeling of the most unusual kind. All fear was for a time at an end and a modest young girl or a country lad, who never before had put two sentences together, would give expression to their religious feelings, lead in prayer, comment on passages of Scripture or exhort acquaintances, whom they thought to be living careless lives, with great confidence and freedom. Religious people everywhere regarded it as a more than common outpouring of the Holy Ghost. Great popular meetings were held at which "the young converts" appeared and spoke with rough earnestness and warm feeling. The people attended the meetings in crowds and listened with such eagerness that they could scarcely be persuaded to go home. When a person was struck down, the people thronged around to sing and to pray and direct the stricken to Christ. Ministers were kept busy in those times. Some ignorant people regarded the physical affection as essential to conversion and some regarded visions and dreams as the evidence of a spiritual change. Ministers who expressed disapproval of these and other false notions were then spoken of as being themselves unconverted and as enemies of the Revival.

The religious movement prevailed mainly among the Presbyterians. Roman Catholics feared or derided it. Episcopalians as a body stood aloof from it. Methodists and Baptists tried to turn it to denominational purposes, but did not succeed to any great extent. The whole heat of the Revival had passed over in six months, but it was fully a year before the excitement had entirely passed away. As might be expected, some who made a high profession that year fell back to their old careless life, but, so far as I had opportunity to observe, many were permanently improved and, although the warm feeling of that time perceptibly cooled, they were more useful and more consistent in practice than they had ever been before. For a time, the

PASTORAL LETTER.

TO THE

CHURCH AND CONGREGATION

MEETING IN THE

BAPTIST CHAPEL, TUBBERMORE.

BRETHREN AND FRIENDS GREATLY BELOVED,

How mysterious are the ways of God! Just at the time when my labours among you seemed most required, I have been called to intermit them for a little season. Never at Tubbermore was there such a harvest to be reaped as now, and yet I have been removed from the field. Had my present indisposition occurred at another time, or under other circumstances, it would have occasioned no surprise; but when scores, nay, hundreds are crying out for the bread of life, to be unable to break to them that precious bread—Oh! is not this mysterious? But stay, my soul! it is the Lord; and sure I am that He doeth all things well. Here let me discover the calm submission—the holy resignation of the blessed Jesus, and say with my whole heart, "Father, not my will but thine be done!"

And yet, beloved, submissive as I desire to be to the will of God, I will not conceal from you the fact that I deeply feel my present removal from your midst. Never as now did I realize the strength of that sweet tie which binds you to my heart. Never as now did I burn with desire to lead you in the green pastures, and by the still waters of the holy Word. O how my soul has thirsted, since parted from you, for your delightful fellowship, and for the work among you. Last Lord's day I wept floods of tears. I felt as David when banished from Jerusalem and from the house of his God. On the 42nd Psalm I needed no commentary: my own deep feelings became its best expositor; and that Psalm is now the very transcript of my soul. But let me not indulge in sad reflections. God, I trust, will soon restore me to your midst, and then for every tear of sorrow I shall have a cup of joy.

But, beloved, if denied for a little the precious privilege of meeting with you, may we not, meanwhile, with ink and pen commune together? To you, members of my flock, and to you, hearers of the Word, I have something severally to say. For your souls I watch—for your souls I must give account. O that I may be enabled once again, though briefly, to address to you all the word of solemn warning.

And what, Brethren of the Church, shall I say to you? Ah! there are many things on which I would delight to dwell; but a word must now suffice, and that word shall respect your duty in relation to the present glorious movement.

Brethren, you will all admit that your eyes never saw, and that your ears never heard such things as you now see and hear every day around you. God in a way altogether unexpected, and to an extent far beyond our utmost hopes, has begun to work in our beloved land. Our own neighbourhood has felt the power of His grace. Already numbers have been humbled before the Cross, and led with open arms to embrace the Saviour; while with many more there seems to be an earnest desire to seek and secure the salvation of the soul. O beloved! need I under these circumstances indicate your duty? Surely the *occasion* has written it. Are you not here called upon as by a voice from heaven, to arise to the work of the Lord? Shall God thus as by a miracle of grace prepare the ground, and shall we refuse or neglect to cast in the seed? Beware, my brethren, O beware that the curse of Meroz rest not upon you. Many of you, I know, are most laborious for the Lord. But are you *all*—yes, ALL as active, as anxious, as earnest as you ought to be? O beloved! let your loving pastor speak to you without fear. Nay, though it offend you he must be faithful. Take care that at the great day of account, the blood of souls be not required at your hands. O the dread realities of eternity! How awful the thought to be found unfaithful! Have you, brother! sister! a relative—a friend—a neighbour now open to the truth, but to whom you have failed to tell of Christ,—how shall you appear with that relative, friend, or neighbour before the seat of judgment? Ah! the thought is enough to arouse the most lifeless. Awake, O awake to your deep—your solemn responsibility. You are "the light of the world"—"the salt of the earth." You are set to reflect the glorious light of Christ—to extend the savour of the Cross, and thus to lead men to heaven and to God. Recognise your position; realise its claims; and let sinners bless you all around as pointing the path to glory.

But for you, attendants upon my ministry, I have also a word. It must be brief, but by God's grace it shall be plain. Some of you I believe to be converted, and some of you I believe to be unconverted. To the former let me speak in all loving fidelity. Let me ask the solemn question, why delay you to follow Christ? Hindrances there may be in your way, but they are hindrances of your own creation. You will not confess the Saviour, lest through weakness you again deny Him. Then will you never confess Him, for while you live and breathe your weakness will continue. Besides, think you has the Christian no better standing than that which self supplies? Ah! ye fearing converts of the Cross, have you not the promise of the aid of Him who cannot be moved? Think you will not your Lord do for you what He did for Paul? 2 Cor. xii. 9. Renounce your fears. Take hold of the strength of Jehovah. Lean upon the arm of the Lord, as the tender little one hangs by its mother's hand, and hell itself shall not move you from the profession of the Gospel.

But perhaps it is *shame*, my converted hearers, that keeps you back. Ah! I blush to suggest the thought. Are you then ashamed of Him, who for you lived and died and lives again? Has the love of Christ so little hold upon you that for His sake you will not bear all reproach? What saith Jesus?—"If a man love me he will keep My sayings." What saith Jesus again?—"He that is ashamed of Me and of My words, of Him shall the Son of Man be ashamed when He cometh in the glory of His Father and of the holy angels." Ponder, I beseech you, O ponder these words of solemn warning, and no longer allow the reproach of the Cross to hinder your confession of Christ.

It may be, however, that mere inattention to the claims of duty is alone the reason of your continued negligence. You are resting upon the Saviour; and your outward conduct is becoming the Gospel; but as yet you have not seriously thought of openly acknowledging Christ. Well, if this be so is it not time you should now begin to think of so doing? Surely you have long enough been inattentive to your Lord's commands? Your want of thought in relation to the will of Christ is without excuse. Ah! how often you have been warned from the Word of God as to the path of duty! But it is not yet too late. Arise, brethren, and let the world know that you are Christ's. Put Him on in holy baptism. Confess Him at His own blessed table. Say of Him, in the devout observance of all His laws, "This is our friend, this is our beloved, O daughters of Jerusalem."

But among my hearers, I must not forget that there are still the *unconverted*; and to you, O my friends, how shall I address myself? Alas! how often have I addressed you in vain, "if it be yet in vain!" Your ownselves will bear me witness that I have not shunned to declare unto you all the counsel of God. I have set before you in language as plain as I could command, your corrupt and ruined condition as sinners before God. I have shown you from the holy Word your utter helplessness. I have tried to bring you to a sense of your danger, to a feeling of the awful peril in which your souls are placed. I have raised in your midst the Cross of Jesus. I have explained how God's own and only Son took the sinner's place, and bore the sinner's punishment. I have taught you that in the sufferings of our bleeding Lord the claims of law and justice have been fully met, and that now "if we confess our sins God is faithful and just to forgive us our sins, and to cleanse us from all unrighteousness." But what shall I now say? Neither your own danger nor a Saviour's love seems to move you. You are dead alike to the thunders of avenging justice, and to the voice of redeeming mercy. By the "terrors of the Lord" you will not be persuaded; by the grace of the Gospel you will not be drawn. O! what can be done that you may not be lost? Here I am powerless, as powerless as a child, except still to testify. But I cannot give you up—O! I cannot give you up. My soul bleeds for your state. I know—fearful thought!—that unless you repent you must inevitably perish. How can I endure to see you lost! How can I abide to witness against you, and behold your torments! O beloved! save me this misery. Compel not your loving minister to rise in judgment against your souls, and to see you depart into everlasting darkness. While yet there is time fly, O fly to the Lord Jesus. You have long neglected Him, but He is ever the bleeding Lamb, the gracious Saviour, and will not, if you now come, cast you out. Your sins may be as scarlet, but He will make them as white as snow; they may be as crimson, and yet they shall become as wool. Come! come! wash and be clean: believe and perish not.

And now, people of my charge—members of my flock, and hearers of the Word, I bid you for the present adieu! May the great Lord bless you all! May these my loving counsels be brought home to your souls! and may I be restored to you speedily in the fulness of the blessing of the Gospel of Christ!

I am, beloved, your tenderly attached and loving pastor,

R. H. CARSON.

Portstewart, July 28th, 1859.

minds of two or three persons were unhinged, but eventually all recovered. Learned physicians spoke of the nervous affection as hysteria. Whether it was or not, I do not presume to say, but, if so, it was accompanied with a religious feeling so intense and so widely extended that I think it could not have been the product of a physical disease.

I was at all times a very diligent reader and kept up my knowledge of Greek and Hebrew until a comparatively recent period. Since completing my 'Theory of a Universal Establishment', I had been reading and studying with a purpose. That purpose was to qualify myself for a professorship, more especially of Church History and my 'Apostolic Church' and 'Scriptural Baptism' were the first fruits of my studies in that line. The latter sprang out of the Revival. The Assembly of 1859 met in Dublin, but the North was in such a state of excitement and ministers were so much needed at home that the Assembly transacted its necessary business and decided to postpone the rest till an adjourned meeting to be held in Belfast in September. On my way home, I travelled with Mr Rogers, then of Comber, and he prevailed upon me to go down with him and to preach. The sermon was designed to give good advice in connexion with the Revival. At the close of the service Mr Rogers and the elders gathered around me, said that such advice was much needed for the time, and urged me to publish. I yielded to their entreaties and it was in a few days issued as a tract, with the title 'Words of Truth and Soberness'. It was circulated widely, particularly in districts where extravagances had begun to appear. In Belfast it was carried round by the town missionaries and a copy left in each house where the missionary called. As the autumn drew near, the Baptists were telling the young converts that they need not expect to enjoy permanent peace before they were dipped and it was reported that some few had acted on the advice or were disposed to do so.

This question of Baptism took many by surprise. Few ministers and still fewer of the Presbyterian people had looked into the subject closely. They had simply followed on year after year in the practice of their predecessors, without inquiring into the grounds on which the practice rested. But I lived on the confines of the Baptist congregation of Tubbermore. I knew the views that they had been taught on the subject. I had studied Dr Carson's large work on Baptism and was quite familiar with all his arguments. Not only so, but, powerfully and plausibly as they were stated, I believed firmly that a satisfactory answer could be given to every one of them. Professor Wilson, some years before, had discussed Carson's arguments in a scholarly way; but, as it appeared to me, something shorter and more popular was now needed, to put into the hands of people who were inquiring on the subject, and that I was the man to do it. The idea of writing on the subject did not strike me till late in the summer. The Assembly was to meet in Belfast on a Wednesday. I sat down on the

Solitude, Carson's home in the townland
of Coolsaragh, Desertmartin

Carson's grave at Desertmartin Parish Church, Dromore

previous Monday and wrote off a tract on the 'Mode of Baptism', copied it out for the press on Tuesday, took it with me to Belfast on Wednesday and on Saturday it was issued from the press. In another week or two this was followed up by a tract on the 'Subjects of Baptism'. A Baptist preacher [Henry?] in Belfast published an answer to the first tract and I replied, but, as I found that he was only making use of my name to achieve a little notoriety for himself and his chapel, I refused to follow him farther. My two tracts had a wide circulation and, after the excitement of the Revival was over, I smoothed them down a little and reissued them in one book, under the title 'Scriptural Baptism'. It was widely circulated in Ulster and in Scotland. It was translated into Italian and printed at Florence for the use of the young Protestant Church of Italy. I have been assured that it has proved useful to many and has kept them steady in their attachment to the ancient and Scriptural practices of the Church, which never made immersion an essential to the rite, nor shut out the household from the ordinance that it administered to the believing parents.

In the autumn of 1859, Dr Robert Wilson, the Professor of Biblical Criticism in Belfast, died. There was not then the same hunger for professorships as there is at present, nor was every man so disposed to believe that he was fit for the highest position in the Church. It was some months before anyone offered for the chair. At length Dr Glasgow, Dr Graham of Bonn, Dr Niblock of Donegal and, I think, one or two more, whose names I forget, came forward as candidates. My attention for some years had been given more to Ecclesiastical History than to Criticism and it did not occur to me at first that I should offer myself to the Electors. But I had read a little on the subject to be treated from the Chair, I was familiar with its general principles, I had formed habits of reading and study and knew that I could in a very short time provide myself with the necessary material to carry me respectably through my first session, after which all would be easy. It was Professor W D Killen who, in conversation, dropped a word that induced me to become a candidate. He did not advise me to offer, nor promise to support me in case I should present myself. But, in my conversing with him at the close of the session 1859-60, he simply said that, if I had seen my own way clear to come forward, his opinion was that I would be elected. I did not say anything at the time, but my mind dwelt on this hint. I went down to Comber and consulted Mr John Rogers, whom I always found to be a kind and faithful friend. He encouraged me to stand for the Chair and promised to support me to the utmost of his power. After mature deliberation, the plan agreed upon was this. My friends in Magherafelt Presbytery were to draw up and sign a requisition, asking me to come forward, on the receipt of which I was to announce myself a candidate.

The requisition was drawn up. My friends, Mr Montgomery of Magherafelt and Mr J M Rodgers of Kilrea,

JOSIAS LESLIE PORTER

JOHN ROGERS

took it to the Synod of Ballymena and Mr Rogers of Comber took it to the Synod of Belfast, in both of which it received a number of signatures. When the news of this proceeding reached Dr Cooke, he immediately started his son-in-law, Rev Josias L Porter, who had some time before resigned his post on the Damascus Mission and who was then out of a situation. I did not expect this move, but it did not discourage me. I drew up my circular and, relying on the acceptance which my little publications had met with from my brethren and the public, I did not solicit a testimonial from any human being, but confidently appealed to the ministers and elders. Beyond issuing my circular, I never asked anyone for a vote. I carried out no canvass whatever, preferring to lose the professorship rather than to do any act which at the time I regarded as degrading to myself. I was anxious to rest my claim on my own character and standing, and not on my personal solicitations. Dr Cooke was reported to be using his great influence, as was natural, on behalf of his relative and, under the circumstances, I was not over-sanguine of success.

Dr Edgar had consented to propose me in the Assembly and I think it was understood that Mr Rogers of Comber was to second the nomination. Speeches were then allowed in proposing candidates and it was judged a good point in a candidate's favour to have an influential proposer and seconder. I did not ask Dr Edgar to do me this favour, but, at the request of Mr Rogers, he had consented to do it. At the last moment, however, a hitch occurred. Dr Nicholas Murray of Elizabethtown was present in the Assembly of 1860. He had been kind to Dr Edgar and other ministers, when, some years before, they had visited America, and Dr Edgar was now anxious that he should address the Assembly. But, after his previous visit in 1851, when he was present on the Fighting Friday, Dr Murray had given a description of the scene which reflected on Dr Goudy of Strabane in an unwarrantable and needless way. The friends of that much-respected minister, who had died in the interval, intimated to Dr Edgar and his friends that, should Dr Murray appear on the platform, they would not permit him to address the Assembly, until he had first withdrawn his offensive remarks in regard to the late Dr Goudy. Dr Edgar took this very ill and, on the morning of the election, after the proceeding had begun, he intimated to Mr Rogers that he would not propose Witherow. I had, of course, nothing to do with the transaction and thought it somewhat strange that I should be punished for the faults of some person or persons unknown. But I did not speak to Dr Edgar on the subject and allowed matters to take their course. When the time came, Dr Brown of Aghadoey, having heard of Dr Edgar falling away from his engagement, arose on the impluse of the moment and proposed me for the chair, a proposition which was seconded by my ever-kind and faithful friend, Dr Clarke Huston of Macosquin. It was kind and considerate in both to come forward in an emergency, but, neither having had time to prepare their remarks, I was merely put before the House and lost any

THE

LIFE AND TIMES

OF

HENRY COOKE, D.D., LL.D.

PRESIDENT OF ASSEMBLY'S COLLEGE, BELFAST.

BY HIS SON-IN-LAW,

J. L. PORTER, D.D. LL.D.,

PROFESSOR OF BIBLICAL CRITICISM, ASSEMBLY'S COLLEGE.

WITH PORTRAITS.

SECOND EDITION.

LONDON:

JOHN MURRAY, ALBEMARLE STREET.

1871.

advantage to be derived from judicious and forcible statement.

There were not perhaps twenty ministers in the Assembly whom Dr Cooke had not at some time or other obliged and it was well known that he had set his heart very warmly on his son-in-law's appointment. He had written letters on the subject to his particular friends. He stated on the day of election that, while he would regret very much that the Assembly should elect an unqualified person on the ground of being related to him, he thought a person so well qualified as Mr Porter ought not to be rejected simply because he was his near-relation. This was understood to be an intimation to all as to what he expected from them. Dr Cooke sat in his own well-known seat in the Assembly and, while the roll was being called, held up his copy of the Minutes and openly marked the names of those who voted on the one side or the other. The result in such circumstances was a foregone conclusion. The only thing in my favour was that Porter was no great favourite with the ministers and that the cleft of feeling introduced into the Assembly by recent controversies had made it more difficult for Dr Cooke to draw after him the same majority as in earlier days. At the first vote, Graham and Niblock, along with others, were left in such a minority that their names were dropped out. The second vote was taken between Glasgow, Porter and myself, the result of which was that Dr Glasgow was dropped. The final vote was taken between Porter and me, and Porter was elected by something like seventeen or eighteen of a majority. When the result was announced, the brethren crowded round me and congratulated me as if I was a victor, one of them humorously, but significantly, saying that if I had married the right woman I would have won the election. He little knew that the woman I had married was more to me than ten professorships. The loss of the election never cost me a thought. I had an attached and kindly people at Maghera to fall back upon, and after, as before, they were never weary of showing me every mark of confidence and respect.

Preaching one day at Portrush in June 1860, I was accosted by a Scottish lady who said that she was struck by my name and wished to make my acquaintance. She ended by asking Catherine and myself to go to her lodgings for tea on a certain evening, which she named. She proved to be a Mrs Wodrow of Glasgow, the widow of Mr Robert Wodrow, a well-known elder of the Church of Scotland whom delicate health had prevented going with Bonar and McCheyne to fulfil the appointment in regard to the Jews in Palestine, which the General Assembly had laid upon them in 1839. We spent a very pleasant evening with Mrs Wodrow and her sister, Mrs Patterson of Montgomery Castle, Ayrshire, who were, as I ascertained, most intelligent Christian ladies. The subject of the former's communication to me was that her late husband's sister, Miss Wodrow of Mauchline, was the last survivor of the historian's family in Scotland,

The Maiden City

that is, the last entitled to wear the name; that she was great-grand-daughter of the historian; that she prided herself very much on her ecclesiastical lineage; that she was under the impression that her name had now ceased to exist among the Presbyterian ministry; and that when she would go home to Scotland and tell her sister-in-law that she had discovered one of the name, for Wodrow and Witherow are only different forms of the same name, I might expect to hear from her immediately. Accordingly, about the beginning of August, some time after the election for the professorship was decided, I had a letter from Miss Wodrow, expressing how much she was interested in the discovery made by her sister-in-law, giving me a whole account of her family, stating how in the published life of his own father, Professor James Wodrow of Glasgow, the historian mentions that the children of his father's younger brother, who was a scrivener and public notary in Greenock, settled in Ireland, and proposing that I should either go over to see her, or that she, notwithstanding her advanced age, would come to see me. It seemed to Catherine and myself the wise thing in the circumstances to invite Miss Wodrow over to Ireland. She accepted the invitation with alacrity, notwithstanding that at the time she was over sixty years of age. I met her in Belfast and brought her down with me to Maghera, where she spent about three weeks with us. She was a most intelligent Christian lady, deeply interested in everything ecclesiastical and religious. She was a member of the Church of Scotland, retaining the old and dear associations connected with her family and not seeing her way clear to leave it at the Disruption. She had never been in Ireland before and everything seemed new to her. I took her down to Portrush for a few days, from which we visited Dunluce and the Giant's Causeway on the one side and Derry on the other.

It was on this occasion that for the first time I saw Magee College, then a completely-finished building, with which in after years my name was to be so closely associated. The car that took us to the College parted us at the foot of Shipquay Street, where we mounted the wall, intending to make the circuit of the city. Before we had reached the Monument, the strength of the old lady was exhausted and she exclaimed in the broad Doric of her native county, "Ka' a Kab". Alas, Derry was not rich enough to own cab or car plying on the streets, for that which took us to the College had to be specially hired from a posting-establishment. The only thing we could do in the circumstances was to cut short our walk and adjourn for refreshments. Our first child, Hugh, was then a baby of six months old and, to Miss Wodrow, as well as to ourselves, he was an object of great interest. The name had come to us from the Chambers family, but I felt that the old lady would have been still better pleased if the name had come from the Wodrows and had been a Robert, or Thomas, or James or John.

Miss Wodrow kept up constant correspondence with us by

letter during the winter and, in the following summer (1861), we paid her a return visit at her residence in Ayrshire. She lived in a large, self-contained house, on the right hand of the road, contiguous to the manse, between the railway station and the town. That whole country is redolent of Burns and Scottish song and she took us to nearly every place in the town and district associated with him or with "Bonny Jean" - Ayr, Tarbolton, Mossgiel and other places, the names of which I now forget. The boxwood manufactory and the humble martyrs' monument in the village were not forgotten. On Sabbath day, to her great delight, I preached for her minister, Mr Fairlie, in the parish church, I being, I suppose, one of the first ministers from Ireland who had preached in a pulpit of the Established Church of Scotland since the Disruption. Dining at the manse during the week, we met Dr Chrystal, the parish minister of Auchinleck, and Dr Rankin of Sorn, both of whom impressed me deeply by their intelligence and urbanity of manners, and both of whom rose afterwards to the Moderator's Chair in the Church of Scotland.

Having, as I suppose, exhausted almost every object that she thought would interest us at Mauchline, she took us up to Edinburgh to see her nephews, John and Charles Thompson, who received us very kindly and with whom we stayed a few days. This was familiar ground to me, the only new places which I saw on this occasion being Hawthornden and its caves, Roslin Chapel and the Prentice Pillar, and the historic battlefield of the Pentlands. We then came down to Glasgow, where Mrs Wodrow, being away on her travels, had in her absence put her house and servants in Garnet Hill at our disposal. From this centre we visited Eaglesham, the ancient home of the Wodrows, and lunched with Miss Hill, the grand-daughter of the well-known professor and theologian, who entertained us hospitably at the manse. Next we visited the farmhouse, then occupied by a respectable family named Craig, that tradition associated with the Wodrow family, but the present occupiers seemed to know nothing of the ancient inhabitants, except that a large stone sunk to a level with the pavement, which, they pointed out, was popularly known as "Janet Wodrow's stone". On returning from the day's drive, we came by Eastwood, where we stood at the historian's grave in the parish where he spent his pastoral life, and called at the manse, where the young minister, whose name I forget, received us kindly.

Miss Wodrow and I, from this time forth, were warm friends and frequent tokens of affection passed between us. In 1862 she again paid us a short visit of eight or ten days at Portrush and in 1863 I went again for a short visit to Mauchline. Her infirmities, however, began to multiply and she died in 1865, about a month before I was elected to the Professorship of Church History in Derry. Her affection only died out with her life. By her will she left a small legacy of twenty pounds to my eldest daughter, Jane, who was called for her. I never knew a more thorough, honest woman than Jane Lilian Wodrow. The interests of the Church of God were very dear to her and her delight was to talk of ministers and martyrs of Scotland. My own tastes ran very much in the same line, and this fact furnished to her new and pleasing evidence that, however the Scottish and Irish branches of the Wodrows had separated in the last century or so, they had both sprung originally from one stock. The history of the family, mostly gathered from the 'Life of Professor James Wodrow' was published in an article written by me and entitled 'The Wodrows of Eaglesham', which appeared in the 'Evangelical Witness'.

The years 1860 to 1865 passed away without much impression left upon my memory, as years of great happiness slip almost unconsciously away. I was happy in the society of one of the best wives with whom any man could be favoured and who made my humble home an Elysium, so far as such can exist in this imperfect world. Four of our children were born in these years and each one, as it made its appearance, was to us a new source of interest and joy: Hugh, born 18 March 1860; Jane, born 18 December 1861; Elizabeth, born 9 October 1863; and Isabella, born 19 August 1865.

During these years I carried on my private studies very diligently, but, beyond an occasional article in the 'Evangelical Witness', did not write much for publication. A small tract on 'The Puritan Worthies of 1662' belongs to that time. My studies now were almost all historical. During that time I compiled the lectures which afterwards I used in Derry. These historical lectures were not satisfactory to myself. There was too little of my own individuality in them. They were in the main compilations from the best historians that might in my opinion be useful to students, but they were not in general the result of a personal examination of the original authorities and the fruit of my own investigations. To this there were some exceptions, such as the lectures on church government, pastoral theology, the Council of Nicea, St Patrick and St Columba, and perhaps a few others, but the greater part was a sort of mosaic, composed of bricks selected from other workmen. The fact is that I started on a wrong plan and did not discover my mistake till I had advanced too far to rectify it with ease. Had I the work to begin again, I would make a brief survey, giving a student, in the course of eighteen or twenty lectures, a bird's eye view of the whole field, something like what I have sketched in my general introduction to my ordinary course of lectures, but at a little greater length. Having in this general way taken in the whole ground, I would then take up particular topics and investigate them to the very depths, so as to introduce some fresh topic, session after session, and to instruct the students on such matters as the circumstances of the times required them to know. By the combination of the two methods, the student would obtain a more general and comprehensive grasp of the whole subject and would be treated at the same time to the results of more original and thorough investigation.

TO

THE REVEREND THE MODERATOR, THE MINISTERS,

AND ELDERS OF THE GENERAL ASSEMBLY.

Fathers and Brethren,

I beg leave to present myself to you as a Candidate for the Chair of Ecclesiastical History in the new College about to be opened in the City of Derry. The warm support which so many of you gave me when, some years ago, I sought a Professorship in the Theological College of Belfast—a kindness which I gratefully remember—warrants me to hope that you will not count me presumptuous now in coming forward again to solicit an appointment of a similar kind;—an appointment which, if you think it right to bestow upon me, I must always regard as a signal mark of your confidence and favour.

Of my qualifications for the office, it is no more than becoming that I should speak with modesty. But I may be permitted to say, that for thirteen years past my private studies have all been in the direction of the subjects with which the Church Historian needs to be conversant; so that the office which I seek would involve no duties for which it has not been my design and endeavour throughout all these years to prepare. Moreover, nearly twenty years spent in active pastoral labour in a large and important congregation, and in frequent and familiar intercourse with my brethren, have enabled me to understand what the duties, sentiments, and requirements of the Presbyterian ministry really are; while on the other hand, they have furnished not a few of my brethren with ample opportunity of becoming acquainted with my character, my principles, my intellectual resources, and my power of conveying knowledge to the minds of others. Further: the Tracts and Treatises which, amid many disadvantages, I have found time to write and publish, have met with considerable acceptance from the general public, as well as from the Presbyterian people; and while I am far from supposing that these productions—the results of such fragments of time as could with propriety be rescued from the engrossing duties of the pastorate, and from professional and more systematic studies—are of such a character as to give me any preëminent claims to the high and honourable office to which I aspire, yet I may be excused for appealing to them as sufficient at least to indicate the tastes and tendencies of my mind, and to illustrate the style of thought and expression which it has been my aim to cultivate.

Should your kindness, Fathers and Brethren, place me in a position where I shall have leisure to devote the rest of my life to study, and to the education of the future Ministry, every effort in my power will be put forth to prove that I deserve your confidence. To have any part, however humble, in the early struggles of a Seminary of Learning, destined, it is fondly hoped, to be a source of blessing to our Church and to our country, I would count no mean honour. But I am ambitious, I must confess, to connect my name with a College whose origin and history will be regarded with interest by the men of other times,—to take a part in training the best minds which our Church can furnish for the grand work which is to be the business and the pleasure of their lives; to confirm the youth of the coming generation in attachment to sound doctrine and to the fine old scriptural principles of Presbyterian polity and worship; to aid in stimulating the minds of the future clergy to a keener taste for theological and historical study; and to help in fanning into vigorous life that love of learning and of literature which deserves to rank as one of the highest glories of a Christian community.

It rests with you, Fathers and Brethren, whether I am to have the opportunity which I thus desire. Should you judge it consistent with your duty to the Derry College, and to the public interests, to confer the Church History Professorship upon me, I will not only be grateful for the honour, but I will give my best attention to the duties of the office, and use every endeavour in my power to do credit to your choice.

With very great respect,

I am,

Fathers and Brethren,

Yours most faithfully,

THOMAS WITHEROW.

[illegible] April, [illegible]

In the spring of 1865 it was announced that Magee College was now ready and was to open in October. I issued a circular offering as a candidate for the Chair of Church History, for which I had so long been making elaborate preparation (see opposite). This time I had no opposition and by the favour of my brethren was unanimously elected to that Chair. This necessitated my resignation of the congregation of Maghera, which I did at the October meeting of Presbytery, exactly twenty years after I had been ordained. Twenty years of preaching the blessed Gospel in such a large and intelligent neighbourhood was a great privilege and serious responsibility. I believe I preached the truth and declared what I regarded as the whole counsel of God and I tried to live consistently and to benefit the people as much as I could. However, no-one knew as I knew myself my great deficiencies, both in teaching and visitation and practice, but the people overlooked my shortcomings and treated me first and last with the greatest respect and regard. I can never, never, forget Maghera and its kind-hearted and generous people. I hope that I won some of them to Christ. My great regret is that I was not able to do them a still greater amount of good.

On the day of my election to the professorship, Catherine and Mr Barkley came up to Belfast, but, as there was no opposition to my election, there was no call of the roll and the election was over before they arrived. The joy of them both was great, for, outside my own family, I had no friend so warm and constant as Mr Barkley. After we had come home to Maghera, he went along with us to Derry and helped us to choose a house in Clarendon Street to be our future residence. This house was our home down till 1880, when we removed some few doors up the street, on the same side, to the house at the upper corner of Princes Street. But the lower house was our home during the remainder of the time that Catherine was spared to me. It was then numbered 23, but while we resided there the number was changed to 39. Now I understand it is numbered 45. On returning to Maghera, we began to make arrangements for removal. I sold off my house and five acres of land and bog, for which I received, if I remember aright, £500, being double the sum for which my father purchased it for me in 1853.

But my preparations for removal to Derry were interrupted by the first great sorrow that fell on Catherine and me from the time we came together. Our dear boy, Hugh, was a healthy and happy child, the comfort and delight of us both. One evening in September he went to bed bright and merry, as children could be, but during the night he took ill, very ill indeed. The doctor was sent for and pronounced it scarlatina. For twenty-one days Hugh fought a fierce battle with the last enemy, his poor mama, not long recovered from her own trial, hanging over him and ministering to him all that gentle hands could do, and I in an agony, scarcely knowing whether I was living or dead. The poor child suffered terribly. We could bring him no

Hugh Witherow's headstone, originally "about ten or twelve yards from the front door", is now to be seen on the far right of this picture

Clarendon Street, Londonderry

relief. We could only pray for him and commend him to God, but God in His wisdom did not hear our prayers. Hugh died on a Sabbath. That day, in fulfilment of a promise, I had to preach at Castledawson. I hurried home and found that my firstborn, the beloved of my heart, was called home to God. Oh, the anguish of that hour to my dear wife and to myself. He was buried about ten or twelve yards from the front door, in the Meeting House green, being the only one who, so far as I know had been ever buried there. His interment was on the day fixed for the installation of the professors at Derry, where I would have been, if death had not entered my home. That was a sad scene to me. My heart and the heart of his mother were bound up in that dear child. God was pleased to give us many other children, all of them precious to us, but our hearts doted on none of them as they did upon Hugh. His mother has long since joined him in the Heavenly Home and no doubt both of them are now "waiting and watching for me". When my work here is done, I hope, by the grace of Christ, to join them.

Next evening, my friends at Maghera held a meeting at which they presented me at parting with an Address accompanied by a gold watch and silver tea-service that cost sixty pounds. I tried to reply, but my words were drowned in tears. What an amount of sorrow and of affection lavished upon me at one time! Perhaps, if I knew it all, my sorrow was a mark of still greater affection. God knows. Next morning, the chaise conveyed me, my wife, and remaining children across the mountains, and we bade adieu to ever-dear Maghera.

(11) Londonderry: 1865–77

Settling down to the duties of a professorship in Derry was like passing from a stormy ocean into the shelter of some land-locked bay. The incessant worry that so wore me down at Maghera was at an end. I had come to live among strangers who knew comparatively little of me and mine. I had no pastoral work to do. I had less business at Presbyteries and Synods. My time could be given to professional duties and to literary work. An amount of domestic bliss, not common in the world, had fallen to my lot and now I enjoyed what to me was the great luxury of preaching the Gospel as often as I pleased in the pulpits of my brethren, without being responsible for any family visitation. Twelve years passed away very sharply and very sweetly. All my other children were born in 39 Clarendon Street, as our dwelling was then called. To save further reference to them, their names may as well be given here: James Milling Witherow, born in Derry on 21 August 1867; Hugh (the second), born on 28 May 1869, but died on 16 December of same year; Emily Catherine, born on 1 November 1870; Mary Lilias, born on 15 March 1874; Agnes Maud, born on 16 November 1875; and Catherine Hill, born on 17 April 1879. The duties of the professorship were light, for the classes were small and my lectures had all been written, at least

Alexander Montgomery

First Magherafelt Presbyterian Church

Union Road Presbyterian Church, Magherafelt

as many as sufficed for my first two sessions, before I left Maghera. The starting of a new educational institution required a good many meetings and at first there was some little friction between the junior and senior professors. But after the undergraduate professors married, and one or two of the more restless spirits had passed away, there was not a more united or harmonious body in the Church than the Faculty of MCD.

One thing only caused us deep sorrow. A charge of writing an anonymous letter, with a view of injuring one of his colleagues, was brought against one of our number, a man of very eccentric habits. His handwriting was so well imitated that we all believed the document to be his. There was an investigation before the Board of Visitors, followed by an appeal to the General Assembly. The Assembly, contrary to the evidence, and without more than a dozen members ever seeing the document on which the case turned, acquitted the accused. Strange to say, in this rough way, substantial justice was done, for I think that nearly all the professors came in the end to think that we were wrong in our belief of our colleague's guilt and that the anonymous letter was not written by him, but by a member of his family who had afterwards to be confined in an asylum. Dr McKee did not live very long after this most unfortunate incident, but the same cordiality never existed between him and us as before. I acted in the whole affair according as I believed at the time, as I am sure so did my brethren. But I am now convinced that we were mistaken and that our unfortunate brother suffered for an act in which personally he had no blame, and of which, had it not been for his own strange statements and eccentricities, we would all have judged him incapable. This is the only thing, in all my connexion with the Magee College, which I sincerely and deeply regret.

In 1866 it came my turn to fill the office of President of Faculty and I opened the second session of the College by delivering a lecture on 'St Patrick', which was afterwards published as an article in the 'British Quarterly Review' for October 1867. This was the first of a long series of articles written by me which appeared in the 'British Quarterly', the 'British and Foreign Evangelical', the 'London Quarterly', the 'Presbyterian Review', and in various periodicals of the Presbyterian Church. I never tried my hand at purely political or literary articles, having a strong taste for historical and theological subjects, and a strong desire to teach and to promote useful knowledge. I mean 'useful' in a religious sense. I was much encouraged in this line of study by the Rev Thomas Croskery, who settled in Derry a year or two after me, and who possessed the most unquenchable thirst for literature and composition of any man I ever knew. We became warm friends and consulted with each other in nearly all cases. He and I were of kindred tastes and both read in the same line. He looked to immediate results and wrote mostly for reviews and newspapers, the effect of which is

James Maxwell Rodgers

The memorial of Thomas Croskery, Witherow's close colleague in Magee

The former Great James Street Presbyterian Church, Londonderry

that the best of his writings are buried to all time and are not likely to be exhumed, except one of his sons, youths of great promise, shall at some future time dig them up from their graves. I was fonder of book production. This brought more reputation, but less money, and it was this latter commodity which would have been most useful to me. He knew the art of turning brains into money much better than I did.

Dr James Denham, whose congregation I joined when I came to Derry, was then a hale, robust man of noble presence, but advancing in years. He went out on a mission the following summer and left me to supply the congregation in his absence. He returned in due time, but, owing, as I think, to the fatigue and exitement through which he passed, he never was able, after his return, to preach with the same vigour as before. During the winter he was struck with paralysis, after which he lingered for a year or two, and then died. He was a kind friend of mine and a most excellent minister, whose death (18 December 1871) I much lamented. When Mrs Denham conveyed to me, through her relative, the Rev Smylie Robson, the wish that I should preach the funeral sermon, I declined, from a sincere belief that, knowing him intimately only late in life, I would not be able to do him justice. But I regretted very much afterwards that I allowed any false modesty to deter me. Owing to the fact that I am always sure to break down and stop when I require to give expression to any tender or pathetic sentiment, it is wise in me to abjure everything in the shape of a funeral address; but I would have been glad now that I had connected my name in some way with that of this eminent minister, next, perhaps, after Dr Morgan, the model pastor of the Church. As it is, I have only to record that I wrote the inscription on the marble tablet, erected to his memory by the congregation of Great James Street in the porch of the church and that Croskery and I started the subscription by which nearly £600 was raised to establish the Denham Bursaries in Magee College.

About two years before Dr Denham died, my friend and co-presbyter, the Rev J M Rodgers of Kilrea, was called to succeed him. It was not the fact, as generally reported, that it was my influence which brought him to Derry. Dr Denham had heard him preach at Portrush and thought him suitable; but, before asking him to preach, he asked me privately if I would have any objection to him as a minister. My answer was, Certainly not. If the congregation were satisfied with his preaching, he would be in every way acceptable to me. The reason Dr Denham put the question to me was that, some time before I left Maghera, there had been a dispute between Mr Montgomery and some members of his congregation, which resulted in the establishment of a second congregation at Magherafelt. In this painful dispute, Mr Rodgers and I took different views and Dr Denham imagined that something had arisen, which would make it unpleasant for me to sit under his ministry. But there was nothing of the kind. Mr Rodgers behaved with

Banagher Old Church

Banagher Parish Church

great propriety in all that painful quarrel at Magherafelt, and, though I did not coincide in the opinions and action of him and his friends, he did and said nothing personally offensive to me. The reason why I experienced some hesitation, as to whether his preaching would satisfy the congregation or not, was that I remembered that at Maghera we were not all agreed upon that point. Some thought him too wordy and diffuse in his discourses. However, Mr Rodgers came and preached and pleased the people. As I was going into the church to meet the Committee of Presbytery, Dr Denham asked me to move that we call him to be the minister, which I did. To my surprise, some opposition was manifested, as I afterwards heard, based on political grounds. It proved unsuccessful and Mr Rodgers was in due time settled as assistant. This was all I had to do in the matter, but I felt, on reflection, that I ought to have declined the responsibility of proposing anyone for a minister, as I was a stranger, who had only come to the city two or three years before. All, however, turned out well and Mr Rodgers proved a most popular and successful minister.

My father lived for two years after I had left Maghera. Once or twice he came to see me in Derry and, on one of these occasions, I embraced the opportunity of having his photograph taken, which I still preserve. He was eighty at his death. I spent a day with him some time before he died, but, as he passed away suddenly, I was not with him at the last. We buried him in Banagher New Church graveyard, with the members of his family, and, after his death, I had a small granite pillar set up to mark his grave. He was an industrious, honest and sober man, highly intelligent, considering his opportunities and station in life, and much respected in the whole countryside. Everyone knew Hugh Witherow of Aughlish. To him I owe more than to any other man. Had it not been for him I would have spent my life in obscurity, in drudgery and without the opportunities of usefulness I have since enjoyed. He lived to see me realise the most sanguine hopes he had ever ventured to cherish. He was my most disinterested friend. No other friend outside my domestic circle was so bound up in my prosperity. Thanks be to God, now that I look back upon it, for such a father. I have the great happiness of thinking that I never did anything to vex him, or to give him on my account anxiety for a moment. When I was a child, I made it a rule to obey every command of his. The same practice I carried out through my youth and manhood, and never had I any cause to regret it. For many years before he died, I was his banker. He carried to me any money he did not require for his business, and it was lodged in the bank or invested in my name. He made no will. At my last visit to him before he died, he told me that he considered he had done enough for me by paying for my education and buying for me the house and little property at Maghera, and that he wished all his money and chattel property to go to my brother Robert. Though I thought this a rather unequal division, his property being

(1)

My brother Robert who inherited all my fathers property died intestate on the 2d June 1885, leaving a widow and two daughters. His farm stock and other property were sold off and the proceeds divided share and share alike among wife and children. The following was the Auctioneers advertisement:-

HIGHLY IMPORTANT & EXTENSIVE SALE OF TWO FARMS, HORSES, CATTLE, 1,300 SHEEP, FARMING IMPLEMENTS, HOUSEHOLD FURNITURE, &c.,

BY AUCTION,

AT AUGHLISH, NEAR DUNGIVEN.

THE Subscribers have received Instructions from the Administratrix of the late Mr. ROBERT WITHROW to SELL BY PUBLIC AUCTION, on the Premises, on FRIDAY and SATURDAY, the 28th and 29th of AUGUST, instant, commencing each day at ELEVEN o'clock a.m. sharp :

LOT No. 1—The Tenant-Right in that Valuable FARM OF LAND, situate in the Townland of AUGHLISH, Parish of BANAGHER, containing 130 Acres, Statute Measure, or thereabouts, held from Year to Year, under Major BRUCE, at the Judicial Yearly Rent of £25.

On this Lot there is a splendid Dwelling-house, Two Storeys high, recently built, suitable for the requirements of a Respectable Family ; the Offices are compact and commodious, nearly all Slated, and in excellent Repair. It is well Fenced and thoroughly Drained, with a never-failing supply of good Water. The County Road runs through the centre. It is situate about Two and a-half Miles from Dungiven and Two from Feeny, and in a quiet and peaceable neighbourhood.

LOT No. 2—The Tenant Right in that most desirable GRAZING FARM, situate in the Townlands of FINGLEN and AUGHLISH, containing 1,868 Acres, or thereabouts, and Four Sums of Grazing on Menard Mountain, held from Year to Year, under the same Landlord, at the Judicial Yearly Rent of £60. Adjoins Lot No. 1. Twelve Acres are Arable, and a large portion can, with a very small outlay, be profitably cultivated. There is a new Dwelling-house on this Lot.

This is a good opportunity for any Person desirous of obtaining Two choice Farms and a comfortable Residence, as such Lands are seldom offered for Sale. The Farms occupy the most picturesque and best position in the Townland in which they are situated, and embrace every modern convenience, the Proprietor having expended about £600 on buildings.

Immediately after the Sale of Farms the following will be Sold, viz :—Five Milch Cows, Three Two-year-old Heifers, Seven One-year-old Heifers, Four Calves, Four Pigs, Eight Hundred Old Sheep, Three Hundred Lambs, Ten splendid Blackfaced Rams, Carts and Cart Harness, Jaunting Car and Harness, Ploughs, Harrows, Grubbers, Threshing Mill, and other Farming Implements, Manure, Lumber, &c. ; Fourteen Acres of superior Oats, Four Acres of Potatoes, Two Acres of T[illegible] Also, the entire Household Furniture, com[illegible] Mahogany Tables, Chairs, Sofas, Presses, Armchairs, Easy Chairs and other Chairs, Carpets, Rugs, Fenders and Irons, Window Drapery, &c. ; the Furniture of Six Bedrooms, containing Albert, Iron, and other Bedsteads, Palliasses, Mattresses, Feather Beds, Drawers, Wardrobes, Dressing Tables, Washstands and Ware, Looking Glasses, Towel Rail, Carpets, Fenders and Irons, together with Kitchen, Pantry, and Scullery Utensils, in great variety.

The Purchaser of the Grazing Farm can have a number of the Sheep at a Valuation, if required. If the Purchaser desires, a portion of the Purchase-Money may remain at Interest for such time as may be agreed upon, at the rate of Five per Cent. per Annum.

Private proposals will be received by Messrs. JOHN M'FARLAND, of Carnanbane, and WM. WITHROW, of Aughlish for either or both of these Farms, up to the 25th August.

ORDER OF SALE—On Friday, the 28th, the Farm in Aughlish, Stock, Crop, &c. On Saturday, the Finglen Farm, Sheep, and all remaining unsold from previous day.

Terms—£100 of a Deposit on each Farm at time of Sale, and the remainder on getting possession, which can be had immediately. On Stock, Crop, &c.—Three Months' Credit on Approved Bills on all sums above £5, and Cash for all sums under that amount.

Purchasers to pay to the Auctioneer One and a-half per Cent. Auction Fees on Farms, and Two and a half per Cent. on all other Lots Sold.

WM. G. SHERRARD & SON,
Auctioneers and Valuators,
Limavady.

August 4th, 1885 [illegible]

at that time valued for more than three thousand pounds, I did not dispute his word, for I knew he had made up his mind and that to complain would be only to vex him. Had I administered, I could have claimed one half of all. Had I chosen to hold what of his was lodged in my own name, I could have done it. But my father's unwritten wish was a command to me. In due time, I made over all the money lodged with me, amounting to about £800, to my brother, and would have done so if it had been ten times the amount.

As I write for the instruction of my children, not for the public, I may record here the death of the second Hugh. He was born in May 1869 and we called him Hugh, as if he had been sent to fill the place left vacant by his eldest brother and to keep up the remembrance of my father. He was a fine and, to all appearance, a healthy boy. Mr David G Barkley, afterwards the Honourable Justice Barkley, son of my old friend at Maghera and now (1888) joint Convenor of the Foreign Mission being then home on a holiday from India, was paying us a visit at Derry in the autumn. Early in October, he and I had gone on a brief excursion to West Donegal. We went to Dunfanaghy and, after a day or two, passed on to Gweedore, where we were shut up by the wet weather for several days. We then turned home. When we went away, the baby was quite well, but, when we came back, I soon saw that something was the matter. Hugh was taken with some internal disorder, the nature of which we did not know, but he cried day and night incessantly and died at the end of a two months' illness. O, the agony of that time! How sad to look into his beautiful black eyes, so soon to be closed in death, to hear his agonizing cries, as if he thought that we could help and would not help, and to feel that we were as powerless to remove his pain as turn the tide of the sea. How my heart bled for the dear child and what a relief I felt when at last he was at rest. Need I say how much the poor mother was to be commiserated? He was seldom out of her arms. Her gentle voice soothed him and her kindly hands (and, O, how kindly they were) did everything for him that could be done. But, alas, in vain. It pleased God to take him away from us. This was our second domestic sorrow. Still, God had given us many other children and had so far spared us to each other. In the deepest trials that afflict men, God is merciful and good. He is keeping the darling boy safely to restore him to me in joy and in glory at a future day. He and his mother are long since reunited.

The first literary work which engaged my attention after settling in Derry, apart from reviews or articles, one of which I usually had on hand, was a commentary, a kind of work for which I had neither gifts nor taste. An American minister named Van Doren, who had published what he called a 'Suggestive Commentary' on the Gospel of John, had entered into correspondence with Dr Samuel Dill, our Professor of Theology, with a view to induce him to contribute a comment on the same plan, in order that it should be issued as one of the series. Dr Dill consented

DERRY AND ENNISKILLEN

IN

THE YEAR 1689:

THE STORY OF SOME

Famous Battle-Fields in Ulster.

BY

THOMAS WITHEROW, D.D.,

PROFESSOR OF CHURCH HISTORY IN MAGEE COLLEGE, LONDONDERRY, AND HONORARY MEMBER OF THE HISTORICAL SOCIETY OF NEW HAMPSHIRE.

Rem coalescere concordia posse.

THIRD EDITION, REVISED AND ENLARGED.

BELFAST:
WILLIAM MULLAN & SON, DONEGALL PLACE.

1885.

THE BOYNE AND AGHRIM

OR

Story of some Famous Battlefields
in Ireland

BY

THOMAS WITHEROW

Professor of Church History in Magee College, Londonderry

WILLIAM MULLAN AND SON
LONDON AND BELFAST
1879

to supply a comment on the Gospel of Mark and spoke to me that I also might aid in the work. I was very unwilling, but Dr Dill urged me much and said that he had obtained the consent of Mr Croskery also to take part. At last I yielded, and selected for my exposition the Pastoral Epistles as lying nearest to the subject of Pastoral Theology, one of the departments which I had to handle in my College lectures. I sat down to work and wrought at it perseveringly. Before I had finished, Dr Dill had died, never putting his hand to paper, as far as I have heard, farther than collecting some material. I persevered until my comment was complete, and then put myself in communication with Van Doren. I found from him that Dr Dill had no understanding with him in regard to remuneration and that I was expected to hand my manuscript over to the projector in the hope that there would be profits, and, if so, that I would get a share. To this I objected and so the whole thing fell through. Van Doren is long since dead. The four manuscript volumes of my comment still repose on my shelves, useless to myself and to everybody else. This was my second literary abortion. The production of them wearied me much more than they would have done, had this kind of labour been more to my taste. Mr Croskery never told me whether he had done anything on his part of the work, but, if he did, it was never sent to Van Doren and was used up in the notes and comments which he afterwards contributed to 'The Pulpit Commentary'.

My next venture was something more successful. The story of the Siege of Derry had been told me at my grandmother's knee and had always for me a sort of fascination. Lord Macaulay's brilliant narrative and the republication of the original records, 'Mackenzie' by Dr Killen, and 'Walker and the Londerias' by Mr John Hempton, combined to awake my interest afresh. Living in Derry, I was more able to study the whole grand event on the field where it occurred, and could tell the whole story with more detail than it was possible for Lord Macaulay to do in writing 'The History of England'. Besides, the subject was abused for party purposes and employed to stir up hatred and strife. If the whole story was told truthfully, it would not be offensive, nor be very discreditable to anyone. With this view, I sat down and wrote 'Derry and Enniskillen', which was published by Messrs Mullan in 1873. Three heavy editions, the last consisting of 3000 copies, have since been published, and the demand for it has not yet ceased. It was received favourably by the public and the London 'Times' devoted three columns to a very flattering notice of it. Friends suggested that it would be a useful piece of work to tell the whole story of the Revolutionary War down to the capitulation of Limerick in the same style. In compliance with this wish, so often expressed, I wrote as a companion volume 'The Boyne and A[u]ghrim', which was also published by the Messrs Mullan. Though written in a more popular style, and forming, in my opinion, a more readable book, it never sold as well as 'Derry and Enniskillen'. The reason I could not say, but I suspect that the Boyne and Aughrim districts are not surrounded by a Protestant population taking interest in the events that occurred on their soil. The sale of 'Derry and Enniskillen' was mainly among the Protestant population of Ulster, who know the localities where the events occurred and who take a pride in the great historical incidents which have made these towns illustrious.

For the first twenty years of my residence in Derry, the College Library was in my charge. I arranged the books, marked them, catalogued them and did all in my power to add to the collection. There were two literary treasures, which, owing to my efforts, were added to the store, which, considering that we had no funds to devote to the purchase of books and were depending entirely on donations, increased wonderfully. One of these was the Greek Fathers. In my bachelor days at Maghera, I had purchased for my own use Migné's Paris Edition of the Latin Fathers in 222 volumes, which I found of great service to me in my historical studies. But the Greek Fathers, with the exception of Irenaeus, Clement and the Apostolic Fathers, were wanting in the College Library and in my own. One day a catalogue of books was sent me from Kelly of Grafton Street, Dublin, offering the Greek Fathers in 108 volumes for forty pounds. Such a chance might not occur again. I wrote without losing a post to one of our trustees, James Gibson Esq, who, except when engaged in judicial business, resided constantly in Dublin, to call at Kelly's, examine the books, and, if he found them to be a perfect set of Migné's edition, to buy them at once, either for the College Library or for me, as I desired to complete my set. Mr Gibson called and purchased the books, had them bound in half-vellum and retained them for the College. This, of course, served the purpose which I had in view, and put a complete set of the Greek as well as the Latin Fathers constantly at my hand.

The other addition was that of seven manuscript volumes, the oldest official records of the Presbyterian Church in Ireland, now known to exist, among them the Minutes of Antrim (two volumes), the Minutes of Laggan and the Minutes of the Presbyteries of Down and Bangor. These documents, once the property of Dr Bruce of Belfast, had been given by his son, Professor Bruce, in the last years of his life, to the Rev Classon Porter of Larne. Mr Porter kindly lent me the Minutes of Laggan, and, in answer to an inquiry of mine, he intimated that, if ever disposed to sell it and its companion volumes, he would let me know. Two or three years after, when Professor Bruce had died, Mr Porter wrote me that he was now willing to sell the seven volumes, and suggested that, while attending the meeting of General Assembly then approaching, I should take a run down from Belfast to Larne and see the books. I wrote him, promising to do so. The great thing was to keep from the Belfast theological professors the knowledge that the books were for sale. I did not give a whisper of it to any human being. Happening to have in my possession a deposit receipt for fifty pounds, lying in my name at the Bank, I took it with me when going to Belfast.

On the appointed day, I went down to Larne, where Mr Porter received me kindly. After tea, he took me into his study and brought down the books. There could be no doubt as to their genuineness, their uniqueness and their value. I said I was afraid to ask him what price he put upon them, lest it should be beyond my means. He answered that he had no difficulty in telling me. The price he set upon them was fifty pounds, and he would not take a farthing less. "But do you not think that fifty pounds is a very high price, Mr Porter?" "Well", said he, "you may think so, but remember that these are the oldest records of Presbyterianism in Ireland; that no copy of them exists; that they are quite unique; and they may never be in your power again." "All that is true", said I, "nevertheless fifty pounds is a long price for seven volumes that I could carry off in a napkin." He then began to take up the volumes and replace them on their shelves. "You need not put them away, Mr Porter", said I, "here is the money", putting on the table the fifty pounds, the very amount which, before leaving Derry, I had resolved to give, rather than miss the lot. The tears trickled down the good man's cheeks as he gathered together the precious volumes and tied them up carefully for me in a parcel. "Many, many a happy hour", said he, "over these old records I have passed. May they afford to you the same pleasure as they have done to me." He then accompanied me and my purchase to the railway station, where he bade me adieu. I often had pleasant letters, on literary subjects, from Mr Porter afterwards, even after he resigned his congregation and retired to spend his last days at Ballygally Castle, but I never saw him again.

For two years the manuscript volumes remained in my house until I had read them through and through. When the time came that I wished to recover my money and deposit the books in the College Library, I adopted the following expedient. I printed a circular, signed by myself and some of my colleagues, stating that the following valuable manuscripts were now offered for sale, that they could be purchased for fifty pounds, that it was desirable to preserve them in Magee College Library, and that, if the person receiving the circular approved, he was to contribute or collect, for the purpose, five pounds, which he was to send to me on or before a given day. The circular was addressed to ten or twelve gentlemen in or near Derry. Mr Gibson, hearing in Dublin of the effort I was making, sent me a cheque for five pounds, telling me to secure the books at any cost. Neither he nor any other knew that, all the time, the books were locked in my own drawer. But I returned Mr Gibson's cheque with thanks, stating that I had made up my mind that no trustee, professor or minister should pay one penny for this object. The lay gentlemen did not fail me, for, on or before the day appointed, all the money had come in. I then paid over the money to the credit of the trustees of the Belfast Bank

HISTORICAL

AND

LITERARY MEMORIALS

OF

Presbyterianism in Ireland.

(1623—1731.)

By THOMAS WITHEROW,

PROFESSOR OF CHURCH HISTORY IN MAGEE COLLEGE, LONDONDERRY.

"Remember them which have the rule over you, who have spoken unto you the word of God: whose faith follow, considering the end of their conversation: Jesus Christ, the same yesterday, and to-day, and for ever."—HEB. xiii. 7, 8.

"Et quidem bonos viros in hac terra fuisse non dubito, signa tamen atque virtutes aut ab eis nequaquam facta existimo, aut ita sunt hactenus silentio suppressa, ut utrumne sint facta nesciamus."—
GREGORII DIALOGI, lib. i.

WILLIAM MULLAN AND SON,
LONDON AND BELFAST.
1879.

HISTORICAL

AND

LITERARY MEMORIALS

OF

Presbyterianism in Ireland.

(1731—1800.)

SECOND SERIES.

By THOMAS WITHEROW,

PROFESSOR OF CHURCH HISTORY IN MAGEE COLLEGE, LONDONDERRY.

"Remember them which have the rule over you, who have spoken unto you the word of God; whose faith follow, considering the end of their conversation: Jesus Christ, the same yesterday, and to-day, and for ever."—HEB. xiii. 7, 8.

"Et quidem bonos viros in hac terra fuisse non dubito, signa tamen atque virtutes aut ab eis nequaquam facta existimo, aut ita sunt hactenus silentio suppressa, ut utrumne sint facta nesciamus."—
GREGORII DIALOGI, lib. i.

WILLIAM MULLAN AND SON,
LONDON AND BELFAST
1880.

The 'Monumenta Presbyteriana Hibernica', not so called

in Derry, intimating to Mr McClure what I had done and stating that, on my receiving from him a cheque in my favour for fifty pounds, the books would be lodged in the College Library. This accordingly was done. Mr Gibson, when he heard the whole story, was exceedingly pleased, saying that I had managed this business well and he went down to the town and purchased a fireproof safe in order to keep them safely. The safe was deposited in the Library and the books remain in it till this day. The secrecy was necessary, lest we should be outbid by the Belfast people, who have unlimited funds at their command.

During these years (1870-77), I was engaged in preparing a very extensive work, afterwards published under the title 'Historical and Literary Memorials of Presbyterianism in Ireland (1623-1800)', but which, if I could have got the consent of the publisher, would have been issued by the name 'Monumenta Presbyteriana Hibernica'. But he shrunk in terror from a long Latin name. The idea was suggested by obtaining, through Mr Croskery, the loan of a manuscript catalogue of works written by Presbyterian ministers, which Dr J Seaton Reid had drawn up for his own private use, when engaged in the composition of his great work, 'The History of the Presbyterian Church in Ireland'. I took a copy of it, to which I was able to add many other names and entries. Chambers' 'History of English Literature' suggested the outward form. The aim was to give a brief notice of every minister in Ireland who had published anything, a short description of the subject of his publication and a short extract illustrative of his style.

The material that I used in addition to the manuscript catalogue already named was the Minutes of the Synod of Ulster (1691-1820), kindly lent to me by that venerable body, manuscript Minutes of Presbytery, so far as I could obtain them, and the pamphlets and books of the writers, whose history I was endeavouring to trace. Many of these have been deposited by Mr Gibson and others in Magee College Library; some were obtained through Dr Killen from the Presbyterian College, Belfast; some were lent me by Mr Porter of Larne; and some I had in my own collection. But, after every effort, many of them were never found, leading me to believe that some at least have perished. I wrought hard, however, at pamphlets, reading, noting and extracting, and, at last, in 1877, the whole work down till 1800 was ready for publication. But the difficulty was to find a publisher. Personally I could run no pecuniary risk. My income was too limited to allow of that. Publisher after publisher declined to undertake the expense. It was too local. It was denominational. It appealed only to an Irish Presbyterian constituency and Irish Presbyterians are not as a rule a literary people. At last, Mr Mullan bought from me the copyright, not only of the 'Memorials', but of 'Derry and Enniskillen', and the 'Boyne and A[u]ghrim' too. All I got for them, counting the first edition of 'Derry and Enniskillen' already published, was a hundred pounds, but I was so much discouraged by the difficulty of getting the 'Memorials' published that I was glad to get anything and to be relieved of all danger. The Mullans drove a hard bargain, but fulfilled their part to the letter and brought out the books in an elegant form. How the 'Memorials' sold I have never heard, but I fear it had not the same extensive sale as 'Derry and Enniskillen', which records a story, the interest of which in the North of Ireland never dies.

My original design had been to bring down the 'Memorials' by adding a third volume, covering the space between 1800 and 1840, but the difficulty which I found in having the earlier volumes published and the limited sale discouraged me from further effort on that line. Mr Mullan told me that the publication of my four volumes required from him an outlay of more than a thousand pounds. How much of this he has since recovered, or whether the firm made any profit on the books, I have never learned. But I desire to leave it on record that both father and son treated me with great kindness and consideration.

Thus it was that twelve happy years in Derry fled rapidly away.

(12) The Moderatorship: 1878-79

I have now reached the most trying and momentous year of my life and enter on the story of it with an amount of dread, and regret, of which I cannot entirely divest myself now at the end of ten years. In the spring of 1878, it became evident from the nominations made by the Presbyteries of the Church, that I ran a chance of being elected Moderator of the General Assembly. It was an honour so far above me, that I never attempted to reach it. I had never taken such a part in the public business of the Church as to entitle me to expect the position. I was a speaker in every way so unready, that I felt myself unqualified for the post. I would have absented myself from the House and allowed another to be elected, had it not been that, so soon as the matter was proposed, my beloved wife, I saw, had set her heart upon it. I could not convince her that I was unqualified for such a high position. She believed me qualified for any post whatever. My refusal to accept office would have wounded her deeply; so, relying on Divine help, I made all the preparation that I could in the circumstances and made up my mind that, if called to the Chair, I would accept the honour that my brethren, entertaining a higher opinion of my talents than they would have done, had they known me better, evidently designed to confer.

Before starting for Belfast on the Saturday prior to the first Monday of June, on which day the Assembly met in May Street Church, I left sealed up in a letter at the 'Standard' office, the address I intended to deliver if called to the Chair, with strict instructions that they should not open it till informed by telegraph that I had been elected. Catherine and I went together to Belfast on Saturday and took lodgings a street or two away from the church. She looked that day in the train so beautiful, so pleased, so happy, that she seemed to have many a year before her yet, and it never occurred to me that my darling was so soon to be taken from me. On Sabbath forenoon we walked out to Newtownbreda and heard an excellent discourse from Mr Workman, and in the evening another equally good from Mr MacIntosh, then minister of May Street in succession to Dr Cooke. On Monday I called at the Mission Office, to obtain from Mr Eakin, Secretary of the Sustentation Fund, a voucher that I had attended the General Assembly, a precaution required by the railway company in order to make my return ticket available. When I stated the object of my visit, Mr Eakin looked in my face and asked, "Are you a minister?" I answered that I was. "Because", said he, "I never saw you before." "Nor", said I, "did I ever see you before, or ever stand before in this house." "Well, that is most extraordinary, that a minister of the General Assembly was never in the Mission Office. To what Presbytery do you belong?" "To the Presbytery of Derry." "May I ask you to favour me with your name?" "My name is Thomas Witherow." "Are you Professor Witherow?" "Yes, some call me by that name." "Oh", said he, "I have heard of you", handing me the voucher.

I mention this little incident to show how rarely of late years I had visited Belfast, and that to many of the younger members of Assembly I was personally unknown. A few hours after, the Assembly met and I was unanimously called to the Chair, Dr Watts having kindly withdrawn in my favour. I had never stood on that platform, except once before, when I went up to sign the Westminster Confession after being chosen a professor. My second appearance was after being elected Moderator. I read my address which was well received by a crowded Assembly. Catherine was present and rejoiced with great joy. Nothing gave her such true delight as anything that did honour to me. At the close, I handed a copy of my speech to the reporter of the 'Northern Whig', but he told me it was already in type, a printed copy having been received in the morning from Derry. The 'Standard' did not act on my orders. What would it have done, in case I had not been elected? Very little of what passed at that Assembly has fixed itself on my memory. The Revised Psalter was, I remember, approved. Mr Simpson of Queenstown took part in the debate on Instrumental Music for the first time, in an address a little coarse, perhaps, in some of its parts, but brimful of ability and force. Sleeping little at night, and in constant excitement through the day, I was glad to see the Assembly over and to retire for five or six weeks to Portrush. My addresses to Deputations were all carefully prepared and read from the manuscript. The Assembly throughout showed me the profound respect that it always shows to its Moderators, and, at the close, my friends overwhelmed me with congratulations.

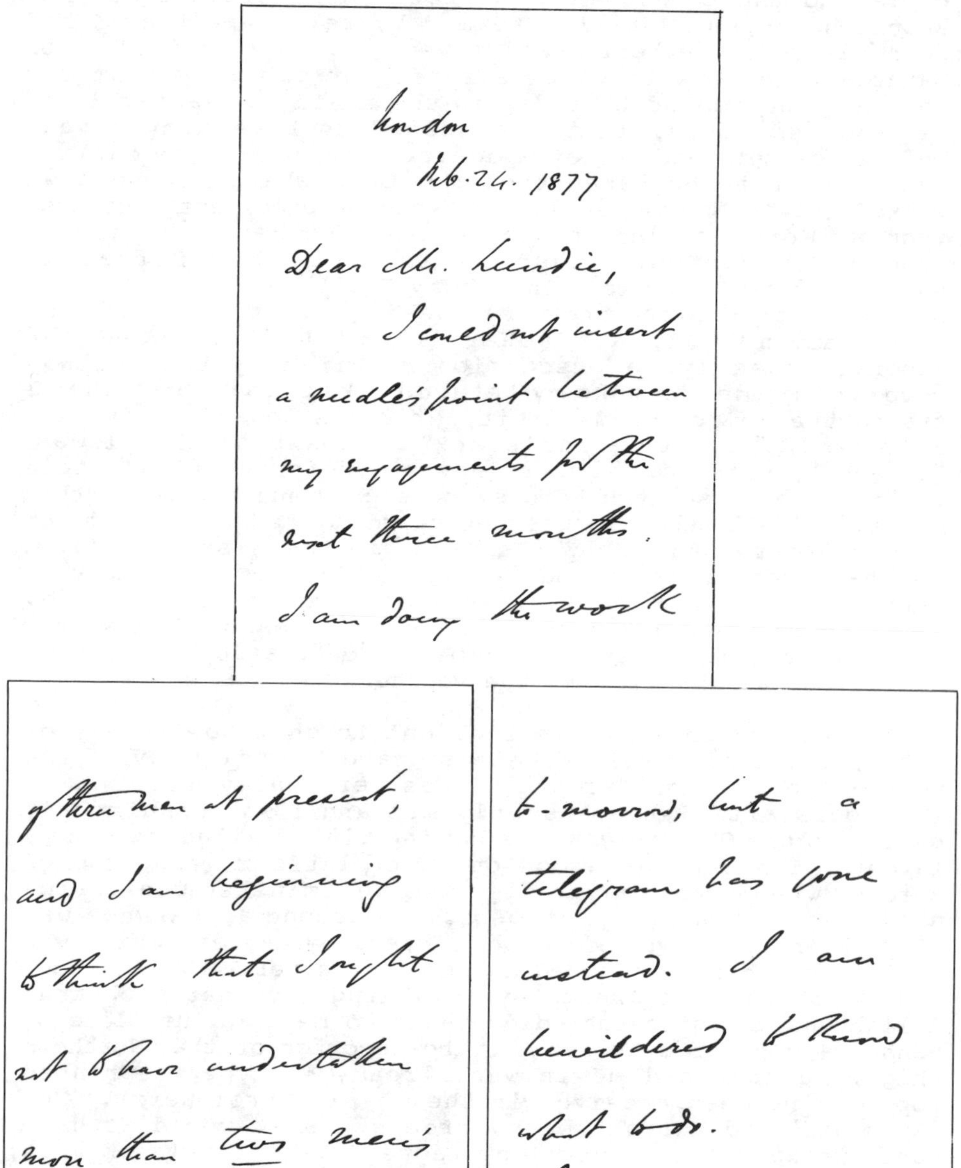

London
Feb. 24. 1877

Dear Mr. Lundie,

I could not insert a needle's point between my engagements for the next three months. I am doing the work of three men at present, and I am beginning to think that I ought not to have undertaken more than two men's work. I should be at Magherafelt to-morrow, but a telegram has come instead. I am bewildered to know what to do.

Yours ever faithfully
Richard Smyth

A telling letter, written within two years of Richard Smyth's early death

That I made no mistakes, I dare not assert, but I believe I made no gross blunder.

Towards the end of August I went for a trip to the Highlands, taking with me Catherine and two of our children, Jennie and James. At Rothesay we joined our old friends, the Rev Joseph Barkley and Mrs Barkley of Carnmoney, and we all travelled north together. Passing up through the Kyles of Bute, we crossed the isthmus of Argyle by the Crinan Canal, and, leaving Islay and Jura on the left, went on to Oban. From this centre we went one day to Iona and Staffa and sailed back in the evening down the Sound of Mull. The next day we went to Glencoe, Fortwilliam and the entrance of the Caledonian Canal. Then, leaving Oban, we returned by stage, passing Dunstaffnage, Loch Etive and Ben Cruchan, till we reached the Pass of Branden, where we took steamer and sailed up Loch Awe to its western extremity. There we took the stage again to Ardrishaig, and, in the evening, reached Rothesay. Next day we started to Helensburgh and Dumbarton, sailed up Loch Lomond, passed down Loch Catrine, went through the Trossachs, and in the night put up at the Bridge of Allan. Here I called on my old friend, Mr Trotter, once the manager of the Belfast Bank, but now retired. The most of that day was spent in visiting Stirling Castle and in the evening we passed on to Edinburgh. Here we rested a few days to enable the children to see the curiosities of that grand city. From this we passed on to see Abbotsford, Melrose and Dryburgh and returned to Edinburgh at night. Next day we came home by Glasgow and Greenock. The weather was superb. We got only two showers during that whole fortnight, one that detained us for about ten minutes at Abbotsford, the other as we were passing through Greenock on our way to the steamer, where we parted, the Barkleys sailing for Belfast and we sailing for Derry. Never before or since did I pass such a pleasant fortnight, the weather so fine, the scenery so grand and the company so delightful. Those beautiful spots I never wish to see again. It would call up the memory of two dear friends that I can never meet in the world again, and, because I do not care to have my memory of those delightful scenes, beheld under the most favourable circumstances, ever disturbed. Iona, Staffa, Glencoe, Loch Awe, Ben Cruchan and Melrose I can never forget, any more than the ever-dear friends in whose company I saw them.

There was none of my colleagues in the Faculty for whom I had a higher admiration than Richard Smyth. On the death of Dr Dill, he had been removed from the Chair of Hebrew to that of Theology. As a preacher, no man since Dr Cooke had evinced similar eloquence and power, while he was also exceedingly popular with the students and his brother professors. Professor Smyth had been Moderator of the General Assembly in the two trying years of Disestablishment and had steered the Church successfully through the breakers. In 1874 he stood for the representation of County Derry, along with the Liberal

Lecumpher Presbyterian Church

Richard Smyth's grave at Dervock Presbyterian Church

Solicitor-General, Hugh Law Esq, QC, afterwards Lord Chancellor of Ireland, and carried the county by a triumphant majority. His period in Parliament was that of the Conservative reaction and his whole time was spent in opposition, but he had charge of the Temperance Question and in adverse circumstances made a most favourable impression on the House. His advocacy made the Sunday Closing Bill for Ireland a success, though, alas, he did not live to see it carried and enjoy the triumph. Dr Smyth MP was never a man of strong physique. His best friends were always afraid that the late hours and wearisome debates of the House of Commons would overtax his powers. But, whether in Parliament or out of it, he never spared himself and was ready at all times to lend a helping hand to any good cause. On a cold November day he left Derry to preach a public sermon for a collection at Lecumpher, near Magherafelt, with the intention to go on to Belfast to attend a banquet given to Lord Dufferin by the Liberals of Ulster. He preached at Lecumpher, went on to Belfast, and, on the morning of the day that the dinner was to be given, called in to see an old Derry friend, who lived on the Antrim Road. He took suddenly ill during the visit and was never able to leave the house. He grew worse and worse and finally died after a few days' illness, on 2 December 1878.

For two years before he died, Dr Smyth had been Editor and joint-proprietor of the 'Derry Standard'. When the news reached Derry that he was so very ill, the office people sent down to me to supply them with editorials, which, of course, I could not refuse. In a day or two more, the sad news came that he was dead. Forthwith I sat down and through all the hours of a damp and dismal day I wrote the biographical sketch of him which filled three or four columns of the local paper. I finished with a heavy heart and thought to have the evening to rest, when in came the Rev A C Murphy, the minister of the First Church in Derry, who had gone to Belfast to be with him in his last moments, to tell me that it was the unanimous wish of the family that I, being the Moderator of the General Assembly that year, should attend the funeral and give the address. This was a kind of thing to which for several reasons I was scarcely equal. Still, a request of the kind could not in the circumstances be refused. I sat down and by 12 o'clock had written an address. Next day, I started by train, in company with many Derry people, met the funeral at Ballymoney and accompanied the sad procession to the churchyard at Dervock. The multitude in attendance was immense. Mr Law, Sir Thomas McClure and many others were present. The corpse was taken into the church, where the religious services were conducted by myself and other ministers. Half an hour after, in that quiet country graveyard, the ground closed over all that was mortal of the quickest and most brilliant Presbyterian minister in Ireland. Had it pleased God to spare Richard Smyth, Dr Cooke would not have been missed so much.

When Dr Smyth died, Sir Thomas McClure Bart, succeeded

LONDONDERRY.

BY THE REV. RICHARD SMYTH, M.A.

DURING several months in the summer of 1859, it was difficult for an eye-witness to describe, with perfect coolness and impartiality, the marvels of Divine grace which were then transpiring in this city. It was no matter of surprise that the judgment was occasionally a little overborne by the fervour of the heart, and carried away by the intensity of the emotions that had been excited. Hence courses of action may have been taken, and statements may have been made, in the rush of enthusiastic joy, which would barely stand the strict scrutiny of a sober retrospect. Where the whole soul was so intensely interested, and the heart so entirely absorbed, it was not a little difficult to give unbiased testimony; and the suspicion sometimes entertained by those at a distance from these scenes was excusable, that facts and figures had expanded under the heat of an unparalleled excitement.

By these dangers a writer is not now beset. The work has had time to be tested; we can survey it calmly and impartially, and no over-sanguine impulses can possibly surprise us beyond the well-defined limits of soberness and truth. Not that the converting and reviving grace of God has ceased to operate upon the churches of our city, but the Church has assumed what may be considered her normal condition—the extraordinary tension of mind and body consequent upon protracted night-meetings and

From Reid's 'Authentic Records of Revival' (1860)

T. & J. McELDERRY,
MILLERS,
GRAIN AND SEED MERCHANTS,
BALLYMONEY.

[ESTABLISHED 1784].
The ANTRIM ARMS Family & Commercial Hotel,
HIGH STREET, **BALLYMONEY.**
EDWARD MOONEY, Proprietor.
THIS Hotel is Furnished and Fitted throughout for the convenience and comfort of Families, Tourists, Excursionists and Commercial Gentlemen. Cars attend all the Trains arriving and leaving Ballymoney. Billiard and Smoking Rooms. Connected with the Hotel is a First-class Posting Establishment. Carriages and Waggonettes for Wedding Parties.

WILLIAM M'AFEE & CO.'S
FANCY EMPORIUM and STATIONERY WAREHOUSE,
Main Street, BALLYMONEY.
In connection with this business is a well-known Posting Establishment. Carriages, Waggonettes and Cars for Tourists, Excursionists and Wedding Parties. ALL FUNERAL REQUISITES.

From Bassett's 'Antrim'

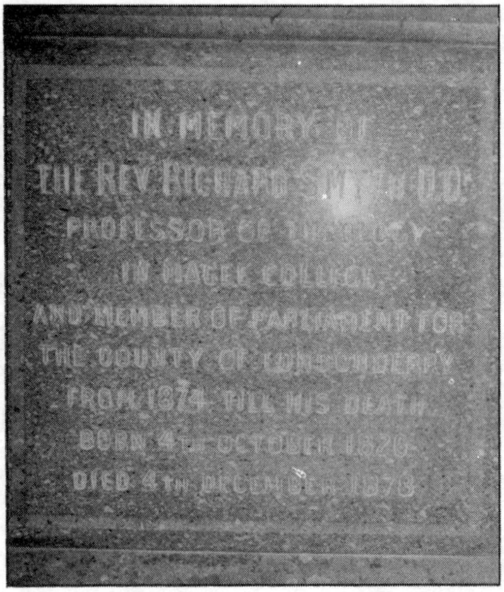

him as MP for County Derry, Dr Croskery succeeded him as Professor of Theology and I took his place as Editor of the 'Standard'. In that capacity I had served for eight months from April till December 1876, during the last illness and after the death of Dr McKnight, so that the duties were not unfamiliar to me. These duties consisted simply in writing the editorials, for neither Dr Smyth nor I, by any chance, ever visited the office. For the next eight years (December 1878 - December 1886), every editorial, with the exception perhaps of half a dozen, written for me by Dr Croskery, at times when I was suddenly called away on business, was written with my own hand. I soon grew to be expert and ready enough at the work. At first, I made a rough draft of the work in shorthand. Then I wrote it out in an extended and improved form for the press. But I had not been long at the work till I was able to write off a long article and send it up to be printed with very little alteration. This facility for composition has since been of great service to me; indeed, without it, I never could have accomplished the little work of a literary kind that is associated with my name.

On the day of Dr Smyth's interment, a number of gentlemen, most of them ministers, dined with me after the funeral at Mooney's Hotel in Ballymoney. I sat at one end of the table and it so happened that every time the dining-room door was opened by the waiter a cold draught of air from the hall, the outside door of which stood open, blew in upon me. I there caught a severe attack of bronchitis which hung around me till the end of March and prevented me from discharging nearly all the public duty usually expected from a Moderator. To add to my misfortune, Catherine took ill of bronchitis too, and, as she was looking forward to her confinement in April, an attack at such a time seriously reduced her strength. The College session was at an end before we had both recovered.

I now have reached the greatest trial of my life, up to the moment at which I write (17 October 1888). When the College session ended, I began to attend more diligently to the public duties connected with the Moderatorship than I had done during the winter. I had returned from some lecture at Moneymore, when I found a letter from Dr Bellis of the Mission Office, requesting me to attend some joint committee in Edinburgh, at which he and Dr Fleming Stevenson could not be present, and at which the Irish Church would not be represented, if I could not attend. Much against my will, I started from Derry on Monday, 15 April, and reached Edinburgh the next morning. The business of the committee was of no consequence. At all events, nothing was done and all was over in an hour. An intense longing for home seized upon me and I resisted all proffers of hospitality coming from the Edinburgh ministers. I started for Derry in the afternoon and after suffering severely from sea-sickness, I reached home about breakfast time on Wednesday. The shadow of some impending calamity was upon me and in this presentiment I was not

S. M. Dill

H. S. McKee

Samuel Marcus Dill, first Professor of Theology in Magee College and formerly minister of First Ballymena, where his successors included his nephew of the same name

Witherow's last resting-place, City Cemetery, Londonderry

mistaken. The doctor was in attendance upon Catherine when I arrived in Clarendon Street and, in two hours after, she was safely delivered of a daughter. She was exhausted in strength after the bronchial attack of the winter, from which she had barely recovered and the doctor would not think of her suckling the baby, as she always desired to do. In other respects, everything looked well for five or six days and she was thinking of rising, when, without any cause that we could see, her condition suddenly altered for the worse. Still I could not bring myself to believe that she was in danger and that God who so often before had brought her safely through a similar trial was about to take her away. I was attending a meeting of the Synod of Derry and Omagh in the First Presbyterian Church when the doctor took me out and said that he could not face alone the responsibility and that he wished professional assistance and advice. The news fell as a heavy stone on my heart, for it was a tender method of intimating to me that there was no hope. Sir William Miller was called in, and, after consultation, they pronounced it to be a case of puerperal fever.

For nearly a fortnight she hung between life and death, not apparently suffering much pain, but very weak and gradually sinking. On 8 May she took formal leave of me and all the children, clinging fondly to James especially, who, as her only surviving son, was the light of her eyes and enjoining him to be wise and good and not to let bad boys carry him away. That scene I can never forget. Friends and neighbours all stood around for every one that knew her loved her. That night the mind began to wander; she relapsed into unconsciousness and about one o'clock pm on Friday, 9 May, her spirit passed gently away.

To me it was a stunning blow. To be deprived of one whom I loved so tenderly and to be left alone with eight children, all of them girls, but one; the eldest not eighteen years old, the youngest only three weeks. It was indeed a heavy burden and for the moment I could have wished that I had been taken instead of her. But in a moment I recovered my senses and my first exclamation was "The Lord gave and the Lord hath taken away. Blessed be the name of the Lord". Why, I thought, should I reflect harshly on my Heavenly Father? Had he not gladdened my house with her presence for twenty happy years and am I to be angry now with Him for taking her home? I prayed for strength in that hour and it was given me. I thought that the best way of showing respect and love for my darling was not to sit down in despair and vain regret, but to put forth double effort to help the eight orphan children she had left behind her and entrusted to my care. I felt that that is what she would have done, had it pleased God to take me away and to leave her behind. On the following Monday, we laid her in the public cemetery at Derry, close by the side of Dr Dill's daughter, who had died while her father was a professor in the College.

Robert Watts,
who sought to make the
Assembly's College an
Irish Princeton, disseminating
Calvinist theology

J S MacIntosh,
Connor's 'Yankee Preacher',
who succeeded
Cooke in May Street

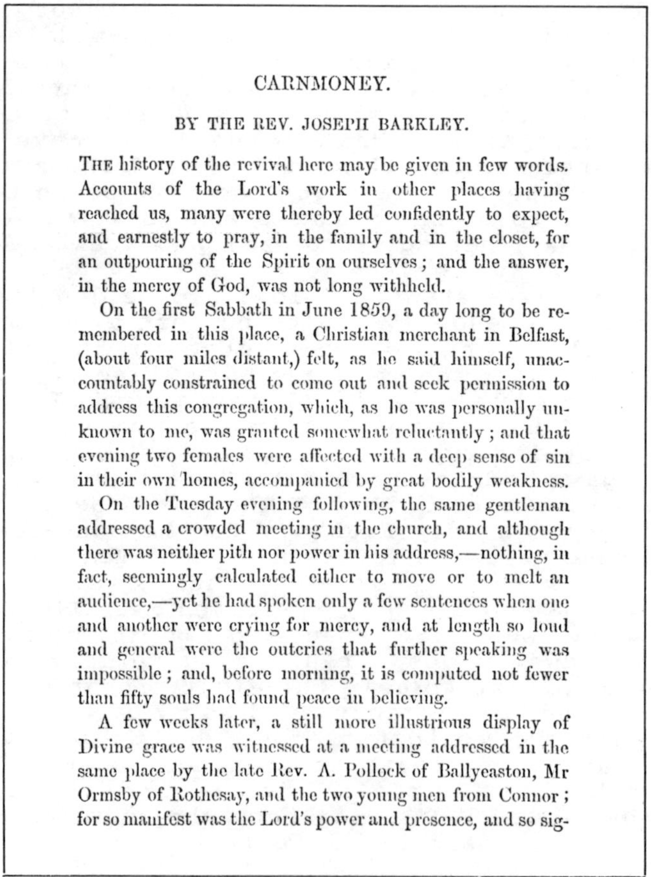

CARNMONEY.

BY THE REV. JOSEPH BARKLEY.

THE history of the revival here may be given in few words. Accounts of the Lord's work in other places having reached us, many were thereby led confidently to expect, and earnestly to pray, in the family and in the closet, for an outpouring of the Spirit on ourselves; and the answer, in the mercy of God, was not long withheld.

On the first Sabbath in June 1859, a day long to be remembered in this place, a Christian merchant in Belfast, (about four miles distant,) felt, as he said himself, unaccountably constrained to come out and seek permission to address this congregation, which, as he was personally unknown to me, was granted somewhat reluctantly; and that evening two females were affected with a deep sense of sin in their own homes, accompanied by great bodily weakness.

On the Tuesday evening following, the same gentleman addressed a crowded meeting in the church, and although there was neither pith nor power in his address,—nothing, in fact, seemingly calculated either to move or to melt an audience,—yet he had spoken only a few sentences when one and another were crying for mercy, and at length so loud and general were the outcries that further speaking was impossible; and, before morning, it is computed not fewer than fifty souls had found peace in believing.

A few weeks later, a still more illustrious display of Divine grace was witnessed at a meeting addressed in the same place by the late Rev. A. Pollock of Ballyeaston, Mr Ormsby of Rothesay, and the two young men from Connor; for so manifest was the Lord's power and presence, and so sig-

From Reid's 'Authentic Records of Revival' (1860)

When the friends who came from Maghera and Magherafelt had gone home and I was left alone in my empty rooms, I sat me down and cried till I thought my heart would break. But I soon saw that this would never do. The children had none to depend upon, under God, but on me and I must do my best for them. The poor things did all in their power to lighten my sorrow and make me forget my trial. But that was almost impossible. To keep me from thinking too much upon it, I sat down afresh to work and never wrought harder in my life, than I did in the years between 1879 and 1887. This, under God, was my only resource. Work, hard constant work, is the best remedy against the evil of brooding over sorrows.

The General Assembly was now drawing near and, according to custom, the ex-Moderator was expected to open it with a sermon. One of my brethren would have preached in my room, had I made the request, but, relying on the help of God, I determined to try it myself. I chose as my text Mark XI: 22-23 and wrote a discourse amid suffering and sorrow and tears. On the previous Saturday I went up to my friend, the Rev Joseph Barkley of Carnmoney, for a visit that renewed my trial, for I remembered that, the last time I had spent a night in that most pleasant of country manses, she had been with me. Mr and Mrs Barkley comforted me all in their power. Next Monday afternoon I went into Belfast and preached from May Street pulpit. God sustained me wonderfully. I studied in my discourse to steer clear of every affecting remark, for, had I touched on any tender point, I would have instantly broken down, as I very well knew. In half an hour, after the service was over, the Moderatorship passed from me to Dr Watts and I descended once more into private life. The kindness of the brethren, one and all, I can never forget. Their sympathy and compassion were overflowing. Nevertheless it was a comfort, nay a positive luxury, to be removed permanently from the fierce light of publicity and to be a private man again. And so concluded this sad and memorable year!

(13) Since 1879

It had been my ambition, all through the year of my Moderatorship, to signalize it in some literary way that would make it worthy of being remembered. It was therefore with pleasure that I arranged to have the second volume of my 'Historical Memorials' and the 'Boyne and A[u]ghrim' published while I occupied the Chair. This was done, so well as I remember, in or about May 1879. No previous Moderator had ever brought out two volumes of the same size during his occupancy of the Chair. But it pleased God to signalize the year to me in a different way from what I intended. The old house, 39 Clarendon Street, now became unpleasant to me. Everything only reminded me of the pure and gentle woman I had lost. At May 1880 I removed a little farther up the street to Number 49, the house at the corner, on the upper side of Princes Street, where I and the children resided until we moved into our present residence at College Hill. The second removal occurred at the beginning of September 1882. The change was very pleasant, for the corner house was cold and I was much annoyed by the constant carting across Princes Street, between the Quay and the Brewery. The quiet warmth and convenience of the College house were all that could be desired. Catherine had often longed for a quiet house in the suburbs, but, when that accommodation came at last, she was not there to enjoy it.

During my residence in the corner house I wrote the 'Bible Class Primer' on the Reformation, at the request of Dr Salmond of Aberdeen. I would have preferred the Ante-Nicene Age, but that subject had been appropriated by another before I consented to write. Dr Given and Dr Croskery each produced a Primer for the same series. The first thing I wrote after coming to College Hill was the 'Principles of Saving Truth', being extracts from the authorized formularies of the Reformed Churches and giving their leading doctrines in systematic order. Had I been still in the ministry, I would have valued such a compilation as supplying me with a course of subjects that I would have tried to expound. But, from this time forward, every minute that I could spare from the newspaper and from other duties was given to the preparation of my work on Church Government, which now under its title, 'The Form of the Christian Temple', is about to appear.

Ever since writing 'The Apostolic Church', my attention had been directed to church polity and I had come to the conclusion that it is not a matter of minor importance, but a portion of revealed Christianity. It grated harshly on my understanding to find it stated by persons affecting liberality, who had attained some degree of distinction in other lines, but who evidently never studied the subject of church polity, that there is no form of ecclesiastical polity contained in the Scriptures, and that every church is left free to adopt or to maintain that which it finds it most for its interest and best suited to the country and the time. It was not so, that I had read the Word of God. Besides, prelatic writers, and notably Dr Charles Wadsworth, Bishop of St Andrews, had invited us to compare notes, and to reconsider the difference between Episcopacy and Presbytery, with a view to their removal. His publisher in Edinburgh sent to me, and to other Presbyterian ministers, a copy of his 'Outlines of the Christian Ministry', merely for paying the postage. It seemed also that the time had come for restating the Presbyterian case and for putting every principle of the system on its Scriptural basis, apart altogether from any polemic purpose. It was with this view that I sat down to prepare the work on which I have expended more time than on any other. My original purpose was to show that each one of these Scriptural principles appears in the uninspired as well as in the inspired ages and so prove how they were nearly all corrupted and lost, until the polity of the medieval age, by a gradual process of innovation, had grown something very different from what it was in the apostolic and primitive time. Had this been done, it would have come in immediately after Book II. Then it was my purpose to consider, in a final and concluding book, how far Presbyterianism was a restoration of the revealed polity of the first ages. I had proceeded some length in the execution of this plan, when it broke upon me that my work would fill two bulky volumes and that no publisher, except at a very heavy cost to me, would undertake the responsibility of ushering my production into the world. It then became necessary to lighten the ship. The five books that I intended were reduced to three. A sharp attack of illness that seized me in July 1887 showed me also that the pressure of study must be lightened, and that my capacity for work was not what it had been. This decided me to curtail. I was done with the work at November 1887, but did not send it to the publisher until I utilized it in the shape of class lectures at Derry during the session 1887-88. It passed through the Edinburgh press in August and September of the present year, and ought to be ready for being issued to the public by 1 November. Messrs Clark of Edinburgh have done me a great favour in bringing it out so nicely.

Of the two great parties in the State, the Conservatives have been more successful than their rivals, account for it as we may, in dealing with the subject of Irish Education. To them we are indebted for the Intermediate System, the Presbyterian Theological Faculty (Ireland) and the creation of the Royal University. The Intermediate System was broached in Parliament and the Act carried through in 1878, principally under the guidance of Lord Cairns, who was a native of Belfast and thoroughly understood the state of parties in Ireland. The details were not all arranged when the Conservatives went out of office, and, when the Liberals came in, the Right Hon Hugh Law, then Attorney-General and MP for County Derry, wrote to me saying that he intended to put me forward as Intermediate Commissioner for the Presbyterian Church. The Assembly's Committee, without knowing this, met that week, and agreed to put before the Government the name of Dr Jackson Smyth. I immediately wrote to the Attorney-General, thanking him for the great honour he intended for me, but saying that I did not care for the amount of travel and loss of time it would involve; that Dr Jackson Smyth had been nominated by the Assembly's Committee; that it would please the church if he was appointed; and that he was the brother of his late friend and colleague, Professor Richard Smyth MP. Dr Smyth was at once appointed. The Assembly's Committee must have been not a little surprised, that for once their recommendation had such a sudden effect upon the Government.

It was in 1879, I believe, that the idea of a theological faculty, with power to give degrees, was first started. The first to start it, so far as I know, was the

THE LIFE AND LABOURS

OF THE

REV. JOHN WILSON,

MINISTER FOR UPWARDS OF THIRTY-THREE YEARS OF
FIRST KILLYMURRIS PRESBYTERIAN CHURCH, COUNTY ANTRIM.

BY THE

REV. WILLIAM IRWIN,
CASTLEROCK, CO. DERRY.

"Behold an Israelite indeed in whom is no guile!"
The Lord Jesus Cnrist
"Remember them . . . who have spoken to you the Word of God."
Heb. xiii. 7.

"A sweete attractive kind of grace,
A full assurance given by lookes,
Continuall comfort in a face,
The lineaments of Gospel bookes."—*Spenser.*

Belfast:
BIBLE AND COLPORTAGE SOCIETY, - LOMBARD STREET.
WILLIAM MULLAN & SON, - - - - - DONEGALL PLACE.
1885.

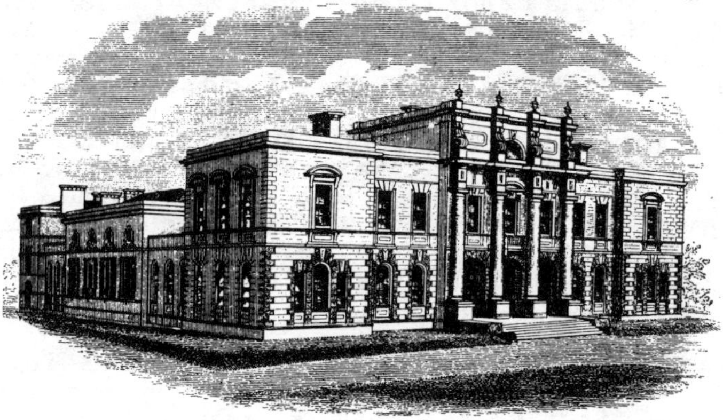

The Presbyterian Assembly's College, Belfast

Rev William Irwin of Castlerock, who complained of it as a grievance, that the Presbyterians were, alone of the great denominations, left without a fountain of theological honour in Ireland. Dr Killen of Belfast and I were stopping that season at Castlerock. The Moderator of the year, Dr Watts, was passing through by train. Mr Irwin captured him for an hour or two, and extemporized a meeting of three professors and two or three ministers in his own drawing-room. It was agreed that we had a grievance and the Moderator undertook at the first opportunity to bring it under the notice of the Government. This was done, and Lord Beaconsfield, to his great credit, conceded our claims and promised to have our wishes carried out. But, before this could be done, the Conservatives had passed out of office and Mr Gladstone succeeded to power. The Liberals, whom most of the Presbyterian ministers supported by their votes, could not for very shame refuse to carry out a promise that the Conservatives had given. The Presbyterian Theological Faculty (Ireland) was thus formed in 1881 and of it the Derry and Belfast theological professors were made members. The Belfast attorney who drew up the Charter charged two hundred pounds for his expenses. My friend, Professor Croskery, and myself were among those who received the degree of DD on the first occasion (1883) that the Presbyterian Theological Faculty exercised its right.

Up till the time of which we now speak, Magee College had been weak and languishing from a variety of causes, one of which was that no student educated outside Trinity College or the Queen's University was by law eligible for a degree in his own country, no matter how great his attainments might happen to be. This limited the number of our students, for it was constantly said, Why should anyone study at Derry, where it is impossible for him to obtain a degree? The same state of things prevailed at all the Roman Catholic colleges in Ireland. Mr Gladstone attempted to remedy this by Supplemental Charter in 1866, but, owing to the opposition of the Queen's Colleges, which were unwilling that their monopoly should be lost, that measure failed. Subsequently the great statesman introduced a Bill for uniting Trinity College and the Queen's University into one great university, but, owing to the shortsighted policy of the Roman Catholic prelates, that grand conception also perished. The O'Connor Don, then an Irish Member, attempted the removal of the grievance, but his well-meant effort did not succeed. At last the Conservatives, I think in 1879 or 1880, carried a measure, establishing on broad lines the Royal University and enabling every student in Ireland, no matter how or where he received his education, to compete if he pleased for its degrees and honours. By a Queen's Letter issued in 1884, I was made a member of the Senate of the Royal University and took my seat in that body on 29 May in that year. From it I received the degree of LLD in the year 1885. Owing to the invigorating effect of the Intermediate Act and of the Royal University, the Magee College which had opened in 1865 with twenty-six students and never had exceeded fifty-one, suddenly took a start and since that time the attendance of professional students has been little short of a hundred.

For the last few years, nothing of any importance has occurred in my pastoral or domestic history. Most of my children are at school, pursuing their education: James is passing through College; Lizzie is living with her uncle, the Rev R G Milling BD,at Ballynahinch; and the youngest, whom poor Mama in her dying moments directed to be called Catherine Hill (in honour of the young lady who, if death had not stepped in so suddenly, was about to marry Professor Smyth), has grown up to be nearly ten years old, without a day's sickness or suffering, so far as is known to me. My only anxiety now is for my children, that they may be wise and useful and good and that they may be able to pass through the world, as it has pleased God to enable me to do, without a stain upon their good name. I do not know that I have anything else to record. How long my life may extend I cannot foresee. Possibly another hand may write the next chapter. Lest that be so, I leave on record here my great thankfulness to God for putting me into the ministry, and thus giving me an office whose very duty is to help sinners to prepare for the Better Life. Nor can I conceal my sense of the privilege that I was trained in connexion with the Presbyterian Church, for, though not blind to its faults, I sincerely believe that in doctrine, polity and worship it comes nearest to the Scriptural model and that no other gives a better opportunity to any soul sincerely seeking salvation. Nor am I ungrateful to my brethren who, by their favour, consigned me to the quiet retreat of a College and then afforded me the opportunity, by writing and study, to bear testimony to truth and to do something, however feeble, to advance the cause of God. With simple trust I rely on Christ alone for salvation and look forward in hope to join at no distant day so many whom I love who have already landed on the Blissful Shore. And my earnest desire is that every one of my dear children may trust in the same blessed Redeemer, cling steadfastly to the same religious principle and live more consistently than I have been able to do. Some of them have given hope already. My fondest prayer and desire is that every one of them may meet me in the Better Land and that we may all stand together around the Throne, without one of us being lost.

College Hill, 18 October 1888

(14) Breaking Down: 1888-89

'The Form of the Christian Temple' appeared early in November 1888 and was noticed favourably in the magazines. Dr John Hall of New York wrote a public letter commendatory of it in the American papers, Dr Warfield of Princeton criticised it tenderly in the 'Presbyterian Review' of April 1889 and, what was to me most agreeable of all, the Irish General Assembly entered on its books a highly complimentary resolution (June 1889). Nevertheless I hear from the publisher that the sale of the book has been slow. Perhaps the price of the volume and the unpopularity of the subject may have had something to do with it. But, whether men hear or reject the message, it accomplished the end I intended. It has put on permanent record my testimony to what I believe to be true on a subject not often understood.

At the end of the session, in April 1889, Dr Killen, Professor of Church History in the Presbyterian College, Belfast, announced his intention to resign at the meeting of Assembly in June. Brethren from many quarters urged me to seek the appointment. I made up my mind, however, not to be a candidate. The reasons which decided me were, that I felt within me symptoms of declining health and did not care to encumber my burden of years with the burden of the heavier responsibility, and, as it was an assistant professor only that was wanted, I did not care, with my large family, to run the risk of a diminished salary. Besides, I was happy in Derry, surrounded by colleagues, brethren and friends, with whom it is a pleasure to associate. The duties were comparatively light and no objection could be entertained to anything, but to the salary, which was always small. Still, there are greater drawbacks than poverty and, as I had borne it uncomplainingly for four and twenty years, I thought I might bear it a little longer. For these reasons, I did not seek out office, which, had it fallen vacant ten or twelve years before, I would without doubt have sought at the hands of my brethren.

The idea of a short supplement to the 'Shorter Catechism', intended to teach the youth of the Presbyterian Church the rudiments of church polity, had always been a cherished idea of mine and I had frequently brought the matter under notice of the Synod of Derry and Omagh. At the meeting of the Synod in April 1888 I was asked to prepare a draft of what I proposed and to submit it to the Synod. This I agreed to do. I found the task very difficult, but, in the end, completed it. Seeing in the papers what occurred in the Synod, the Sabbath School Society entered into correspondence with me and induced me to send them my manuscript. They retained my manuscript for months, without letting me know whether they intended to accept or reject it. The first intimation I obtained of its rejection was when, in April 1889, the Rev Henry Osborne of Holywood sent me, in proof, another catechism which he had prepared at the request of the Society. I attached no blame to Mr Osborne, but felt that this was not nice treatment from the Society. It was simply tying my hands in regard to publication until they would be able to forestall me in the field. This they effectually did. I prepared another manuscript copy, submitted it to the Synod, and, having been revised by a Synodical Committee, it was issued in July 1889, under the auspices of the Bible and Colportage Society. It is intended for advanced pupils leaving Sabbath School and entering the Bible Class and

Death of Mr James Barkley

The Presbyterian Church has sustained a loss of no ordinary kind by the death of Mr James Barkley of Maghera, an event which occurred there on Saturday last, 12 May, and which it is our melancholy duty to announce this morning. He was a native of the town in which he spent most of his life, having been born there about 180[4] or very soon after. Having served his apprenticeship in Kilrea, he started in business for himself at Ballybay, in County Monaghan, but owing to the unexpected death of his brother George, which left the old home at Maghera vacant, he removed there from Ballybay in 1840. For the last forty-nine years he has resided in that town and has attended diligently to his mercantile affairs up till March last, when he was seized with that mortal illness under which he slowly sank and which in the end of last week carried him away in a ripe and honoured age.

Mr Barkley was the type of man not often met with, even in the best of churches. On no occasion throughout a long life, except from illness or other necessity, was he or his family ever absent from their pew in the house of prayer during both diets of the Sabbath worship. He usually took copious notes of the sermon and spent a due portion of the afternoon in examining the children and young people in his employment upon the discourse which they had heard in the morning. This strengthened the habit of attention on the part of the young and enabled them to retain in memory the truths which they had heard. He never could be induced to accept the office of the eldership for his business engagements required constant attention and he shrank from undertaking duties which he knew he would not have time to perform. The result was that he never sat as a member in any Session, Presbytery, Synod or General Assembly. But all the energies of his nature found full scope in other departments of usefulness. For over sixty years he took a prominent part in Sabbath School work, first as teacher and then as superintendent. He was never absent, except in a case of urgent necessity. In early life he often went to England to purchase goods, but on these occasions he always managed to reach home on Saturday, that the work of the Sabbath School next day might not be interrupted. In addition to the numbers of young people who thus came under his religious influence, the whole financial concerns of Maghera congregation were under his care for nearly forty years. He kept the accounts and dispersed the payments during all that time without fee or reward, but with as much accuracy and order as could be done in the best banking establishment in Ulster. He never took part as a speaker in any public meeting, religious or otherwise, for he felt and knew that his true sphere was not talk but action.

Mr Barkley was a man of sound judgement, kindly feeling, and upright and consistent life. He took deep interest in the Church and her ministers, and especially in

→

will, I hope, do good. Our Church has suffered much in past years for want of clear and definite teaching on that subject, systematically given.

My dear friend, Mr James Barkley of Maghera, died on 18 May 1889. A brief notice of him that I sent to the Belfast 'Witness', and which I reproduce hereafter makes it unnecessary to describe his life in detail. His son, the Judge, afterwards wrote me to say that I was inaccurate in one or two of my statements. His father was younger by nearly two years than I had made him. He served his apprenticeship with his uncle, David Graham, in Magherafelt and he first set up in business in the town of Kilrea. With these exceptions, the family accepted my statement as a true statement of facts.

Mr Barkley was my intimate friend for four and forty years. During the twenty years of my ministry I took scarcely any important step without consulting him. His judgement was always sound, his motives the very highest, his conversation edifying and his conduct upright. The interests of the cause of Christ were at all times uppermost in his mind. During all my time in Maghera he stood at my right hand to aid and befriend me. When I was prostrated by fever in 1852, he read and prayed at my bedside. When I was elected to the professorship in Derry, he came to this city, along with Catherine and me, to assist me in the choice of a house. And, afterwards, when I received my degree of DD from the Theological Faculty, he travelled all the way from Maghera to be present on the occasion. When my dear wife was laid in the cemetery at Derry, he stood at her grave and strengthened me under my trial. During the four and twenty years which have elapsed since I removed from Maghera, he was my faithful correspondent.

I would have gone to see him in his last illness, but, knowing that my own health was not very good, he wrote from his dying bed, specially requesting me not to do so. In his death I lost a true friend. No man I ever knew approached so close to the model of a perfect Christian as James Barkley. My desire is that in God's own time I may follow him to that world where he now is and that the friendships of earth may be renewed before the Great White Throne.

During the Christmas holidays (1888) I was confined to bed for a week, with a violent attack of indigestion, and, although I recovered in some degree and discharged all my College duties as before, I never have enjoyed since the same buoyant health as before. After the session ended, my illness increased, producing not only flatulence, irregularity in the action of the bowels, and pain in the stomach, but, in the month of May, a difficulty of breathing which was very painful and made everything in the shape of work impossible. Professor Bigger and other friends, without my knowing what they did, raised among themselves sixty-four pounds and sent it to me, saying it her missionary and charitable enterprises. There was no waste in his establishment, yet his money was always ready when he was convinced that the Gospel or its ministers needed help. He was fond of reading and from his long experience in the religious instruction of the young, he acquired a deep and extensive knowledge of the Scriptures and came to be an intelligent and well-read theologian. Though a modest and unassuming man, instinctively disliking all fuss and parade, his clear intellect, quiet humour and readiness of reply made him a formidable antagonist to any man who would venture to draw him into controversy in private life. He used to say humorously that he had helped to train three ministers in his time and to make professors of them, referring, we suppose, to Professor Gibson, once of Ballybay; Dr Witherow, now of Derry; and Professor Leitch. There was really more truth in the remark than appears on the surface. Not one of these men would deny how much he owed to the intelligent conversation, the high principle and good example of James Barkley. It is not in every congregation that a young minister, in his days of rash youth and inexperience, meets with so judicious a counsellor and such a true and unselfish friend. Though intimation was given that the funeral would be private, the Sabbath School children could not be kept from attending in large numbers on Monday last and the Sabbath School teachers of Maghera bore him to his grave. He gave special directions that no funeral sermon should be preached in his honour and, though we have scrupulously endeavoured to write within the lines of truth and justice, we doubt whether even this meagre notice of his life and work would have met his approval had it been possible to consult him.

Mr Barkley trained a large family, all of whom that now survive are out in the world filling useful and honourable positions in society. Many of our readers are of course aware that the late Rev Joseph Barkley, minister of Carnmoney, was his youngest brother and that his eldest son is Dr David Graham Barkley, recently a judge in the Supreme Court of the Punjab and now one of the conveners of the Assembly's Foreign Mission.

New St Lurach's with James Barkley's grave in the centre

was their wish I should go to Harrogate, take a course of the waters there and try to recover my strength. In company with my eldest daughter, I went there on 1 July and in the following week I was joined by my daughter Lizzie from Ballynahinch, who had not yet recovered her strength after an attack of illness which she had had in the spring. The treatment at the Hydropathic weakened me very much. In fact, I was ill all the time I was there, but, since coming home, I feel better, my pain very much diminished and my physical vigour increased. Whether any permanent cure will result remains to be seen. I desire to trust in God and to leave my case in His hands. But I never can forget the unselfish, kind and thoughtful conduct of the beloved friends who, with their generosity, made it possible for me to enjoy for a season the recreation and hydropathic treatment at Harrogate and opened up to me a new experience of life.

The books that an author writes are usually the only means of doing good which remains after he himself has passed out of sight of men. Sometimes what a man has actually produced is never known and sometimes what he never wrote is fathered upon him, so that his name goes down to other generations, weighted with opinions that he never entertained and which he would in his lifetime have repudiated. In order, so far as is in my power, to prevent this injustice being done me, I append a catalogue of my literary productions, great and small, simply saying that, with the exception of literary and historical mistakes to which every man is subject, I adhere at this moment to every statement and opinion expressed in them, and that, looking back upon them, they do not contain a single line that "dying, I could wish to blot". The exception of most importance to this statement is my juvenile, unprinted, 'Theory of a Universal Establishment', every word of which, at the time of composition I believed to be true, but which I am now convinced broaches a theory visionary, and impractical, in such a world as this. I regard it now myself as more a curiosity than anything else and would not wish to see it quoted as giving my mature opinion on the true relations of Church and State.

List of Writings of Rev Thomas Witherow DD

Published Books

(1) 'The Apostolic Church' 18mo 180 pp Belfast 1856
(2) 'Scriptural Baptism: Its mode and subjects' 24mo 72 pp Belfast 1864
(3) 'Derry and Enniskillen in 1689' 368 pp Belfast 1873
(4) 'The Boyne and A[u]ghrim' 335 pp London 1879
(5) 'Historical and Literary Memorials of Presbyterianism in Ireland' first series (1623-1731) London; second series (1731-1800) London 1879
(6) Primer 'History of the Reformation' 93 pp Edinburgh 1882

Assembly's Tribute

At Belfast the eleventh day of June, one thousand eight hundred and eighty-nine years, which day the General Assembly of the Presbyterian Church in Ireland being met and constituted, the following deliverance with reference to Dr Witherow, Professor of Church History and Pastoral Theology in Magee College, was adopted with the acclamations of the House:

The Assembly conveys to the Rev Thomas Witherow, DD, LLD, Professor of Church History in Magee College, Londonderry, its warmest thanks for his treatise recently published on the constitution of the New Testament Church, entitled "The Form of the Christian Temple". By this production of his prolific pen Dr Witherow has rendered highly important service not only to the Presbyterian Churches of Christendom but to every one who seeks by the careful study of the Word of God to know the constitution of the Church, as set up by Christ and His inspired Apostles. He has successfully combatted the theory that no system of Church government is laid down in the New Testament, demonstrated that the great principles of Presbyterianism are Divine; and established in the clearest manner that Prelacy, as exhibited in the three great ecclesiastical corporations of the present time, the Greek, the Roman, and the Anglican, is a human addition.

The Assembly cordially congratulates Dr Witherow, the Professors of Magee College, and the whole Presbyterian Church, on the completion of a work so distinguished for literary merit and so valuable in the elucidation of Divine truth, and earnestly desires for it a wide circulation.

(Extracted from the records of the General Assembly of the Presbyterian Church in Ireland by John H Orr DD, Clerk of Assembly)

(7) 'Principles of Christian Truth' 88 pp Edinburgh 1883
(8) 'Life of Dr Goudy' (continuation) Dublin 1887
(9) 'The Form of the Christian Temple' 8vo 468 pp Edinburgh 1888-9
(10) 'Two Diaries of Derry in 1689' (with introduction) Derry 1888

Unprinted Books

(11) 'Theory of a Universal Establishment' 1853
(12) 'Suggestive Comment on the Pastoral Epistles' 1869

Unfinished MSS (1859)

(13) 'Theology of the Celtic Church'
(14) 'Historical Sketch of the Reformed Churches'

Reviews

(15) St Patrick 'British Quarterly' October 1867
(16) Montalembert on St Columba 'British & Foreign Evangelical' July 1868
(17) Presbyterians and the Irish Church 'British & Foreign Evangelical' 1869
(18) The Two Testaments in their Relations 'British & Foreign Evangelical' 1870
(19) The New Testament Elder 'British & Foreign Evangelical' April 1873
(20) Confession and Absolution 'London Quarterly' Jan 1874
(21) History of the Vatican Council 'British & Foreign Evangelical' April 1874
(22) The Vatican Dogma 'British & Foreign Evangelical' April 1875
(23) Ultramontanism and Civil Allegiance 'British Quarterly' April 1875
(24) The Three Creeds 'British & Foreign Evangelical' April 1876
(25) The Origin and Growth of Episcopacy 'British & Foreign Evangelical' 1877
(26) Why did the Reformers reject Episcopacy? 'British & Foreign Evangelical' Oct 1878
(27) Was Aerius a Heretic? 'British & Foreign Evangelical' Oct 1883
(28) Presbyterianism in Canada 'Presbyterian Review' April 1888

Printed Lectures

(29) 'Three Prophets of Our Own' Belfast 1855
(30) 'The Sabbath not a Church Holiday' Belfast 1871
(31) 'John Knox and His Times' Belfast 1872
(32) 'Address at Cooke Centenary' Belfast 1888

Unprinted Lectures

(33) 'Life and Works of Calvin' 1860
(34) 'Dr Cooke' 1868

(35) 'Siege of Derry' 1874
(36) 'Martin Luther' 1884

Pamphlets and Printed Addresses

(37) 'Defence of the Apostolic Church' Belfast 1857
(38) 'Historical Sketch of the Presbyterian Church in Ireland' 1858
(39) 'Words of Truth and Soberness' 1859
(40) 'Reply to Rev R M Henry on Mode of Baptism' 1860
(41) 'The Puritan Worthies of 1662' 23 pp Belfast 1862
(42) 'Address at Gortnessy Jubilee' Derry 1889
(43) 'A Short Catechism of Church Polity and Worship' Derry 1889
(44) 'College Address on Difficulties in Confession of Faith' Nov 1881
(45) 'College Address on Revision of the Confession' Nov 1887 and May 1888

(44) and (45) were printed in the newspapers at the time.

Articles Contributed to Magazines and Newspapers

(46) The Force of Scripture Example 'Irish Presbyerian' July 1853
(47) The Old Church of Ballynascreen 'Irish Presbyterian' November 1854
(48) Study of Ancient History 'Evangelical Witness' June 1862
(49) Irish Protestantism: Why it is Divided 'Evangelical Witness' August 1862
(50) Churchmen of the Past 'Evangelical Witness' May 1862
(51) Papers on Baptism 'Evangelical Witness' 1862 and 1863
(52) Guinness and Tertullian 'Evangelical Witness' Oct 1863
(53) One Church and all Dispensations 'Evangelical Witness' June 1864
(54) James Bryce of Killaig 'Evangelical Witness' June 1864
(55) Notes on Dr Bryce's Letter 'Evangelical Witness' Sept 1864
(56) Lifeand Writings of Sedulius 'Evangelical Witness' Feb 1864
(57) The Wigton Martyrs 'Evangelical Witness' Oct 1867
(58) The Magherafelt Book 'Evangelical Witness' Feb 1868
(59) History of Maghera Congregation 'Evangelical Witness' March 1868 and Dec 1868
(60) Minutes of Laggan 'Evangelical Witness' July 1868
(61) Adam Murray, the Hero of the Siege 'Evangelical Witness' 1868
(62) King William's Minister 'Evangelical Witness' Feb 1870
(63) Teaching our Distinctive Principles 'Evangelical Witness' 1871
(64) Mr Froude and the Earl of Belmore 'Evangelical Witness' for 1873

(65) Hundred Best Presbyterian Books 'Derry Standard' 2 April 1886
(66) History of the Ruling Elder Four articles in 'Witness' July 1888

Memorial Sketches

(67) Sketch of Dr John Brown of Aghadoey 'Derry Standard', 23 April 1873
(68) Dr S M Dill 'Derry Standard'
(69) Rev William McClure 'Derry Standard' Feb 1874
(70) Rev Richard Smyth DD MP 'Derry Standard'
(71) Rev Thomas Croskery DD 'Witness' 8 Oct 1886

Sermons

(72) Salvation in Blood Acts 4:12 Printed in Sinclair Seaman's Prayerbook
(73) Synodical Sermon 1878 John 21:15 Religious Education Schools (MS)
(74) Assembly Sermon 1879 Mark 11:22-23 Strength of Faith (MS)
(75) Lecture on Psalm 97 Maghera 12 Nov 1859 Reasons for Praise (MS)
(76) Peter's Temptation Luke 22:31-32 April 1876 (MS)
(77) Inconsistency of Christians 1 Sam 15:13-14 Sept 1880 (MS)
(78) What is Truth? John 27:38 (MS)
(79) Baptismal Regeneration John 3:5 16 Oct 1880 (MS)
(80) The Seal of Baptism Rom 4:11 12 Dec 1880 (MS)
(81) Important Uses of Baptism Acts 22:16 5 Dec 1880 (MS)

Omissions and Additions

(82) Ireland in Some of its Aspects Six Carey Lectures, 1880 (MS)
(83) Essay on Church Legislation 1889 (MS)
(84) Essay on Christian Missions Historically Considered (MS)
(85) Autobiography (MS)
(86) The Wodrows of Eaglesham 'Evangelical Witness' Sept 1869
(87) Jerome Savonarola - Review of Villari's 'Life' 'Witness' June 1869
(88) Church Polity a Part of Christianity 'Theological Monthly' Jan 1889
(89) Sermon, The Power of the Keys
(90) Antiquity as a Test of Truth in 'The Church' edited by Gavin Carlyle
(91) St Columba and the Early Monastic System of Ireland MS Lecture 1873
(92) Home Rule for Ireland 'Derry Standard' 4 April 1886 Scrap B Vol 11

The foregoing catalogue does not include mere sermons or skeletons of religious addresses, of which I have produced fourteen volumes bound, and as many unbound as would make a fifteenth volume; nor class lectures, of which I possess a great heap; nor ordinary newspaper editorials, of which I wrote a great number from March till December 1876, during which time I supplied the place of Dr McKnight on the 'Derry Standard', and from December 1878 till December 1886, during which time I was sole Editor of that paper. The sermons, when written at all, were very hurriedly prepared; the lectures, though compiled from the best sources, were not in general the result of personal and original investigation, and the editorials were called out by the politics of the times and the exigencies of the hour. The works entered in the catalogue received more thought and consideration and, should a time ever come when my opinion on any subject shall be deemed a matter of any importance, I desire that the words containing that opinion shall be taken from the writings named in the present catalogue, and not from the hasty and ephemeral products of the hour.

College Hill 9 August 1889

POSTHUMOUS TRIBUTES

Death of Professor Witherow DD, Magee College

'Derry Standard', 27 January 1890

In the early part of July the deceased went to Harrogate in the hope that its salubrious climate would be beneficial, but on his return to Derry towards the end of August it was found that, while his residence at Harrogate had relieved other complaints, it seemed to have aggravated the heart infection. For the last six weeks Professor Witherow was confined to his house, but he was, on the whole, cheerful and hopeful. It is only about three weeks since a paragraph written by him appeared in our columns, requesting information as to whether the statement was true that the late Robert Browning, the famous poet, was, as stated by a Scotch contemporary, a direct descendant of Micaiah Browning, a hero of the Siege of Derry. It will thus be seen that, almost up to the last, his mind was active and his desire for historical information unabated. On Thursday the 16th of this month Professor Witherow retired to bed early in the evening and on the following day, when Dr Brown called, he found his patient weaker and evidently sinking rapidly. The family saw that the end was approaching and that end, to him the beginning of a new and brighter life, came on Saturday morning, when he passed peacefully away to his eternal rest and reward, from the presence of the members of his family. Professor Witherow was pre-deceased by his wife several years ago and their children who remain amongst us will have a double measure of the sympathy of the Christian people in their irreparable bereavement. Their loss is great and the loss of the Presbyterian Church and of Magee College is only secondary to theirs. The name of Witherow is known and revered in every quarter of the globe where Presbyterianism has a footing and the regret at his demise will therefore be world-wide. Their loss, however, is his gain.

'Londonderry Sentinel', 28 January 1890

After a painful, protracted illness, Dr Witherow, Professor of Church History and Pastoral Theology at Magee College, passed away peacefully at 10 o'clock on Saturday morning. For nearly eighteen months Dr Witherow suffered from a painful form of heart disease which brought affections of the other vital organs in its train and assumed an acute form about three months ago. In earlier stages of the disease he visited Scarborough [or Harrogate?] and some other health resorts without much, if any, benefit. He was confined to his room latterly and during five days preceding his death was in a prostrate condition and unconscious. He was assiduously and affectionately nursed throughout his illness by members of his family and Dr Brown, his medical attendant, was indefatigable in his exertions to alleviate the sufferer. Dr Bernard and Professor Cumming, Belfast, were called in consultation, but could do nothing more but confirm Dr Brown's treatment. The deceased gentleman was in his sixty-eighth year, having spent a busy life; first as minister of a large congregation and latterly as professor in Magee College, where he produced several theological and historical works of great merit, evincing literary ability of a high order.... In private life, he was one of the most congenial of companions; his conversation exhibiting practical discernment and knowledge of the world, side by side with a happy humour which added to the attractiveness of his society. In his death the Presbyterian Church has lost one of its ablest theologians and controversialists and the Magee College a learned and indefatigable teacher whose place will not be easy to fill.

'The Witness', 31 January 1890

The Rev Thomas Witherow DD, Professor of Church History in Magee College, Londonderry, died at his residence, College Hill, on Saturday at ten o'clock. This announcement which we make with very great regret, will be received with sadness in every home of the Presbyterian Church in Ireland, as well as in all Presbyterian circles the world over. Dr Witherow has been failing in physical health for the past six months. By the advice of friends in August last, he sought a change of scene and a respite from self-imposed labours at Harrogate, but he returned nothing better, but rather the worse. Symptoms of a serious kind manifested themselves, which indicated that he was suffering from heart disease, and, notwithstanding all the efforts of medical skill and filial affection to prolong a valuable life, the end has come, and death has released a true man from the pains and labours of life, has transfigured a character splendidly furnished and a career devoted in all its stages to the service of God and man. The death of Dr Witherow is a very serious loss to the cause of Presbyterianism and to everything it represents. His mental powers, his time, his life were consecrated to the service of his Church, and splendid service he rendered in the defence and exposition of the policy and principles of a faith which has done so much to preserve and extend the light of Scriptural truth, and which has been a main factor in the advancement of civil and religious liberty. A more loyal or more competent servant of Presbytery has rarely existed. By his death Magee College sustains an uncommon loss. That institution, which has trained so many of our ministers, he served with boundless energy for nearly a quarter of a century as a professor who was an exceptionally good teacher and who was an inspiring model of dignity, integrity, punctuality and conscientiousness. The students who came under his wand learned much from his lectures which were the production of a vigorous, cultured mind, but they gained more from the penetrating influence of the man, for they felt that the workman was greater than his work, stimulating and effective as the work undoubtedly was. Historical investigation will miss the services of one of the most conscientious and competent exponents of the forces and facts of the past. The community has lost in Dr Witherow a man of great simplicity and firmness of character, a man whose honesty of purpose, purity of life and motive strength of common sense, generous candour and intellectual gravity were so conspicuous that he was reverenced by all who knew him and respected by opponents who felt the keenness of his weapons of war. Few men will be more or longer missed than Dr Witherow, few deaths make such a void as his, few lives have been so fructuous in good and so glorified by hard, faithful work; he was a great teacher, a ripe scholar, a stimulating preacher and a most capable professor. The Presbyterian Church in Ireland has to bewail the fall of a defender of the faith, and not a defender only, but a brilliant expounder, who could give a reason for the faith he held, and who showed in many a tractate that the creed which embraced the stronger half of the Protestant world was not only reasonable but Scriptural, not only intellectually defensible, but steadied, purified, enriched and developed, in all God-like, man-like graces, the souls it set on fire...

Dr Witherow was very happy in selecting titles for his works. We venture to affirm that no author of modern times has ever hit on so many really expressive, beautiful titles. The very heading of his first publication is a wonderful tribute to three great men. If he avoided in his selection of titles of his works everything that savoured of clap-trap, his wares were all sterling metal. His smallest publication was a valuable contribution on the subject treated. He wrote because he had something to communicate. His pamphlets were all chips from a good workshop. They are clear, with the facts marshalled in logical order, the arguments all clenched, and he never fell into the mistake of that class of authors who sometimes in their zeal hammer the head of the nails they drive in. Some think that he was rather too much a controversialist, but they quietly forget that a great number of Scriptural truths had to be rescued from the hands of the Philistines, that the just claims of Presbytery as the Scriptural form of Church government has been persistently denied, and that the honours to which Presbyterians were entitled in connection with the memorable Siege of Derry had been given to others. To set things right in this crooked world necessitates consecration. He rescued stolen property; he did divest some jackdaws of the peacocks' feathers in which they had arrayed themselves; he did mercilessly handle preposterous claims. But his works show that he never used a poisoned arrow in his warfare, and such was the natural gentleness of the man that he abstained from all personalities even under great provocation. His style was individual - it was, in truth, the man. It was nervous, chaste, vigorous Saxon. His meaning was never clouded with words or mystified with purple patches. It was the style of a strong, honest mind, which saw things clearly, a flexible, forcible, fitting vehicle for conveying his convictions and conclusions to his readers.

Dr Witherow's professoriate of twenty-five years in Magee College, like his pastorate at Maghera of twenty years, was successful, because he brought to his duties to the Church and to the students for the ministry the same conscientiousness, the same loyalty to truth, the same resolve to do faithfully what was required which characterised all his actions. He had ample knowledge of his subject, gained by patient investigation; a true grasp of the principles of the New Testament polity; sympathy with students' difficulties, and a power of expression which made him the easiest of teachers to follow. Church history, like any other history, may be treated in such a manner as to be either the most barren or the most fruitful of studies. It may be treated as a string of facts, which make it as profitable for spiritual nourishment as sawdust to a hungry man; or a narrow-minded man may treat it as illustrating a few cut-and-dried maxims which he foolishly imagines are Scriptural principles. Dr Witherow was not narrow in his views or contracted in his sympathies. His lectures were not a string of dry facts or barren discussions about metaphysical knots. He had considerable dramatic power, a fresh way of looking at things, and the faculty of making the past a living reality. His students not only learned much, but they got an impression of the grandeur of the story of the Church. They were interested as well as instructed. In private life he was the same as in public - honest, frank, blunt, companionable, full of information, a good talker, and, what is more difficult, a good listener, an excellent storyteller, and a man whose laugh was an inspiration. His talk was not a preachment, it was crisp and free, a compound of good sense and hearty humour. His use of words was just and picturesque. His face was very attractive, for it betokened kindliness, determination, honesty, power, veracity. A straight, kindly, scrupulously just man was he, and at the root of all, and feeding all the gifts of nature and graces of character, was a piety which, if not of the self-advertising type, was genuine and genial.

Our first and last thought about him is that he was a Christian man, and that is everything. It will make his work lasting and his memory a heritage to his Church and to his children. He leaves behind him seven daughters and one son, who promises to perpetuate the abilities of his father, as well as to keep untarnished the traditions of an honoured name. Dr Witherow's talents and industry, his rare powers of mind and rarer powers of concentration, would have ensured his success in any earthly calling. He was led to choose Church life as the sphere of his labours, and he leaves behind him a name which shall be remembered for good. With the exception of the venerable President of the Assembly's College, who inspired him with a desire to study Church history, no man in our communion has done more or better work in that field, and no man has done more to preserve the memory of the silent makers of Ulster's pre-eminence. He was a lover of Presbyterianism, and of all that was good and venerable in any of the Churches of Christendom.

The Funeral

On Tuesday the remains of Professor Witherow DD, of Magee College, were removed from his residence, College Hill, Derry, for interment in the Borough Cemetery. The funeral cortege was very large and representative. The hearse was preceded by the students of Magee College, walking two abreast. After the hearse came the Faculty - Revs Professor Petticrew DSch; Professor Dougherty MA; J L Bigger BD; Professor Graham, Professor Leebody and Professor McMaster. The Trustees of the College were represented by Revs J M Rodgers and R McMorris, Mr John Cooke JP and Dr Barclay. Then followed mourning carriages with the family and other friends of the deceased. The Bishop of Derry and the Dean were present. Among those attending the funeral we noticed a number of ministers of the General Assembly and of other denominations. At the grave Rev Dr Ross led in prayer, after which Rev J Maxwell Rodgers, with whose congregation Dr Witherow was connected as an elder, delivered a short address, referring to the qualities of the deceased professor as an author, a minister and a Christian gentleman, and also to his services rendered to the Church. Rev Dr Orr offered up prayer and the grave was closed.

A meeting of clergymen and other friends of the deceased gentleman was held in the Union Hall, Derry, Mr A Baxter JP, Mayor, presiding. A resolution was passed to the effect that it would be a fitting tribute to the memory of the deceased, and an appropriate recognition of the great services he had rendered to the Church in this country, America, and the colonies, to raise a sum of money on behalf of his children, and to perpetuate his memory in such other way as might be deemed necessary. The motion, which was proposed by Mr W J Bigger JP and seconded by Mr James Harper, was unanimously passed. Mr Tillie DL proposed a committee with power to add to their number, consisting of ministers of the Presbyterian Church, to give effect to this resolution.

[We ('Derry Standard') understand that Mr J M Witherow BA, has been appointed to continue the Church History lectures in Magee College till the end of the session.]

Notable Figure

The death of Dr Witherow, which we chronicle today, will be no surprise to many of our readers. For some months it has been widely known that the President of Magee College was in failing health and for weeks past the sad announcement we have now to make has been expected by a multitude of friends who knew how rapidly his strength was sinking. The regret that all who knew the late Professor of Ecclesiastical History in Derry will feel, will be none the less keen, though it may be mitigated by the knowledge that the best which human skill could do to arrest a hopeless malady was done, and that he has been spared a more protracted term of suffering in the grasp of an incurable disease.

With Dr Witherow there has passed away a notable figure of our generation. A prince and a great man has fallen in our Presbyterian Israel. Our readers will find elsewhere a sketch of his life that will well repay perusal; and our task in this column may be discharged by paying a well-earned tribute of respect to the memory of one who, by his labours as a professor and an author, has laid the whole Church under lasting obligations; and by pointing out one or two of the lessons that may be fitly drawn from a life of rare nobility of aim and purpose, and of strenuous endeavour in the service of the truth. The most striking feature of Dr Witherow's character was, perhaps, his single-minded devotion to duty. No man ever lived a more earnest life. Devotion to his work was with him an absolute passion. He could not put his hand to any task into which he did not at the same time throw his whole heart. Whatever he attempted was sure to be done as well as he knew how, and the humblest task was dignified by the spirit which he carried into all his work. He asked no thanks; he claimed no praise from anyone for anything which he ever did. The consciousness of duty well and truly done was sufficient reward for one who never "sought his own" in any unworthy or ignoble sense. A transparent honesty and simplicity of character impressed all who ever came within the sphere of his influence. To him all pretence was hateful. It was impossible to surprise him trying to be taken for anything but what he was; and men whose ways were widely different from his instinctively paid homage to the unbending firmness of righteous purpose that they well knew no bribe could prompt, no threat could force to do any act that was not right, or speak any word that was not true. Of anything that was false or mean he had an inbred loathing. His lofty spirit was incapable of leaning to a dishonourable or even a doubtful course of action. He was emphatically an honest man, a man of principle; one to whom, if need were, you felt instinctively that you might trust your life.

It does not need to be written here how true a son he was of the Church of his fathers, to which he had rendered service beyond most, service loyal, ungrudging, capable, valiant. For five-and-twenty years he had helped the students trained under his care to a fuller insight into the principles of our Church polity and to a firmer grasp of the Scripture truth upon which, as on a rock, our Presbyterian Zion stands. In the region of ecclesiastical controversy he had spoken with an authority that commanded respect even from those who differed most widely from his views, an authority based upon wide and accurate knowledge of the questions in dispute. Possessed of a singular gift of lucidity in thought and style, he had made the discussion of themes that are sometimes supposed to be the monopoly of specialists attractive to men with little time or taste for such discussions. He was understood of the common people. Our very children, when the occasion called, he could teach how to give good reason for their attachment to their Church. And yet he was no bigot, no narrow-minded controversialist, who could see nothing good beyond the bounds of his own denomination. The view he had matured by patient thought he held with tenacious grasp. He had not a particle of the spurious liberality that leads weak men to hold all earnest convictions cheap. For friend or foe, for flattery or threat, he would not bate a jot of what he believed to be the truth. But he could rejoice in goodness, wherever it appeared, and all good men, though they followed not with him, he could admire and love. One useful lesson in these distracted times we may learn from his life: that the firmest adherence to principle, the most fervent zeal for truth, is compatible with great breadth of sympathy; that Christian principle of the purest metal is not the enemy, but the friend and the natural ally of courtesy and kindness towards opponents, of gentleness towards all men.

By the grace of God he was what he was; and that for which he would most desire to be remembered, now that he is gone, is, we may well believe, his simple faith in that redeeming Lord who has now for him in very deed abolished death and brought life and immortality to light. "These blessed truths", speaking of a simple statement of the Gospel, in the very last letter he ever wrote, he said "are very dear to me. I have cherished them all through life, and it is my desire to die with the belief and love of them in my heart." The death of such a man is no common loss to the Church he loved and served so well. To many in this and other lands who have never seen his face the tidings of his removal will come like the stroke of a personal bereavement. The Presbyterians of Ulster and of Ireland, with many of our kinsmen in lands beyond the sea, will join with us to-day in tendering heartfelt sympathy to the orphan children who have lost the kindest and best of fathers, and to the College which has been deprived of a President who was a strength and ornament to the institution he has served so well.

'The Irish Presbyterian'
(in which the 'Autobiography' was serialised, 1936-38)

I regret that my own acquaintance with Dr Witherow and knowledge of him was so meagre, but this 'Autobiography' reveals the quality of the writer so patently, and his attractive and lovable personality with such absolute unself-consciousness that no tribute of mine, or indeed of any other friend is necessary. Those who read these rich chapters understandingly and with sympathy will get a clearer and more adequate conception of the essential goodness and lofty character, and the kindly nature of Dr Witherow than could be obtained from any biographical details or personal estimate that a friend might write. The disclosure of his sterling worth is self evident and unintentional.

I was familiar with the appearance of Dr Witherow. My recollection of his person is: medium height, stout, dark complexion, round faced, genial, but reserved. Looking at him, one could understand the affection that he evoked from those who were privileged to know him. He gave me the impression above all of trustworthiness, competence, steadfastness. I was in his class only once, as a visitor. On the one occasion on which I listened to his lecture, a sentence of advice to his students was memorable, and remained with me helpfully through the years. He advised us earnestly never to make a will for any member of one's congregation. He said, if I remember aright, "Will-making is a lawyer's business, not a minister's", and he added, with twinkling eye: "You would not wish to take the bread out of a poor lawyer's mouth!" He impressed the fact that minister's will-making had often led to endless disputes and enmities in congregations, and many ministers are sadly aware of this. I have often spurned or failed to take good advice, but this wise counsel of Dr Witherow's I obeyed throughout my ministry in two congregations with untellable advantage.

This tribute to Dr Witherow of a well-known Belfast citizen, a solicitor, distinguished in law and literature, is worth recording. He informed me that,when he went to the Londonderry college many years ago,he was unacquainted with the people, and unaware of the best method of procuring suitable lodgings. He summoned courage to call on Professor Witherow, and to ask him for advice on this (to him) important matter. Dr Witherow received him kindly, immediately put on his hat, and, taking the student's arm, conducted him to the manse of the late Rev Dr Maxwell Rodgers, whose acquaintance with suitable rooms was wide, and who also accompanied our young friend to

Daughters of Thomas Witherow

comfortable lodgings in which he remained during his stay in the city. On their first meeting thereafter Dr Witherow halted the student and solicitously enquired about his welfare, in which he continued to take an interest, inviting him to his home occasionally, entertaining him, and following his career with a fatherly regard.

D B Knox

Family

Dr Witherow was happy in the surviving members of his attached family, to whom he is a vivid and beloved memory. His daughters who are alive [1936?] are Mrs W Adams, Mrs D Craig, Mrs A Gilchrist, Mrs Dr Hamilton, Mrs H M Knox and Miss J Witherow. A daughter (Emily), who died, was Mrs James Louden (Ballysillan). His only surviving son (two died in infancy) was the Rev James Milling Witherow MA, DD who had a brilliant and successful career in the ministry and in literature. The main facts of his life-history are recorded in his brief biography which appeared in a Scottish journal at the time of his greatly-regretted death in 1933.

Dr J M Witherow studied theology at Magee College, and later at the New College, Edinburgh. Ordained at Wallace Green Church, Berwick-on-Tweed, in 1892, Dr Witherow, six years later, became colleague and successor to Dr Drummond, of Belhaven U F Church, Glasgow. He remained in Glasgow for five years, and then went to London to become minister in Upper Norwood Church. For more than twenty years, Dr Witherow remained in London, resigning his charge for health reasons in 1923. For some time afterwards he travelled in Canada, where he also did ministerial work. When he returned home in 1927, he was appointed minister of Trinity Church, Bridge of Allan, on a five years' basis. His work was appreciated so much, however, that the charge was later made a permanent one. Dr Witherow was keenly interested in literature, and wrote for British and American periodicals. He was sixty-six years of age, and is survived by his wife and a family of three sons and three daughters.

The Rev W W Boyle BA, Tillicoultry, in a tribute to Dr J M Witherow, said: "He was by far the ablest scholar and clearest thinker of his contemporary students. He graduated MA with first-class honours. He kept up his omnivorous reading, and we were often surprised at the variety and accuracy of his information. In Wallace Church, Berwick-on-Tweed, he maintained the traditions of that famous church until he was called to Belhaven, Glasgow, where his name is still fragrant. Anyone who had to go to him for advice knows how sound his wisdom was, and in his preaching he never offered God what cost him nothing, but put his best into every sermon he preached and every task he undertook. As a man and a friend he shone. He had no use for duplicity, but was as sincere a man as I ever knew, with a rare affection and goodness of heart."

TWO DIARIES

OF

DERRY IN 1689.

BEING

RICHARDS' DIARY OF THE FLEET,

Now first Printed from the Original M.S.,

AND

Ash's Journal of the Siege,

Reprinted from the Edition of 1792.

WITH INTRODUCTION AND NOTES

BY

THOMAS WITHEROW, D.D., LL.D.

LONDONDERRY:
PRINTED BY WILLIAM GAILEY, WATERLOO PLACE.
1888.

Sketch

In the 'Irish Presbyterian' for May 1903, Dr Witherow's son, the Rev J M Witherow MA, DD, wrote a biographical sketch of his father:

"As a professor, I have heard it reported that my father was stern, and I believe that this was true enough. He demanded close attention and hard, serious work from his students. He had little sympathy with any kind of athletics. At the same time I have heard more than one of his old pupils declare that no professor was kinder or more eager to help them when they went forth to their ministerial work. As a historical lecturer, he confesses himself that he began with a wrong plan, and that his work suffered in consequence. But, in the contributions which he made to historical literature, it is obvious that his ideals were high. Every authority for the Siege of Derry mentioned by Macaulay he read through himself, learning French in order to master the despatches of the French ambassador. And one important MS authority, which Macaulay never saw, was unearthed by him in Dublin, and printed for the first time. In the study of documents and estimating their comparative worth to the scientific historian, he was chiefly guided by the principles laid down in Sir George Cornwall Lewis's book: 'The Influence of Authority in Matters of Opinion'. This book led him to be, perhaps, unduly severe in the handling of all writers not contemporary with what they narrate, and to be very sceptical regarding every tradition that was mere tradition, even when comparatively early in its origin. Still, anyone who has studied, for example, the original authorities for the lives of St Patrick and St Columba will grant that, within the severe scientific limits which Professor Witherow set himself, he gave in his lectures on these saints a wonderful reconstruction of their thoughts and circumstances.

As a reader he was insatiable. His reading, however, was restricted to certain well-defined departments, biography and history, especially the history of Christian institutions. Very rarely would he look at a volume of poetry in his later years, though his Byron and Shelley and Coleridge are pencilled throughout, and he knew much of Shakespeare, Scott and Burns by heart. He was fond of Dickens and the Waverley Novels, but George Eliot to him was tainted and Thackeray was dull. Often I tried to get him to read Ruskin, but after a few pages he would laugh and lay the volume down. As a worker, he was systematic and tireless. For nine hours of every week-day, winter and summer, he was reading or writing in his study all the years that I knew him. I doubt whether he ever really enjoyed two days consecutively, if spent away from his books. His face never brightened at the word 'holiday'. I know he would have been delighted to see foreign countries, especially the scenes of famous events; but he was always too poor. He never was out of the British Isles all his life.

Appreciation

The biographical article by Mr Armour was considered by Dr Witherow's son to be the ablest and most appropriate of all the public references to his father's character and career. He wrote to a friend on 21 November 1934: "I can never forget the fine appreciation of my father's works and character which he contributed to 'The Witness' thirty-eight years ago. It was much the best of all the biographies that then appeared."

From a tribute by the late Rev J B Armour MA

Death has released a true man from the pains and labours of life, has transfigured a character splendidly furnished and a career devoted in all its stages to the service of God and man. His mental powers, his time, his life were consecrated to the service of his Church, and splendid service he rendered in defence and exposition of the policy and principles of a faith which has done so much to preserve and extend the light of Scriptural truth, and which has been a main factor in the advancement of civil and religious liberty. Dr Witherow's penmanship, which, in Dr Cooke's opinion, was the best of all the members of the General Assembly, so neat and beautiful to the last day of his life, so peculiar, so dear to the heart of printers, he obtained from his teacher, formerly an old soldier. His Sabbath schools were a model for the district. He visited his congregation, which was large, very systematically. He allotted a certain time for this work, and then, when it was over, he settled down to the reading and manufacture of books.

Dr Witherow's professoriate of twenty-five years in the Londonderry college, like his pastorate in Maghera of twenty years, was successful, because he brought to his duties to the Church and to the students for the ministry the same conscientiousness, the same loyalty to the truth, the same resolve to do faithfully what was required which characterised all his actions. He had ample knowledge of his subject, gained by patient investigation, a true grasp of the principles of the New Testament polity; sympathy with student difficulties, and a power of expression which made him the easiest of teachers to follow. He was not narrow in his views or contracted in his sympathies. He had considerable dramatic power, a fresh way of looking at things, and the faculty of making the past a living reality. His students not only learned much, but they got an impression of the grandeur of the story of the Church. They were interested as well as instructed. In 1884 he was made a Life Senator of the Royal University, a distinction which he prized very highly, as it was the recognition by the Government of the day of the services he had rendered to literature and civil liberty. Honours never spoiled Dr Witherow. He was without the vanity outward distinctions tickle. He lived the simple, single-minded life of a student. He consecrated his powers to the service of God;

he led a noble life to good purpose. He hit hard at times, but he could not strike an unfair blow, and he never used an argument that he knew was unsound for the sake of gaining an immediate advantage over an opponent, because he possessed an innate courtesy and sense of justice, and "his ruling instinct was to pierce through falsities to find truth".

In private life he was the same as in public, honest, frank, blunt, companionable, a good listener, an excellent storyteller and a man whose laugh was inspiration. His talk was not a preachment; it was crisp and free, a compound of good sense and hearty humour. His use of words was just and picturesque. His face was very attractive, for it betokened kindliness, determination, honesty, power, veracity. A straight, kindly, scrupulous, just man was he, and at the root of all, and feeding all the gifts of nature, and graces of character, was a piety which, if not of the self-advertising type, was genuine and genial. Our first and last thought about him is that he was a Christian man, and that is everything.

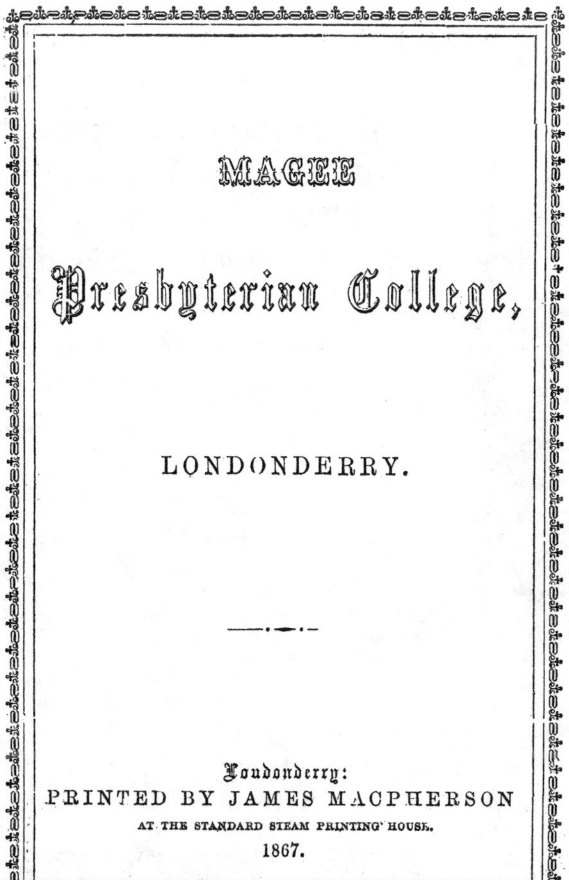
MAGEE

Presbyterian College,

LONDONDERRY.

Londonderry:
PRINTED BY JAMES MACPHERSON
AT THE STANDARD STEAM PRINTING HOUSE.
1867.

Cooke's grave in Balmoral cemetery, Belfast

THE COOKE CENTENARY.

Commemorative Addresses

ILLUSTRATIVE OF THE LIFE, CHARACTER, AND DISTINGUISHED PUBLIC SERVICES OF

The Rev. Henry Cooke, D.D., LL.D.,

ON THE

CENTENARY OF HIS BIRTH,

11TH MAY, 1888,

WITH A BRIEF NARRATIVE OF THE PROCEEDINGS.

BY REV. ROBERT CRAWFORD,

BELFAST.

"His name will be a venerable tradition in the Church in generations to come, as long as the Presbyterians of Ulster shall reverence and adore the name of Jesus."—PROF. WALLACE.

BELFAST:
W. MULLAN & SON, DONEGALL PLACE;
C. W. OLLEY; AND
THE RELIGIOUS TRACT AND BOOK DEPOT, ROYAL AVENUE.

PUBLISHED BY THE CENTENARY COMMITTEE:

The Profits to be given towards the erection of the "Cooke Centenary Church," Ormeau Road.

PRICE THREEPENCE.

Commentary

by Rev John Brown
sometime minister of Draperstown Presbyterian Church and formerly Lecturer in History, Magee College, Londonderry, and the New University of Ulster, Coleraine

In the early afternoon of 11 May 1888, in May Street Presbyterian Church, Belfast, on a platform 'covered with crimson cloth and decorated with choice plants', stood a stoutish, round-faced man of 'dark complexion' and medium height. From this platform, ordinarily used at the annual meetings of the General Assembly of the Presbyterian Church in Ireland, he delivered a lecture to mark the beginning of the centenary celebration of the birth of Rev Dr Henry Cooke. To keep all in mind of the subject, if that were needed, 'in the forefront stood the much-admired bust of Dr Cooke, the pedestal of which displayed a pretty wreath of evergreens and rare exotics'.[1] The lecturer was the Rev Thomas Witherow DD, LLD, Professor of Church History and Pastoral Theology in the Magee College, Londonderry, and sometime minister of the Maghera congregation within whose bounds Cooke had been born, baptised and reared. Witherow was well-fitted to impart to the audience which thronged May Street Church his 'Thoughts on the Life, Work, and Character of Dr Cooke', and this commemorative address has much value as a source for examination of Cooke's career and his influence in Ulster during the mid-nineteenth century. Perhaps Witherow himself valued it little enough. He did not even mention his share in the Cooke celebrations when he wrote the final pages of his 'Autobiography'.

Thomas Witherow died one hundred years ago, and the Ballinascreen Historical Society has done well to commemorate the centenary of his death by publishing in full Witherow's account of his own life. For Witherow knew the district well. It was not very far from Ballynascreen that he was reared, in Aughlish, on the other side of the mountain. Most of his active ministry took place in neighbouring Maghera. As Clerk of the Magherafelt Presbytery he had much to do with the Presbyterian congregations of Draperstown and Swateragh. He knew a good deal of the history and traditions of the district which especially interests the Society, and it was probably John MacCloskey, later master of the classical school at Tirgarvil, who suggested to Thomas Witherow's father that his son should have a classical education.[2] That course of learning, so vividly described by Witherow in his later days, led to the ministry and to Maghera.

On 1 October 1845, in Maghera Presbyterian Church, Witherow listened to his former teacher and close friend, the Rev Andrew Todd of Finvoy, County Antrim, preach an appropriate sermon based on First Corinthians, chapter 9, verse 16: 'Woe is unto me, if I preach not the gospel!' Witherow publicly declared that he believed 'the

1 Cooke Centenary Commemorative Addresses Belfast [1888?] p6
2 MS 'Autobiography' p3

Westminster Confession of Faith to be founded on and agreeable to the Word of God'; as such he subscribed it as the confession of his faith, signing his name carefully and clearly in the Presbytery record. And then 'Mr. Witherow was set apart to the Pastoral Office in the Congregation of Maghera', with the laying-on of hands of the Presbytery.[3]

There could be more than one interpretation of the formula he had signed, for it was a compromise reached ten years before, after long disputing, but Witherow seems to have understood it in a strict sense. For him the Westminster Confession was the best systematic and logical setting-out of the 'plan of salvation' which, he fully believed, was revealed in the Bible. This plan of salvation through Christ, as set out in the moderate Calvinism of the Confession, was the foundation of his theology and personal religion. His preaching was based on it. His Presbyterianism, which he was always ready to defend, had divine warrant in Scripture. For him a relevant Biblical text settled any argument. His view of history depended on his belief in the over-ruling Providence of God, and in his private life he submitted to what he believed to be its all-wise ordering.[4]

So, aged 21, Thomas Witherow took on himself the heavy responsibility of ministering to the estimated 375 families and 1875 souls of the congregation of Maghera. Sinclair Lewis once cynically wrote that 'the life of a small-town preacher, prevented from engaging even in the bucolic pleasures, is rather duller than that of a watchman at a railroad crossing', and that his listeners 'understood him only when he promised Heaven as a reward for monogamy and honest chicken-raising, or threatened them with Hell for drinking hard cider'. This may (or may not) have been true of some sides of church life in parts of the American Mid-West in the early years of the present century, but Witherow would hardly have agreed that this was his fate in Maghera.

There, in the mid-nineteenth century, he had little time to enjoy boredom. The 'Autobiography' sets out his duties in detail. Statistics cannot measure the influence and success of his ministrations, but official returns to Government show that, for the year before he left Maghera for Magee, there were 340 families and an estimated 1700 individuals under his pastoral care.[5] This was in spite of the Great Famine, and of emigration during the past seventeen years. The 'Autobiography' might be misread as implying that his income was only £60 a year. But the records show that for the year before he went to Londonderry his congregation paid him £106:17:9. Also, throughout his time in Maghera, he received each year his Royal Bounty (Regium Donum) from the State. This gave him another £75 a year. At no time was he paid as little as £60 by the congregation. If Maghera had possessed the same endowments and grants as Magherafelt, Witherow would have

3 Magherafelt Presbytery Minutes 1:10:1845
4 MS 'Autobiography' pp 37-39; 'Mode of Christian Baptism'(Belfast 1859) p3
5 Magherafelt Presbytery Minutes 4:4:1865

have been the best-paid minister in the Presbytery.[6]

Witherow's account of affairs in Maghera congregation when he arrived is rather too simple. Trouble did not begin with the 'warm dispute over the choice of a minister' that Witherow mentions, but with the departure, in April 1844, of the Rev Smylie Robson to be a missionary to the Jews in the Middle East. Some of the congregation took it very ill that he should leave Maghera after a ministry of only nine months and appealed to the Magherafelt Presbytery to refuse him permission. It finally agreed with the General Assembly's Board, which had issued the Call to Robson, to leave him to decide. Robson decided to go, probably for the best reasons as he saw them. A fine scholar, he did well abroad, and showed great courage during one of the customary massacres in that part of the Turkish lands. In different circumstances, he is said to have attended the historian Buckle on his death-bed and to have thought rather poorly of the chances of the deceased.

There had been serious threats that, if Robson were allowed to go, many would leave the congregation. Not many seem actually to have done so. But the great majority stayed to engage in 'warm dispute over the choice of a minister'. Witherow's account is perhaps just a shade over-flattering to himself. In fact, not only one, but two candidates finally refused calls from Maghera, and it may have been battle-exhaustion, rather than an exaggerated report of Witherow's popularity in Magherafelt, that induced them to give him a 'hearing'. No doubt there were such reports, but some of them probably came from the Rev James Wilson of Magherafelt, who seems to have been impressed by Witherow, and was active in the matter. Witherow, himself cool-headed and sensible, though sensitive, and reared a countryman in a not dissimilar district, was well-advised. He depended on James Wilson of Magherafelt and neighbouring co-presbyters to keep him right, as well as on the Rev Andrew Todd of Finvoy. The difficulties of his earlier days in Maghera were soon mostly overcome and he was acceptable to the congregation as a whole. But it seems odd that in his 'Autobiography' Witherow says so little about his immediate predecessor.

The Rev Charles Kennedy had poor health for twenty years before his death in 1855, but was often well enough during much of Witherow's time to attend such Presbytery meetings as were held in Maghera. It seems indeed probable that Witherow was referring to Kennedy in the curious passage relating 'a tradition that an old minister of Maghera once said, on the occasion of some brethren being troubled for putting their schools under care of the National Board, that "he thanked God that <u>he</u> never took anything to do with education"'. Witherow took care to add 'whether such words were actually used I do not know', but the implication was that Kennedy was responsible for the poor state of education in the congregation when Witherow himself came to Maghera.[7]

---

6 Ibid 29:1:1844; 5:2:1844; 20:2:1844

7 MS 'Autobiography' p75

What the relations were between these men is not very clear. Kennedy had come to Maghera in 1801. His was the task of restoring order in the congregation after the rebellion of 1798, and this was not easy. There were serious divisions. The idea, still widespread amongst the less well-informed in some quarters, that 'the' Presbyterians were all United Irishmen in the 1798 is wrong. Probably more than one-third of the Presbyterian men in and around Maghera may at least have taken the United Irish Oath of Secrecy, mostly perhaps for their own safety. Probably less than one-third were active loyalists.[8] The rest were crypto-loyalists or indifferent. The inhabitants of the town and townlands were divided amongst themselves. This extended even to families and households. The effects of these divisions lasted for years, reinforced by local differences and animosities.

Since Charles Kennedy was a loyalist, his influence probably helped on the reaction against anything tending to republicanism and rebellion in Maghera, after the events of 1798, though there was a secession from the congregation in 1803 or 1804, when a Seceding congregation was founded in Culnady. But this may have had nothing to do with Kennedy's politics. He got a good deal of publicity when he was tried at the Londonderry Assizes in the eighteen-twenties for firing his gun outside his house when a riot took place in Maghera. He was acquitted of any ill intent. It is not impossible that he or a relative of his was mentioned in a very scarce Orange ballad of that period called 'The June Fair Fight in Maghera': 'Here's a health to Brother Kennedy, he did his part right well'.[9] Not that this would have pleased Thomas Witherow very much. He had decided by the time he came to Maghera that he was a Liberal. So far as one can make out, his political views were of the Whig brand, and he was not the advocate of any far-reaching schemes of constitutional or social change. 'Amelioration, not reconstruction' might describe his notions.

Tradition says, with what truth may be in it, that Kennedy was in the habit of attending evening service occasionally in the local Episcopalian Church. It also maintains that, after he died, his wife became a member of the Church of Ireland. If so, it reinforces the suspicion

---

8 PROI, Rebellion Papers 620/23/134: Clotworthy Soden to Cooke, Maghera 30:5:1796, on Watty Graham's brother; ibid 620/23/167 Soden to ?, Maghera 11:6:1796. More than one-third of the male members were absent from communion in the Presbyterian Church after McKeever's arrest.

9 A more accurate version of this line, from Tobermore: 'And likewise Brother Kennedy and Forrester, who proved to me a friend'. Robert Forrester Esq of Cloverhill, Maghera, was Deputy Grand Master of County Londonderry Grand Orange Lodge.

that relations between Witherow and his senior minister were at best rather formal, whatever may have been the cause. Witherow's attitude to the local Church of Ireland clergy seems to have been at best wary. Referring to the dinner after his own ordination, he comments acidly on the 'very magniloquent terms indeed' in which the rector, the Rev J Spencer Knox, 'with a great flourish', proposed his health, though it had been agreed that there should be neither toasts nor speeches. This is the only mention by name of Knox (which is rather peculiar, since he seems to have been very much an evangelical) in Witherow's account of his days in Maghera. That Witherow knew any of the Roman Catholic clergy well looks rather unlikely.

There is good reason to think that, in the Maghera district, Knox was much closer to the community as a whole than was the scholarly Witherow, who was happiest when living quietly amongst his books, and was neither a magistrate nor the son of a bishop.[10] But the young minister of Maghera was far from being a nobody. He had the respect of his congregation and served it to the best of his much more than considerable ability. He was efficient and painstaking in dealing with its affairs, and, as Clerk of the Presbytery, his conduct of business and his minutes of its proceedings were accurate - and discreet. He had patience and common sense. Earlier he had had the sense to learn a system of shorthand that served him well in his clerical and literary work. He knew much about human nature. As a boy he had gone with his cattle-dealing father to fairs and markets. When still little more than a boy, and then as a young man, he had lived much alone in Belfast and avoided disaster. He learned a lot more in Maghera.

It taught him something about politics. In the account of his life he does not include in his list of writings the 'Address to the Presbyterian Electors of Maghera and its vicinity' which he records that he issued in July 1852, in support of Samuel McCurdy Greer. Greer stood for the 'Presbyterian and Tenant Right interest' against the Conservative landlords, Bateson and Jones. As an historical document, the 'Address' deserves to be better known. It is a clever, lively piece of electioneering, and as good in its own way as anything Witherow ever wrote. It tells us something about Witherow himself. Is he perhaps just a trifle over-anxious to safeguard himself against any possible charge of unfairness to the Conservative candidates? And when he suffered a severe reaction, after the election, how much of it was caused simply by over-exertion, how much by old troubles in Maghera bubbling to the surface when the minister stirred the boiling political pot? Elections themselves rarely give people typhoid fever. But excessive fatigue, excitement and great anxiety might reduce one's natural resistance.[11]

---

10 If the 'Pastoral Annals by an Irish Clergyman' (London 1840) be indeed Knox's work

11 MS 'Autobiography', p65

In a later election, when James J Clark Esq, JP, of Largantogher, upheld the Conservative interest, a canny side of Witherow appeared. A good landlord and an upright man, though with a good sense of his own importance, Clark had been a member of Maghera Presbyterian Church, and of its Committee. He was its spokesman when he declared that certain members would leave the congregation should Robson be allowed to go to evangelise the Jews.[12] In the end Clark had himself done so. But he had no quarrel with Witherow, and had worked with him very well in setting up a school. Witherow settled the electoral problem by the ingenious, but possibly over-elaborate device of contriving 'to be absent' on a visit in Monaghan, coming back just 'in time to vote for Mr Greer'. It may be some measure of how deeply Witherow felt the results of his earlier safari into the political jungle.

He had already, though, dared to venture into another area, sometimes jungle-like enough in its own way. It was that of authorship and publication. But he was later glad that his first effort, intended to provide a rational scheme for the subsidising of Churches by the State, was not accepted by the publisher. Theology and History, and especially some judicious mingling of the two, were more to his mind and he read continually. Witherow would hardly have agreed with a good deal of the theology expounded by Thomas à Kempis, but we may think that he did understand the earlier Thomas's confession that he found it most restful just to sit in a corner with a little book.[13] We may wonder, though, when we consider the curious miscellany that Witherow read in his early days, what he made of Byron's 'Don Juan'.

The conscientious and methodical minister of Maghera read with purpose, as well as for enjoyment. His reading was meant to enable him to preach and write more 'usefully', as he would have put it. And what, to his mind, could 'do more good' than to defend, maintain and propagate Presbyterianism? He fully believed that history, if properly interpreted, proved that Presbyterianism best set forth the 'Divine plan of salvation' and came nearest to the teaching and practices of the early Christian Church.

The 'Autobiography' is of great interest in helping towards some understanding of Thomas Witherow's personal religion. It sets out vividly his early, rather passive, accepting of the religious notions of his family and denomination, as compared with his later active and firm acceptance of salvation through the substitutionary sacrifice of Christ, made by Him on Witherow's behalf. This depended on his conviction of the essential inerrancy of the Bible, which set forth the plan of salvation as contained in the Gospel of Jesus Christ. He was convinced that he had entered into a personal relationship with Christ, and that he was bound to witness to this. The Witherow who, as a young fellow, had begun to drift,

---

12 Magherafelt Presbytery Minutes as cited above (note 6)

13 Credited to à Kempis in a copy of his 'Imitation of Christ

almost, into the Presbyterian ministry, was different in important ways from the enthusiastic minister who came to Maghera to preach the Gospel, expound the Scriptures, administer the Sacraments, attend to the needs of the people and take part in the work of the various Church courts. One must lose no opportunity to instruct and edify.

So Witherow encouraged the Maghera YMCA by his lecture, on a cold winter evening in early 1855, on 'Our Local Celebrities'. It celebrated Adam Clarke, Alexander Carson and Henry Cooke. Divided in opinions and denominations, all three had local origins and, especially, 'evangelical' opinions. The discourse was published later that year as 'Three Prophets of Our Own', its section on Cooke being expanded as the basis of the Centenary Lecture in 1888. The success of the 'Three Prophets' encouraged Witherow to continue research into Church History. An attack on him by R H Carson, the Baptist, of Tobermore, because of what he thought was derogatory to his father in 'The Apostolic Church' (which was published as a result of such research), inspired Witherow's 'Defence of the Apostolic Church' in 1857.

One may perhaps find in Witherow a much more sensitive man than might at first appear. In his account of this affair he seems to congratulate himself rather excessively on his overthrow of the daring Carson. But we may be grateful for his recording of an interesting version of the attempted flight of Hudy McGuigan from the top of Craignashoak.[14] Whether the 'religious public' was quite as shocked by Carson's father's comparison of the controversial efforts of William Brown of Tobermore to Hudy's flight we know not. But Witherow gives so much space to his overthrowing of R H Carson that we may suspect that Carson's attack had hurt him more than a little.

By this time Witherow was gaining a good idea of his strength - and of his weakness. In his own account, we can perhaps note a certain self-distrust that lasted all his days. Able and competent, he could manage well in some situation and at the same time wish that he had never got himself into it. This seems very noticeable in the case of his activity in the rough-and-tumble of the political elections in Londonderry County in the mid-fifties. A 'loner' in some ways, one thinks, he had an instinct still to seek support. Witherow was independent-minded enough. He was no enemy of real reforms in Church and State, but his instinct was always to favour cautious and gradual change, and to be happiest with plenty of support for his activities. He had no wish for unnecessary trouble or martyrdom. One might say that whereas Cooke was a liberal Conservative, Witherow was a conservative Liberal, so far as politics went.

In religious affairs, it was Cooke's stand for the conservative interpretation of doctrine in the Synod of

---

14 MS 'Autobiography' p70; see 'Hudie McGuigan' by 'Benroe' Moyola Books 1989

Ulster, and his defeat of Arianism in the great debates of the late 'twenties that had deeply impressed the young Witherow. To fit himself to explain the interpretation of religion, and defend the Church whose life-blood it seemed to him to be, was of increasing importance to him during his time in Maghera. The success of his 'Three Prophets', and the attention he had given in it to Cooke, very likely put the notion of becoming a professor into his head in 1855.

There were other reasons. Witherow never fancied himself as a great preacher, though he was not a poor one. But the composition and laboured committal to memory of sermons, two on each summer, one on each winter Sabbath, took much of his time and energy. The rather formal visitation of the nearly 400 families under his care he appears to have endured, rather than enjoyed. As a student, this future professor had spent his summer vacation back in Aughlish. He got peace to work, he says, partly because 'association with uneducated people whose ideas and habits were so far different from mine had no charm for me'.[15] May we cautiously surmise that he brought something of this aloofness with him to Maghera? He could always 'pass himself' with people, and had a genuine and practical interest in their welfare. But though he could be relaxed and even quite jovial in company with chosen friends, especially clerical ones, one senses that, to use the old country phrases he must often have heard, he 'aye keepit a wee thing tae himsel'.

According to himself, the Rev Mr Witherow managed to keep from the Maghera folk the knowledge of his forthcoming marriage to Miss Catherine Milling, daughter of a local businessman, until all was over and the couple quietly off to Sandymount. But we may be allowed to wonder, knowing small-town and rural Ulster, whether it was quite such a surprise to the neighbourhood as he thought. At least his illusion, if it be such, shows a pleasing innocence of mind. This romantic episode did neither the minister nor the congregation any harm. During the following year, Maghera congregation actually increased from 328 to 350 families, which paid Witherow £116:0:10 1/2 as stipend. In the previous year it had been £105:5:10 1/2.[16]

Mr and Mrs Witherow came back to find curiosity deflected from them by an election which did not greatly concern Thomas. But on Thursday, 2 June 1859, the 'Great Religious Revival' of that year crossed the Bann from the County of Antrim and came by way of Culnady to Maghera. Witherow took note of what he saw of it, and wrote an account of its progress and results in the Maghera area for the benefit of the Rev William Gibson, who published it in his 'Year of Grace'.[17] Now William Gibson, Professor of

---

15 MS 'Autobiography' p29

16 Magherafelt Presbytery Minutes 3:5:1859; 1:5:1860. But the Revival of 1859 had something to do with this increase.

17 W Gibson 'The Year of Grace' 2nd ed (Edinburgh 1860) pp 224-230

Christian Ethics and Moderator of the General Assembly in 1860, found no favour in the sight of the Rev Isaac Nelson. Nor did his 'Year of Grace', in any of its editions. Nor did Witherow's contribution to it, though Nelson let him off a good deal more lightly than he did many others. 'Honest Isaac' contented himself with pointing out Witherow's inconsistency in claiming that the early 'prostrations' at Culnady 'could not have arisen from animal excitement' (implying that they were the result of direct interposition by God the Holy Spirit), and his statement that 'the body of the people soon learned that animal excitement is a different thing from spiritual life', without setting out how later prostrations and other physical 'phenomena' differed, if at all, from the cases in Culnady? In other words, when is 'animal excitement' not 'animal excitement'?[18]

Whatever he may have done later, Witherow seems not to have thought things out very thoroughly before he put pen to paper for Gibson. It seems likely that this flick of the whip from Nelson made the victim smart. There is no mention of the affair in Witherow's own record and he may have consoled himself by reflecting that his advice that the proper way to deal with revivals was to go along with them, cautiously, had been well received by very many of his brother ministers. He had published this advice in 'Words of Truth and Soberness'.

Maghera had certainly gained something from the greater earnestness and religious feeling aroused by the Revival, and this helped to account for the record number of 40 new communicants admitted that year to full membership in the congregation. But Witherow candidly allowed that, apart from the organising and renewing of prayer-meetings, greater attendance at public worship, more family worship, and improvement in conduct generally, the Revival had made little impact on most of the people. But credit must go to Thomas himself for much of all this. There had been pretty steady improvement in these respects all through his ministry. He was worried, though, that the Revival could be exploited by sects for denominational purposes. There were signs of this in places near to such centres as Tobermore, where the Baptists were strong. Hence his tracts to warn against what he saw as Baptist error and proselytism. 'The Mode of Christian Baptism' and 'The Subjects of Christian Baptism' were later published together, 'smoothed down a little', as 'Scriptural Baptism'. In its day it had a considerable popularity, at least in Presbyterian circles. These tracts reveal a Witherow, acute and ingenious, who knew his Bible and his Greek and Latin. He understood the essential points in dispute and had studied the beliefs and methods of his opponents. He was a skilful tactician, but was not unfair or rude towards those who differed from him, though he used the weapon of ridicule to effect against their logical fallacies committed in argument, as he saw and interpreted them. At times some of his own analogies seem a trifle

18 I Nelson 'The Year of Delusion' III (Belfast, 1860) pp 49-73

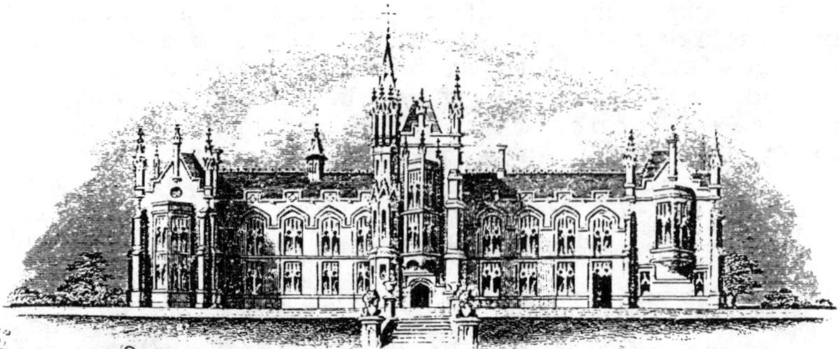

Magee Presbyterian College, Londonderry

MAGEE COLLEGE,

LONDONDERRY.

THE Trustees of Magee Presbyterian College, near Londonderry, beg to present the following brief account of its origin, and statement of its present condition and requirements, to which they respectfully invite your favourable consideration:—

In the year 1846, Mrs. Magee, widow of the Rev. Wm. Magee, Presbyterian Minister of Lurgan, left £20,000 for the erection and endowment of a Presbyterian College. This sum was allowed to accumulate for some years, during which discussions took place between the Trustees and the General Assembly as to the site and constitution of the proposed College. These matters were referred to the judgment of the Lord Chancellor, who sanctioned a scheme for its building, endowment, and general management. The Rev. Richard Dill, of Dublin, the Rev. John Brown, of Aghadoey, D.D., and James Gibson, Esq., Barrister-at-law, were the original Trustees appointed under the will of Mrs. Magee. By the decree of the Chancellor they were authorised to select a convenient site at or near the city of Londonderry. The number of trustees is limited to three, until the removal by death or otherwise of those originally appointed, after which the number shall consist of nine—six ministers, and three elders. The appointment of Trustees is vested in the General Assembly. The curriculum of the College embraces Literary, Scientific, and Theological Education, consisting of the following branches:—1st. Latin and Greek; 2d. Logic, Belles Lettres, and Rhetoric; 3d. Metaphysics and Ethics; 4th. Mathematics and Natural Philosophy; 5th. Oriental Literature and Hermeneutics; 6th. Church History and Pastoral The-far-fetched. But the tracts were quite effective.

The favourable reception of Witherow's pamphlets during that exciting year of 1859 may very well have helped to encourage him to seek the Chair of Biblical Criticism in the Belfast Presbyterian College in 1860. His account of the election of the Rev Josias L Porter to the Chair, with himself as runner-up, defeated by only 17 or 18 votes after a remarkable contest, is highly interesting. Witherow did not feel altogether qualified for that Chair, and was probably glad enough not to have to make up enough material during the summer to lecture respectably on that subject during at least part of the next session. But he gives so much space in his reminiscences to that election that it seems reasonable to suspect that he felt his rejection more deeply than he says. As Thomas Witherow sat on the platform in May Street Church on 11 May 1888, waiting to be called on to eulogise Henry Cooke, did he picture him in his 'own well-known seat in the Assembly' in those days of open voting, marking the names of those who voted for his own son-in-law, Porter, as against those who voted for Witherow? Certainly he remembered it vividly when he described the scene for his family's benefit.[19] Perhaps his own final judgement of Cooke may have been much the same as that made by a later minister of Maghera who also in his time held a professorial Chair, that in some ways 'Cooke was a man of whom the world was quite worthy'.[20]

Anyhow, Witherow was elected without opposition to the Chair of Church History and Pastoral Theology in the new Magee Presbyterian College, Londonderry, in 1865, as one of its seven orginal professors. That a professor should have what amounted to two Chairs was a luxury not uncommon in those days and for long afterwards. It was enjoyed in the Queen's University of Belfast until 1909, and lasted in practice in Magee until 1947, and nominally for another six years.

In some ways to go to Magee was a kind of gamble for the new professor. Its situation was rather curious and its prospects in some doubt. As long before as 1844, the new General Assembly of the lately united Presbyterian Church in Ireland was in an expansionist mood and decided that it must have a 'College for the purpose of affording a liberal education in both Arts and Divinity'. A main object in this was to have provision for and control over the general and theological education of its Divinity students, but the Arts Department was to be non-sectarian. In 1846 Mrs Magee of Dublin died. She was the widow of the Rev William Magee, minister of Lurgan, and bequeathed £20,000, 'in trust, to apply the same to the building and endowment of a College for the education of young men in preparation for the Christian ministry in connexion with the General Assembly'. The trustees could determine the site, and could determine the rules, regulations and discipline of the College 'subject to the advice and directions of the General Assembly'. After a more than

---

19 MS 'Autobiography' pp 83-87
20 He later tended to modify this opinion.

ology; 7th. Theology. The Chairs of Latin and Greek, of Logic, Belles-Lettres, and Rhetoric, of Metaphysics and Ethics, and of Mathematics and Natural Philosophy, constitute the Literary and Scientific department; the Chairs of Oriental Literature and Hermeneutics, of Church History and Pastoral Theology, and of Theology, the Theological department. The Literary and Scientific education is open to persons of all religious denominations. The General Assembly have the appointment, from time to time, of all the Professors, no person being eligible to any Chair who shall not sign the Westminster Confession of Faith, in order to secure orthodoxy of religious sentiment. The internal government of the College is entrusted to the Professors, who, for that purpose, have been constituted a Board of Faculty. The General Assembly have power to prescribe the course of study for such students as are candidates for the Christian Ministry, and to appoint a Committee, who, together with the Trustees, form the Board of Visitors, and have the general superintendence of the College. Every donor of £50 is entitled to the free education of one student through the Literary and Scientific course; every donor of £100 is entitled to the free education of one student through the entire curriculum; and every donor of £200 has the same privilege for one student in perpetuity. Any corporation, company, congregation, or other community or association, who shall contribute any of the above sums, or land, or annual grant of equal value, shall, through their representatives, enjoy the same privileges as single donors of similar amount. The Rev. Richard Dill, who died on the 8th December, 1858, devised real estate, consisting of houses and tenements in the City of Dublin, producing an income of about £250 per annum, and bequeathed also about £6,000 secured in Mortgages, &c., to establish Professorships and Scholarships in connection with the College, as well as all his books, to form a nucleus of a library. At its meeting in Dublin in 1859, the General Assembly appointed the Rev. William M'Clure as Trustee, in room of the late Mr. Dill.

In addition to the original bequest by Mrs. Magee, and the property left by the Rev. R. Dill, the Honorable the Irish Society have made a grant of £250 per annum in perpetuity, for the endowment of one chair in the Literary and Scientific department, to be called the Irish Society's Professorship, and have given a further grant of £250 per annum for five years, towards the annual expenditure.

The Trustees having reported that the College was ready for the reception of Students, and that endowments were secured for the several Professors contemplated in the scheme, the Assembly, at its annual meeting in Belfast, in July, 1865 (the largest ever held in Ireland), appointed Professors to the various Chairs.

The grounds, which are extensive, overlook the broad waters of the Foyle, and are memorable in the annals of the Siege of Derry as having been the scene of many a struggle, and the death-bed of many a warrior. The College was formally opened by the Moderator of the General Assembly, on the 10th October, 1865, in the presence of the Mayor of the City, a great number of magistrates and clergymen, and a vast assemblage of the inhabitants of the City and of the neighbouring counties. Twenty-six students were then enrolled—a number which has been increased to forty during the present session.

The following is a list of the present Officers of the College:—

TRUSTEES:

The Rev. John Brown, D.D., Aghadoey, Co. Derry.
James Gibson, Esq., A.M., T.C.D., Barrister-at-Law, Chairman of Co. Donegal, Dublin.
The Rev. William M'Clure, Londonderry.

PROFESSORS:

Latin and Greek, - - - Rev. Henry Sheil M'Kee, M.A., D.D., LL.D., Hon. M. and F.R.S.L.

Logic, Belles-Lettres, and Rhetoric, - - - - Rev. Joseph Thoburn M'Gaw, B.A., Q.U.I.

lively controversy and a suit in what Professor Killen of Belfast called 'that kind of earthly purgatory', the Court of Chancery, the well-meaning lady's intentions were carried out by her victorious Trustees, and the Magee College built on the west bank of the Foyle on the outskirts of the city of Derry.[21]

It was a 'complete' college, with both an Arts and a Theological Department, as orginally determined by the Trustees, as opposed (in more senses than one) to the college which the 'Belfast' party had managed to have built there. This latter, called the 'Presbyterian' College, often the 'Assembly's', and now the 'Union' College, associated for some purposes with the Methodist 'Edgehill', partly represents the orginal 'Magee' of Thomas Witherow. At least it has inherited endowments, various books, and the name of 'Magee' for certain of its functions.

The death of his eldest child, Hugh, prevented Witherow from being installed at Magee along with the other professors in the autumn of 1865. His description of the child's illness and death is vivid and touching. But the entry of his academic career and settling down at No 23 Clarendon Street gave him much to do. Once again the 'Autobiography' helps towards fuller understanding of the man and his career. The Witherows had bidden 'adieu to ever dear Maghera' and Thomas at once remarks that to get to Magee was 'like passing from a stormy ocean into the shelter of some land-locked bay'. No more 'incessant worry'. He had 'no pastoral work' to tire him. And a rather revealing statement expresses pleasure that he had come 'to live among strangers who knew comparatively little of me and mine'. Could it be that, even though Thomas and Catherine had been presented at parting with an 'Address accompanied with a gold watch and silver tea-service that cost sixty pounds' (and that was no small gift for those days), they had not been entirely comfortable in her home town?

He soon found in Magee that though he was now released from his demanding task of Clerkship of the Magherafelt Presbytery, he was considered the obvious person to be Secretary of Faculty at a difficult time. The College was staggering to its feet, very gradually. Lecturers and various underlings had to be recruited. The Secretary had to explain to excitable foreigners that the Faculty, as soon as it heard of their existence, had not at once decided to appoint them to teach languages. If it offered them the job, they often tended to explain that the pay was not good enough, and what was the best that the College could do? If one recollects the legend correctly, one gentleman of this kind seemed to consider himself insulted and wished to fight a duel with somebody. For all his interest in the wars of the seventeenth century, such things were not exactly in Witherow's line.[22]

---

21 R Dill 'Prelatico - Presbyterianism, (Dublin 1856) passim; J R Leebody 'A Short History of McCrea Magee College, Derry' (Londonderry 1915)

22 MS 'Autobiography' pp 93-95; Leebody op cit; tradition; information from J S Macmaster

Metaphysics and Ethics, -	JOHN PARK, Esq., M.A., Q.U.I., (Dill Professor).
Mathematics and Natural Philosophy, - - - -	JOHN ROBINSON LEEBODY, Esq., M.A., Q.U.I., (The Hon. the Irish Society's Professor).
Oriental Literature and Hermeneutics, - - -	Rev. RICHARD SMYTH, M.A.
Church History and Pastoral Theology, - - -	Rev. THOMAS WITHEROW.
Theology, - - - - - -	Rev. SAMUEL MARCUS DILL, M.A., D.D., (Dill Professor.)

LECTURER:

Modern Oriental Languages, Rev. JAMES GLASGOW, D.D.

TUTORS:

Modern Continental Languages, - - - - - -	Mons. RENCZYNSKI.
Elocution, - - - - - -	Mr. JOHN HEMPHILL, B.A.

It will be observed that this College provides for its Students a complete curriculum both of Science and of Theology.* *It is the only complete College under the entire control of the General Assembly of the Presbyterian Church in Ireland*, in which that Church has full security for the proper training of its future ministers.

The friends of this institution have great reason to be gratified with its past progress. When the peculiar difficulties with which it has had to contend are considered, it has prospered far beyond their most sanguine expectations; but, for future success, all that has been already accomplished will be of little avail without the means of affording pecuniary rewards to deserving students. The College must enter into competition with old and richly

*It thus includes what would be called in America the College and the Seminary.

endowed universities; and it is vain to suppose that this can be done successfully without adequate funds, or that all the learning and ability of the Professors in Derry will be found sufficiently attractive to students apart from that powerful metallic influence which is elsewhere brought into operation. Necessity is laid on very many of the best students to resort to those localities where they are certain to have the means of supporting themselves by their own honourable exertions. The only means by which these antagonistic influences can be counteracted are to be found in the establishment of *Scholarships* on a permanent foundation. Such Scholarships would perpetuate the names of the donors, and thus be enduring monuments of their public spirit and Christian liberality, while, at the same time, they would stimulate the students in their literary pursuits, and add to the importance and dignity of this youthful establishment.

An active friend is endeavouring to secure a number of annual subscribers of a moderate amount, for a period of *ten* years—say fifty subscribers at £2, and one hundred at £1, *per annum* each, thus realising an annual income of £200 for a period of ten years. The sum thus realised would produce Eight Scholarships of the value of £25 each. These, with the Two "Dill Scholarships" of £25 each, and the "Adams Bursary" of £10, would make a fair beginning, but more numerous Scholarships, and of a larger amount, are necessary for the success of the College.

Another requirement is a good *Library*. There have already been obtained from various sources three thousand volumes, but many of these are not such as would have been selected for a college. Some books have been received from America, and several friends of the Institution have sent large and valuable contributions; but there are many others interested in the welfare of the College who could enrich it by donations of books which would be very useful as works of reference, although of comparatively little value to them. Still, there are many new books published from time to time

Luckily for him and his colleagues, the Irish Society of London, local folk growing wealthy from the growing trade and industry of Derry, and various sympathisers, contributed a good deal of money to endow Chairs and to support and equip the College. It had no grant from the State until it was absorbed by the Royal University of Ireland in 1879 - and then it got a grudged one with just one endowed professor. Witherow became a Senator in 1884. With a limited range of subjects and few scholarships, the College had to compete with the Queen's Colleges, especially those in Belfast and mid Galway. It had also to compete with the Presbyterian Theological College, founded through the 'Belfast' party's influence in the early 'fifties.

When the new Professor of Church History and Pastoral Theology arrived in 1865, he found 26 students at the College, 16 of whom at least were 'theologicals', either then or later. After the first three years numbers fell. In 1871 only three entrants appeared. It was not until 1882 that the new connection with the Royal University caused a big increase. Women were admitted in 1883, and numbers were well maintained until the odd events of 1909, when the College was marooned by Augustine Birrell and then taken off by Trinity College, Dublin. What Witherow would have made of these events we do not know, for he had been in the City Cemetery since 1890. But he might have been shocked by certain suggestions that a certain person, originally connected with Magee, had perhaps tendered certain advice (for reasons not unconnected with a disappointment suffered by a certain relative) to the receptive Birrell.[23]

Witherow would perhaps have been hard to shock by anything that a Liberal Government did. He had taken so ill Gladstone's effort to pass an Irish Home Rule Bill in 1886 that he became a thorough-going Liberal Unionist. His previous active support for the Party in Londonderry had not gone much farther than mentioning its doings with some approval in the editorials he wrote from time to time in the 'Derry Standard'. Nor does he seem to have been much concerned with local affairs outside the congregation which he joined and in which he became an elder. Great James Street Church was but a few yards from the two houses which he occupied in Clarendon Street. A few minutes' walk more took him along the Northland Road to the College. Tradition has it that he spent much the greater part of his time there; that not much more than one hour passed in lecturing each morning, and that the rest of the day, apart from meals, was mostly given to work in the Library. As Librarian, Witherow served the College well. By 1870 the Catalogue ran to 132 pages. In 1887 the Pamphlet Catalogue contained 79 pages. Both were carefully set out with the items arranged in alphabetical order and systematically indexed and marked. A great many books and pamphlets were the gifts of benefactors, for the College had limited means. A good many were gathered in, and many presented by

---

23 Information based on the recollections of a former President of Magee.

which donations are not likely soon to bring in, but which it is most important that Professors and Students should have an opportunity of consulting. A few hundred pounds devoted to this object would be of incalculable service, especially at the present time. It may also be mentioned that additional apparatus is much required in the department of Natural Philosophy.

There are also requirements in reference to *Endowments*. Moderate salaries have been secured from the bequests already referred to, for the seven Professors mentioned above; but these, though supplemented by fees, are far from being an adequate compensation to these learned gentlemen for the important work they have to do. It would be exceedingly desirable if the Trustees were enabled to afford higher inducements, in the shape of larger salaries and free residences, in order to secure their permanent services, and to obtain suitable successors on their removal by death, or otherwise.

In addition to the Chairs already endowed, *new Chairs* are necessary, since, in some cases, one professor is at present required to do the duty of two. For instance, the Professor of Greek has to teach Latin; the Professor of Mathematics has to teach Natural Philosophy, including Chemistry, &c.; and the Professor of Hermeneutics has to teach Hebrew. There are as yet no Chairs of Natural Science, English Language and Literature, or Modern Languages. The endowment of such Chairs would be an immense accession of teaching power, and would draw young men from various distant parts, not only of Ireland, but of the United Kingdom, to pursue their studies within the College walls.

Such is a brief statement of the establishment, and of the present state and requirements of Magee College. It has its seat in the metropolis of the North-West of Ireland, which, already renowned for its defence of Civil and Religious Liberty, will also, if this institution succeed, be distinguished in the future annals of the country as a place of learning, and a source of light and knowledge to many coming generations.

This College derives no assistance from the State.

It owes its existence and present means of support to private liberality, assisted by the generous contributions of the Hon. the Irish Society, of London. Animated by the desire to carry out to the fullest extent the intentions of its founders, and believing that not only amongst their fellow-citizens at home, but amongst their countrymen abroad, as well as the many descendants of Ulster emigrants to be found in all the United States of America, and throughout Canada, there are not a few who will take a deep interest in such an institution, and be ready to promote its prosperity and success, the Trustees venture to lay before all such their present appeal, trusting that it will be favourably received by every friend of Ireland, and every well-wisher to the Irish Presbyterian Church.

JOHN BROWN.
JAMES GIBSON.
WILLIAM M'CLURE.

Magee College, Londonderry;
April, 1867.

Witherow himself, with his name carefully signed in those which he had written himself, and with precise lists of contents entered on the fly-leaves of those containing several pamphlets.

Witherow published little during his first two years in Magee. This was natural enough, but he had had the foresight to prepare a good few lectures in advance of taking up his duties. From 1867 he wrote steadily. Some of his work was rather slight, reviews and such for papers and magazines popular with the 'religious public'. He gave occasional lectures and addresses to outside audiences. But he was searching steadily for materials with the intention of doing greater things and serving his Church thereby. His mind was concentrating on history, and on the historical approach to religious topics, especially those connected with the past, teaching and organisation of Presbyterianism in Ireland.

This search and the writing it fed were just beginning to produce important results when Witherow suffered two great sorrows. His colleague and close friend, Richard Smyth MP, died unexpectedly in the winter of 1878. In May 1879, just twenty years after their marriage, Catherine Witherow died of puerperal fever, having borne Thomas ten children. He had to rear eight as best he could, with the aid of friends and relatives. But, rightly or wrongly, one has the notion that the shock of these bereavements, and the cares that the death of his wife caused him to contend with, made him lose heart greatly. He was still to write much, and never wrote badly; still, the best part of what he wrote was done by 1879. Anyhow it is by that part that he is most remembered an an author.

In late 1873 he published the best known of his works, 'Derry and Enniskillen'. To himself it was not the most important of his writings. Nor was 'The Boyne and A[u]ghrim', which followed in 1879. His paternal grandmother had told him 'over and over again' at her knee the story of the Siege of Derry and of the Battle of the Boyne.[24] When he left his books and looked out of the east window of the College Library, he could see the City of the Siege. He could see where, on the far side of the Foyle, Jacobite guns had been emplaced to bombard it. To the front was Ross's Bay and down the river to the left was the place where the boom had been broken when the Mountjoy and her fellows had relieved the famishing defenders. It is not impossible to think that, as he gazed through this window, Witherow may have remembered Cooke's dismal prophecy that, should the Magee College be built in Derry, the day would come when the 'foxes of Innishowen would be grinning out of its deserted windows'. In those early days the Professor may indeed have considered that the College, its staff and himself were under siege. That would have quickened his interest in the earlier event.

Witherow did what he could to maintain its existence. Quite a number of students came from the area covered by

---

24 MS 'Autobiography' p101

his old Presbytery. By 1870 he had given at least 45 books to the Library, and had bound at his own expense, and presented, many pamphlets. He encouraged others to do the same. Certainly one accepts his statement in the Introduction to 'Derry and Enniskillen' that he wrote the book to 'teach his countrymen......to look at the past in a calm and kindly spirit, to rise superior to the passions of an evil age'.[25] Unfortunately neither that, nor succeeding even more evil ages, have given overmuch attention to this excellent sentiment. Still, Witherow's book was well received and did Magee no harm. It appealed to very many and gained a good amount of money and reputation for the Magee professor and his publisher, Mullan, who then persuaded his author to continue with the 'Boyne and A[u]ghrim' in 1879.

The earlier book is rather the better. In both Witherow did tend to rely rather much on Macaulay's versions of the Siege and of the later events and battles, as well as on his depiction of James II and other characters, and on his estimates of their aims and actions. But Witherow's local knowledge, and his careful examination of recently-unearthed sources, enabled him to correct and add to earlier accounts. (Still, even in the 4th edition of 1914, Lundy was leaving Londonderry with a load of 'matchwood' on his back!')

W D Killen, Professor of Ecclesiastical History in the Belfast College, had an important influence on Witherow. Killen's lectures had had 'peculiar charms' for him, as a student, and 'were calculated', Witherow says, 'to interest and instruct, as well as to communicate an impulse'.[26] This impulse was not only towards Church History, but also towards a very critical, if not exactly hostile, attitude to the Church of Ireland as established by law. Another strong source of this attitude was the 'Plea of Presbytery', a controversial work published in 1843 by Killen and others to demolish claims made for Episcopacy by a Londonderry curate. And in Thomas Witherow's mind were the tales of the Scottish Covenanters and the persecutions which they had undergone in the seventeenth century. And there was also the memory amongst Presbyterians of the disabilities they had suffered in Ireland during the previous century, and their resentment at the continuing remnants of these. So Witherow was prepared to accept and stress Killen's view of the Rev George Walker and his activities during the Siege of Derry, as Killen had expressed it in his introduction and notes to MacKenzie's 'Memorials of the Siege of Derry', published in 1861. This started controversy which will probably never be settled, but has diverted attention from the many merits of Witherow's book, based as it was on original research and making a real attempt to be fair to both sides in the conflict. His whole-hearted acceptance of Macaulay's view of James II, though, perhaps tends to give a rather incomplete and too harsh view of James's character and

25 'Derry and Enniskillen' (Belfast 1873) p vii
26 MS 'Autobiography' p35

actions.

Witherow's attempt to give 'The Boyne and A[u]ghrim' more popular appeal than 'Derry and Enniskillen' was no great success. He suggested that in the places to which it mostly referred there were few Presbyterians to buy copies. But he was hardly quite so simple as to imagine that his earlier 'debunking' of Walker's claims to renown would not have upset some folk. Did he really expect his rather critical attitude towards the Church of Ireland to have been happily noted by all? It is possible too that the dash of Liberalism, moderate enough in itself, mixed into 'Derry and Enniskillen' was little to the taste of many Conservatives, both Episcopalian and Presbyterian. But perhaps the professors of that age were more apt to be surprised by denunciation of their works than are our contemporaries? Still, the later book is far from being a bad one. Its author had learned enough from wide reading to have a fair understanding of the strategic and political problems of the times. Matters of military organisation, recruitment, arms, training, discipline, supply, hygiene and morale, as well as tactical doctrine and practice, were not much in his line, but the same might be said of many of his successors, even of the great Macaulay. So far as he could, Witherow had gone to original sources for information, and showed good judgement in interpreting them. He had perhaps a tendency, as in his account of the Battle of the Boyne, to put together details gathered from various documents and to consider the result as a sufficient and explanatory account of what had happened. But his common sense did enable him to have some idea of what was in the mind of the resolute William on that well-celebrated day. This may also be said of his accounts of the Sieges of Limerick and of the decisive Battle of Aughrim; his description of that engagement brings out more clearly some of the reasons for the defeat of the Jacobites than does the section on the Boyne.[27]

In the new library at Magee, overlooking the Foyle, Witherow wrote in praise both of the defenders of Londonderry and of the Jacobites who had held out in Limerick. He visited the Boyne where William's men had crossed under heavy fire and counter-attack, and where their enemies' cavalry had sacrificed themselves to cover the retreating infantry. He recorded the fierce fight at Aughrim where that Irish infantry had redeemed its credit, and where the Huguenot Ruvigny's horse and the Derry and Enniskillen regiments had turned the battle in favour of the Williamites. Witherow did his best to be fair to both sides, whilst making it clear that he believed the Williamite cause to be the better. For him, as for his great exemplar, Macaulay, the victory of that cause ensured the ultimate survival of civil and religious liberty in the British Isles.

The stamp of his clerical profession was indelibly on Witherow. He was a preacher and a moralist. He was also a

---

27 He seems to have had a clearer idea of the use of the cavalry and dragoons at Aughrim.

Presbyterian by conviction and a Liberal in politics. A little ingenuously it may be, he had used a section of 'Derry and Enniskillen' to denounce the wrongs suffered by Presbyterians and Roman Catholics in eighteenth-century Ireland, in spite of the principles, as he saw them, of the Glorious Revolution. It may be that he had forgotten, or never known, that Episcopalians had, in the eighteenth century, suffered much the same disabilities in Presbyterian Scotland. A shade gratuitously, he had included a set of instructions for what he recommended as a better way to celebrate the Revolution, the memory of William III and the Relief of Derry than by maintaining the local traditional customs. But it was his assault on the reputation of the Rev George Walker, and his insistence that Adam Murray was the true hero of the famous Siege, that aroused anger and even bitter controversy that has not quite burned itself out even yet. It is not surprising that the first sentence of the Preface to 'The Boyne and A[u]ghrim' declared that 'when 'Derry and Enniskillen' was published, it was not the design of the Author to return to the subject again. He had told his story, drawn the moral, and had no personal wish to touch any more a matter of which Ireland has had perhaps quite enough.' But he had yielded to 'kindly pressure'.

Witherow was already busy on what he considered to be a much more important work. This was what he had wished to call 'Monumenta Presbyteriana Hibernica', but Mullan & Son very sensibly thought that 'a Latin title might repel ordinary readers and limit the sale'. So the two volumes appeared in 1879 and 1880 as 'Historical and Literary Memorials of Presbyterianism in Ireland'. The change of title was part of what Witherow described glumly as the 'hard bargain' the Mullans drove. Young Mullan had declared that he had 'little confidence in the support from Presbyterians'. They had foreseen that this publication would hardly cause much obstruction by queues outside their bookshop. Sales were slow, and Thomas was glad enough to escape without financial loss to himself.[28] According to Witherow, the 'Memorials' were the best effort he could make to 'illustrate the history and principles of the Presbyterian Church in Ireland'.[29] He did it through short biographical sketches of those ministers who had written between 1683 and 1800, and by illustrative extracts from their works. These 'Memorials' are also a monument to his own single-minded industry and to his zeal for the preservation of the records of his Church's past. They are still a useful guide to the existence and whereabouts of these records. They set out much of value about the lives, circumstances, abilities, characters, customs and achievements of 141 Presbyterian ministers in Ireland during the seventeenth and eighteenth centuries. There are often vivid and particular accounts of their theological and political opinions and influence, of the social and economic conditions of their times, of their influence on their Church and community.

---

28 MS 'Autobiography' Ch XI

29 'Historical and Literary Memorials' 1st Series Belfast 1879 Preface p x

Witherow would hardly have expected reviews of this work to be as favourable as the three columns that the London 'Times' had given to 'Derry and Enniskillen', praising it as 'an excellent work on a subject of enduring interest' and as 'natural, candid, and lifelike'. But he may well have been unprepared for some of the criticism that the 'Historical Memorials' received. Sales were not likely to have been much increased by a private review from the Rev Robert McKinney, of Mahurangi, New Zealand, who was a friend of Thomas and had been his neighbour in Swateragh. 'While recognising the merit of all his work', wrote McKinney, 'we should like to see him engaged in a somewhat wider field - a book, for example, on some department of Apologetics....better than....the 'Presbyterian Memorials' can afford - a vain effort to rescue poor old creatures from that oblivion for which God and Nature designed them'.[30] That Mr McKinney was not a very sensitive man we may deduce from his later actually quoting this passage in full in a letter of sympathy to Witherow's daughter after her father's death.[31] But he was vague about what he may have meant by 'Apologetics', for Witherow's 'Memorials' were meant to record the lives, actions and writings of the 'poor old creatures' as illustrations of a justification and defence of the existence, doctrines and organisation of his own Presbyterian Church in Ireland - a legitimate (and often suffering) branch of the Church of Jesus Christ. Presbyterians had to endure severe religious, legal and social discrimination in seventeenth and much of eighteenth-century Ireland. And the last religious test in Trinity College, Dublin, was abolished only six years before the 'Historical Memorials' were published.

The two volumes, though, contain more than sharp criticism of Episcopalian works and ways. Ballinascreen and Tobermore folk may find here Robert Sinclair, minister at Larne from 1755 till 1795, son of William Sinclair, near Tobermore, of the 'old and respectable' family still represented in the Sixtowns of Ballinascreen. Here he is in Witherow's pages, 'fresh and venerable in his old age, with a white bushy wig, a good complexion, and noble aspect'. He has not forgotten the customs and enjoyments of his folk and loves best 'the favourite airs' of travelling harpers and treats them kindly on their visits. He sits in his parlour, amusing his family with lively talk, while 'his little wife', who reaches 'but a little above his elbow', peeps up at him 'with her black admiring eyes' and 'devours' his discourse. And he has tales to tell, for, a tall handsome man, has he not worn the uniform of the famous Volunteers of Ireland, and reviewed them on Ballygally Hill, and published 'Fortitude Explained and Recommended; a Sermon preached before the Larne Volunteers, the 1st of August, 1779, from Philippians ch. 4 v. 8'? [32]

Maghera has its notice too, in the short, discreet

---

30 Private information

31 Do

32 'Memorials' 2nd Series Belfast 1880 pp 221-225

account of the eloquent Rev John Glendy DD, who fled to America when the rising of the local United Irishmen collapsed in June 1798. And, Witherow says, 'he sympathised warmly in the political movements of the United Irishmen', implying that he did not sympathise with the 'foolish march of the country people' into the town.[33] The rector of Maghera, the Rev Clotworthy Soden, would hardly have agreed with this view of Glendy. As a magistrate, he reported on 16 November 1796, enclosing 'a paper taken down from the Tree of Liberty at a popish Chappel [sic] near Maghera last Sunday', and his opinion of both it and Glendy. 'It is truly a Glendy production and at the bottom of every Mischief and Villany [sic] in this Country is that horrible Rascal.' The rector of Kilcronaghan, the Rev William Bryan, also forwarded two copies of threatening 'notices', sent to men in his neighbourhood, proving 'how much that Villain John Glendy's instructions have prevailed here'. These reports were not available to Witherow, and he seems to have relied much on some local traditions, both in this work and in the Cooke Centenary address.[34]

It is not impossible that Glendy had actually taken at least the oath of secrecy about the affairs of the United men, but had not given much more than advice and encouragement, both directly and indirectly. The actual pressure to rebel at the particular time seems to have come from Watty Graham, William Harper and William McKeever. In the old ballad, Graham declares:

> O William McKeever, it's you that's to blame,
> For you are the cause of my sorrow and shame.[35]

McKeever escaped and Graham was hanged. Harper seems to have got away. His father, minister of the Burger Secession Presbyterian Church at Knockloughrim, was tried by court-martial, but evidence was weak against him, and he got off to America, to which Glendy went too, having evaded arrest and trial. Tradition maintained that Mrs Clark insisted till her dying day that the woman she met near Maghera one evening in the gloaming was Glendy dressed in a woman's gown.

Tradition also said that Glendy owed his escape to Colonel Leith of the Aberdeen Fencible Regiment, in garrison at Maghera after the rebellion, who was supposed to have ensured that he was not captured. There is quite possibly truth in this. Leith was a Scot and his Aberdeen men mostly Presbyterians. The court-martial records are interesting. The sentences had to be confirmed by him. As much responsible as any man for the rising at Maghera was Charles Wallace of Tobermore, a Presbyterian licentiate. He had been Adjutant of the local United Irish regiment, and seemingly eager to rise. His sentence was 800 lashes 'to be inflicted in the usual manner in the town of Tubbermore', after which he was to be transported for life.

---

33 Do p 313
34 Rebellion Papers PROI Carton 620/26/61/a d e
35 R M Young 'Ulster in '98' Belfast 1893 p 60

Leith remitted the sentence of flogging, 'the Prisoner having been stripped', for flogging, 'in the town of Tubbermore opposite to his own chapel' and sent to Belfast for transportation. He was not the only prisoner to have his sentence lessened by Leith (who later distinguished himself in the Peninsular War), though the hanging of William Cuddy is still something of a mystery.[36]

Witherow may tend to minimise Glendy's share in the events of 1798, but he does give more information about him as he was later in America. Minister in Second Baltimore, which had been built for him, Glendy was close to such men as Jefferson and Madison. The University of Maryland gave him the degree of DD. Neat and even elegant he was, with his hair curled, and 'powdered as white as the snows of Mont Blanc'. A Baltimore elder remembered him as 'pale, his eyes intensely blue, his gesticulation animated and graceful, but somewhat profuse'. He had to use an eyeglass or spectacles to read in the pulpit, but his 'sermon was a perfect torrent of Irish eloquence. His voice was as sweet as the harp of David, but as unlike as possible to the horns that demolished the walls of Jericho. The whole impression produced by his preaching was at the time perfectly delightful, though I cannot say that it was very enduring.'[37] All this seems to agree well with the Glendy of a report in the United Irishmen's 'Northern Star', sent in by James Graham, Session Clerk of Maghera congregation, on 5 December 1792. 'A few individuals excepted, on whom the breath of aristocracy had shed its baleful influence', had assembled at their meeting-house to celebrate the victory of the French revolutionaries over the invading Austrian and Prussian armies. 'The Rev John Glendy exhibited.....distinguished abilities in a manly, disinterested and public-spirited manner, having displayed with peculiar energy the signal interposition of heaven on behalf of the French nation.' This was the congregation which in 1801 gave its call to Charles Kennedy to succeed John Glendy in Maghera.[38] Though there are signs in the Cooke Commemoration Address that Witherow may have known more than he wrote about these affairs, he could not examine the Government papers of that period, and consult various other unpublished sources of information. The 'Memorials' are still of great value, but must be used with care, always allowing for his honest objections to Episcopacy and Roman Catholicism, as well as to what he looked on as dangerous heresy in his own Church.

Perhaps there <u>was</u> just a trace in Witherow of what the South African Boers would have recognised as being rather 'slim' - not exactly 'artful' or 'cunning', nearer to 'crafty'. It may have been partly a result of his early expeditions with his cattle-dealing father to the fairs and markets of Mid and South Derry. We note that his Clerkship of the Magherafelt Presbytery and his Secretaryship of the Magee College Faculty were hardly accidental honours; they needed business ability, thoroughness and discretion. As

---

36 Rebellion Papers PROI Carton 620/1/2/19/7/3
37 'Memorials' op cit 2nd Series supra pp 314-315
38 S McSkimin 'Annals of Ulster' p 38 n(c)

Moderator of the General Assembly in 1878, when debates were more full-blooded and hotter than in our relatively polite days, Witherow presided, calm and dignified, and ruled as it suited him, uttering no opinion on the merits of the use of Instrumental Music in church services. But he calmed the meeting by allowing a popular 'comic turn' to spend some time telling funny stories. He took care shortly after, at an ordination dinner, to declare his opinion that it was a great pity to divide the Church by introducing such music into public worship. He thus indirectly (and indeed correctly as Moderator, though unofficially), gave a public vote for the 'status quo'![39] It was very skilful. That he does not mention it in the 'Autobiography' may show that this kind of cautious diplomacy was simply a habit of his.

That Witherow remembered little enough about this Assembly when he wrote his 'Autobiography' is not surprising, for it was during his time as Moderator that his wife died, as well as his brilliant friend, Professor the Rev Richard Smyth MP. Heartbroken and bewildered, Witherow describes his wife's happiness when he became Moderator, and the tour in Scotland they had had that summer, with simple, genuine emotion. Still, it never seems to have struck him that to have borne him ten children inside nineteen years, and to have had to care for the house in Clarendon Street that she did not like, might not have been entirely blissful for the late Mrs Catherine Witherow. It might indeed have lowered her resistance to the fever that killed her.

The family had now to be split up, some children going to one set of relations, some to another. To the best of his ability Witherow did what he could for them, writing letters, for instance, full of the best advice possible to James, who hoped to enter the Indian Civil Service, and relying much on the daughter who stayed at home in the new house in College Avenue, which was such an improvement on Clarendon Street. He had also been writing steadily enough for various periodicals in favour with religious folk, but his mind turned now to what he seems to have believed would be his greatest work, more important and 'useful' than his books on the Williamite Wars and the 'Memorials'. So he laboured on 'The Christian Temple', which appeared at last towards the end of 1889. Those (and they are few) who have at least dipped into this work are not surprised to learn that the author was obliged by his publishers to reduce its contents from five sections, called 'Books' by him, to three. These were, hoped Witherow, 'to bring under the eye of the inquirer those passages of the Holy Scriptures, which are supposed to bear directly or indirectly on the subject of Church Polity; to find out the principles or facts which these passages underlie; and to combine such facts and principles, with a view of ascertaining whether they do or do not, contain the outlines of a form of Church Government'.[40] This process was ingeniously compared to the successive stages of the building of the 'Christian

---

39 Belfast Newsletter 8/6/1878 and seq

40 'The Form of the Christian Temple' Edinburgh 1889 Preface p v

Temple'. Each section of the book depends on what are considered to be the relevant Biblical texts, and Witherow accepts the full inspiration of the Bible. Granted his premises, the argument is generally logical. It has all the marks of the lecture-room in Magee where the author originally treated his students to it. But, again granting the premises, Witherow's conclusions are moderate enough and he presents a Presbyterianism that he believes to be more in accord with original Christian organisation and doctrine than are other systems, but he does not deny that these may contain important elements of it. Within the framework which he sets out, he accepts the possibility of change in matters not essential. He was gratified by favourable reviews, but 'the hue was not the wear' and sales were slow.

In an important section of his 'Autobiography' Witherow describes how the lawyer and enthusiastic Magee Trustee, James Gibson of Dublin, helped him to secure the great Migné collection of 108 volumes of the works of the Greek Fathers of the Church, which he used in the writing of the 'Temple'. It was also Gibson who helped him in the somewhat complicated foray that he made to secure the Rev Classon Porter's collection of Irish Presbyterian manuscript records on which he based much of the 'Memorials.' We may note with interest that the Rev D B Knox, who was responsible for the serialisation of Witherow's memoirs in the 'Irish Presbyterian' in the late nineteen-thirties, did not publish Witherow's comment that 'the secrecy was necessary lest we should be outbid by the Belfast people, who have unlimited funds at their command'. Some 'slimness' there perhaps? And not too much love between the Colleges, in spite of Witherow's regard for Killen, whom he eulogised when the Belfast Professor retired?

To help Smyth, Witherow had found time to edit, nominally, the 'Derry Standard' for a time in 1876. He became Editor himself in late 1878. He seems to have rather enjoyed journalism, especially as he had only to write the editorials. The 'Standard' supported Presbyterian and Liberal interests. So in 1886 Witherow found himself having to decide the 'Standard's' attitude to Gladstone's conversion to Irish Home Rule. It was a time of anguish for many Ulster Liberals. Witherow does not seem to have had as much trouble in making up his mind as did a successor of his in Maghera, the Rev R H F Dickey, brother of the late Rev C C M Dickey of Draperstown. The Maghera minister is said to have disappeared into his Manse on hearing the news of Gladstone's 'about turn', was not seen for a fortnight, and came out an ardent and active Liberal Unionist to oppose Home Rule. It was an interesting change for Thomas Witherow to find himself denouncing a Liberal Government in the 'Standard', and also to be in private correspondence with the Duke of Abercorn about the representation of the County of Londonderry in Parliament.

Witherow was already anxious about his health and resigned his editorship in 1888. The loss of his wife and dispersal of his family affected him. His father's death had also saddened him. It is a matter for the psychologist, but one may possibly consider that he had been 'father-dominated' in his earlier day. It appears to have shocked him when this father left the bulk of his property to Thomas's brother, who had stayed on the farm and his account shows some signs of brooding about it. But the work in College, so far as the academic side went, was not too heavy. Even marking examination papers was no great burden. For much of Witherow's time the Magee campus was not exactly thronged with students, and the papers set in those days often demanded little more than verbatim acquaintance with the content of set books. It appears that, at least in his later days, Professor Witherow was kind enough to inform first-year students beforehand of the actual content of the paper!

His task as Secretary of Faculty in a new College that had to make its way was much more burdensome. In his carefully discreet way Witherow recorded just as much as was strictly necessary of its doings, but enough remains to show that personality clashes and cabals are no modern phenomenon in university institutions. Funding was a continual problem. There had to be recruitment of students. There were powerful 'interests' that were no great friends of Magee and they had to be countered. Professor Witherow was quietly responsible for much of the goodwill towards Magee that gradually grew, but it took worry and anxiety in those early years for the College to survive, let alone grow.

There was some recognition of his work. When the Royal University of Ireland was established, he became a Professor of the University and a Senator. In 1889 he became President of Magee College and people said many pleasant things about his character and achievements, even if they had not all bought his books. But Thomas Witherow was wearing out. The sorrows and troubles of his past years and the sedentary life he had lived for so long were having their cumulative effect on a sensitive and vulnerable man. His excessive weight was a deadly foe, and his heart was failing. Sent to Harrogate by kind friends to take the waters, he found himself the worse for it. The Thomas Witherow who rose in May Street Church in the early afternoon of 11 May 1888 and came slowly forward to give his estimate of the work and worth of Henry Cooke was a man marked for death. He died on 25 January 1890.

The Witherow Memorial Window in Magee Library